Miracles with My Master, TARA SINGH

Applications of A Course in Miracles

Miracles with My Master, TARA SINGH

Applications of A Course In Miracles

By
Markus Ray

Immortal Ray Productions
3000 Vanderbilt Place #118
Nashville, TN 37212
www.ImmortalRay.com
ImmortalRayProductions@gmail.com

Editorial Supervision: Tajinder Chana and Lia Schultz

Library of Congress Cataloging-in-Publication Data
Ray, Markus.
Miracles with my master, tara singh / Markus Ray with Sondra Ray

   p. cm.

ISBN: 978-0-9916277-3-8

1. Auto-Biography. 2. Relationships. 3. Self-Help: Miracles. 4. Mind-Body-Spirit. I. Ray, Markus. II. Title.

1st Edition, December, 2015

ISBN: 978-0-9916277-3-8
ISBN: 978-0-9916277-4-5 (ebook)

Immortal Ray Productions
Nashville

❖ *Table of Contents* ❖

❖ *Acknowledgements* ❖

I am very grateful for Tajinder Chana who helped me with this book. Her dedication to *A Course in Miracles* and her editorial skills greatly contributed to *Miracles With My Master* flowering. Lia Schultz continues to be supportive of Immortal Ray Productions, which makes this book possible.

I would like to thank all the students and staff who formed Tara Singh's Foundation for Life Action, that later transformed into The Joseph Plan Foundation in 1993. To name a few—Charles Johnson, Aliana Scurlock, Jim Cheatham, Barbara Michael, William McClintock, Leslie McClintock, Johanna Macdonald, Melanie Coulter, Ted Ward, Frank Nader, Rachel Logel, Lucille Frappier, Dr. Bill Kelly all provided the key support for the workshops and publications of books and tapes to be presented to the public.

There were many more, too numerous to mention, who helped Tara Singh bring deeper awareness to students of *A Course in Miracles*. I was the beneficiary of their dedication and hard work. They prepared the seedbed of possibility for the Teacher/Student relationship to unfold in my life. Without them this meeting with my master could not have taken place. Without them I would have missed the opportunity to make contact with this great soul, Tara Singh, who helped to liberate me from my self-made limitations, and put me in touch with my God created Self.

7

Miracle of All Miracles

Oh Great Mother of all Mankind,
to Your People, Masses of Millions,
now would I write my dedication
to that Miracle of all Miracles,
to that Meeting of Minds that joined
Me with my Master,
through Life's Meander of Movement
toward a Marriage beyond Measure,
From My West to My East and back again,
now would the Vision of One World
grow in my heart because of Him,
now would my true Marriage be Manifest
because of Him, My Master,
now would the Magnificence of my Mission
be made clear because of Him.
"Into His Presence" did I enter on Easter of 1989,
and would I now endeavor to tell this story,
My Miracles with My Master, My M & M's,
My Meeting with a Marvelous Man, the One
Ordained to make *A Course In Miracles* truly
known to the world, and to me, His student.
To this Man of Life Action would I dedicate myself,
and this book, to God's "Star Lion", Tara Singh.

"Surely all art is the result of one's having been in danger, of having gone through an experience all the way to the end, to where no one can go any further. The further one goes, the more private, the more personal, the more singular an experience becomes, the thing one is making is, finally, the necessary, irrepressible, and, as nearly as possible, definitive utterance of this singularity—Therein lies the enormous aid the work of art brings to the life of the one who must make it,—that it is his epitome; the knot in the rosary at which his life recites a prayer, the ever-returning proof to himself of his unity and genuineness, which presents itself only to him while appearing anonymous to the outside, nameless, existing merely as necessity, as reality, as being —." Page 4

RANIER MARIA RILKE—in Letters on Cezanne.

❖ *Preface* ❖

Having Your Consciousness Awakened by A True Master Like Babaji

Markus spent 17 years with his master, Tara Singh, studying *A Course in Miracles*. The holy relationship with a master transcends all other relationships in life. My master was, and still is, Babaji—the immortal yogi-Christ of Herakhan, India. I feel very fortunate to have a husband who had already surrendered to Tara Singh before we got married. Markus feels very fortunate to have a wife who had already surrendered to Babaji before we married. When you surrender to a master, your whole way of looking at the world changes.

With a true master, your eyes will discover the beauty of creation. Your ears will hear divine words. You will taste heavenly food. Your feet will bear you throughout space. Your hands will learn to create in finer higher worlds of the Soul. A true master gives you victory over your weaknesses, which will give you real power.

The true master emanates beneficial elements for his group. His sole care is to give you elements of higher nature in harmony with heaven. You find nothing but blessings near your master. He corrects your mistakes. He encourages you;

and under His guidance you can end up becoming a virtuoso. With him you cannot fall back into inertia, you feel continually stimulated forward. He draws you upward by his words and his example. Your consciousness is awakened by him or her.

How can you meditate on heavenly subjects when you have no high ideal, which will lift you above your ordinary life?

The master may have to be severe on his disciples by telling them certain truths for their progress and advancement. (When you are ill, you think it makes perfect sense to swallow disagreeable remedies). Most people are afraid to tell you the truth. The master is not. The master has to give several injections and a few operations! His motive is never to demolish someone, but to help him change to become beautiful and to be saved. He wants only the best for you. He wants you to be liberated, rich and loved by all. Every day I am grateful to Tara Singh even though I never met him. I receive the benefits because Markus' Holy Relationship with him brings enlightenment to our marriage.

For me, there was nothing that could surpass receiving initiation and wisdom from Babaji. I know Markus feels the same. The master will give you love you never found even in your own family. The invisible world sends Masters like them and if you don't accept them, then you might get other teachers in the form of illness, misery or difficulties. (If you have to go through these things then there is probably a karmic reason for it—which means you have thought forms that are stuck.)

11

The true master will lead you to real freedom so that you are strong despite all difficulties. He will warn you about what awaits you if you continue on your present path. He can open doors for you, but it is up to you to walk through them. He is an essential tuning fork—you must tune yourself to him. You end up vibrating quite differently.

You must always love and serve a higher being than yourself so you can perform miracles (thanks to him) and do good, which is doing what is natural to your true nature. There is an osmosis that goes on between you and the master. You benefit greatly from his light. It does not matter what form his existence takes. You can tune into these masters and they can guide you from other dimensions.

You also have available to you the mind of Jesus directly in *A Course in Miracles*. He is right there guiding you in a step-by-step process towards enlightenment. And you have many books by Tara Singh to help you. You also have Ammachi right now, in the form of the Divine Mother. And there is Babaji, who said, "My love is available." Take advantage of all these true spiritual masters for your own sake. Their love is available. Why not receive it? At any moment you can choose a new life.

Love, *Sondra Ray*

❖ *Introduction* ❖

My meeting with my *master*, Tara Singh, and the miracles I experienced with him form the subject of this book. Generally we think of miracles as something supernatural and outside the normal realm of everyday life. In fact, miracles occur naturally all the time. Especially when two minds meet and give their combined attention to overcoming the limitations we have been conditioned to believe, miracles become facts. Limitations are never facts, as I grew to understand through my relationship with a man who was never bound by them. If thinking "outside the box" was ever a subject meritorious of mastery, Tara Singh was a master of this kind of thinking. I had the good fortune of meeting him in the spring of 1989 in Stony Point, New York, at a workshop he was giving over the Easter weekend on *A Course in Miracles.* My relationship continued for seventeen years with him until his passing in 2006. In fact it continues even now, beyond the limitations of time, place, history, and physical existence we normally associate with relationships. A relationship with a master is not bound by these limitations, as I would come to know with Tara Singh.

I suppose this meeting had its precedents that are appropriate to mention. I had studied art at the Cleveland

Institute of Art, and later at the Tyler School of Art in Philadelphia, where I lived at the time. "Artists are spiritual by nature," I remember one of my art professors saying. So after graduating with a Masters degree (MFA) in Painting in 1982, I was launched into a life that was inherently spiritual by nature. In addition to seriously pursuing the life of an artist in the years preceding my meeting with Tara Singh, I studied yoga with a Sikh master, Yogi Bhajan. I also had gone through a series of "Rebirthing" sessions during this time. Rebirthing is a consciously connected breathing process that helps people clear some very deep seated subconscious thought patterns that are holding them back in life and relationships—due to their conditioned beliefs.

Rebirthing uses the breath as a tool for clearing the past, identifying and forgiving the negative thoughts in the mind, and facilitating a process of inner awakening. When one of the main voices of the rebirthing movement came to town, Sondra Ray, I took her *Loving Relationships Training*, the LRT®. Among many of the jewels of wisdom given in this weekend workshop, one of the most impressionable jewels Sondra offered lit up my consciousness like a lighthouse in a fog. It was her introduction to *A Course in Miracles*. I had a vague notion that the books existed—perhaps I even had an unexamined copy in my home library at the time. But when Sondra Ray uttered with perfect certainty, "This is the most important book written in the last 2000 years," I felt my attention wake up to red alert. It was one of those moments when you feel the hair on your arms stand up on end.

Sondra Ray would influence me quite profoundly in the next few years. Between 1985 and 1989 I attended many of her seminars and retreats—and even became a practitioner of the Rebirthing/Breathwork process. I started studying *A Course in Miracles* with a passion, reading the Text and doing the daily lessons in the Workbook for Students. The words of Jesus flowed into me and I became grateful for the alchemy that was happening in my mind. I did not understand the depth of it in the beginning, but I knew something profound was taking place beyond my own conditioned thinking.

As the clarity of Sondra Ray's simple but direct teachings entered my outlook on life, it was no accident I would travel with her to India in 1987 and 1989. We journeyed to Herakhan, Babaji's ashram in the Himalayas. Babaji was first mentioned by Paramahansa Yogananda in the West. In chapter 33 and 34 of Yogananda's famous classic, the *Autobiography of a Yogi*, Babaji is described as a *Yogi Christ* figure who is an original Maha-Avatar, the Master of his masters. Sondra had met Babaji personally in Herakhan on many occasions during His last manifestation (1970-1984), and she continues to take a group of students there annually to participate in the Divine Mother Festival, the Navaratri. When one of my rebirthing colleagues asked me if I wanted to go with Sondra to India, I thought he was asking me to "go to the moon." It felt like *that* big of a stretch. So I was startled when I heard myself say, *"Yes!"*

New Delhi in 1987 was another world. The common notions of India being filled with masses of poor people seemed apparent as soon as we stepped out of the airport after midnight, and witnessed hundreds of people sleeping on the ground up and down the pick up areas and taxi zones. Whole families were "camped out," and small groups of begging children tugged on our clothes for a rupee or two. But luckily, the taxi driver soon whisked us off. After a suspenseful ride through the smoke filled atmosphere due to open cooking fires, we were safely deposited at a five star hotel that was far beyond the beauty and luxury of anything I had ever seen in the West. Clad in white marble it approached the majestic, like a palace, with high domes that reached all the way up to the 20th floor. The contrast was startling. From the hoards of beggars to the kingly palace—this was my first experience of India—a country of *very high contrast*.

Sondra Ray had the India Quest down to a well-organized transformational pilgrimage. She had been to India many times by then, and had the local contacts and the certainty of her program, which made the whole experience seamless for the participants. We had our orientation, and a few days in New Delhi to explore the sights, do some shopping, and buy some Indian clothes that we would wear in the ashram in Herakhan. It was a miracle I was even there. Traveling half way around the world was quite a stretch for me back then. Sondra was like a Nordic high priestess in her impeccable flowing gowns and erect poise of always being so *present*. She held the space for us to come so far on a journey the likes of which we had never known—to not only receive a strong and authentic dose of Indian culture, a country imbued with spirituality and the importance of God-realization—but to be focused on our own process of awakening with the help of her spiritual masters.

The notion of a spiritual master was still very new to me. I had met Yogi Bhajan at various yoga retreats, the Sikh master who brought a form of kundalini yoga to the West, but I was now in the motherland of the Master/Student relationship. The sole purpose of this relationship is the inner liberation from all illusions and personal problems. I was beginning to wake up to the reverence a student must have to receive the boon of enlightenment. I was becoming aware of the fact that associating with one who is fully awakened to his/her own God nature was a necessity in my life. There is a different aura around such a being. I noticed with Yogi Bhajan he imparted something more certain, more true, more purified and lofty than any of my teachers in college had done. It was something beyond intellectual knowing. It was a *Presence*. I experienced the same with Sondra Ray.

Now on the India Quest, the reverence for the master was the defining theme of the trip to Herakhan. Herakhan, in the Kumaon foothills of the Himalayas, is the home of the Maha-Avatar Babaji who comes and goes in various forms throughout history for the sake of humanity's evolution. He does not come through the womb of a woman, but through the direct manifestation of His divine will. Like Melchizedek in the Bible, he has "no father and no mother"—He is a "priest for all time." In 1970 He manifested a body from a ball of light in a cave at Herakhan. In 1977 Sondra Ray met Babaji for the first time. And in 1987 I was taken by remarkable events to the feet of the Guru myself on Sondra Ray's India Quest—by then

He had been departed from His body for three years, but the energy of *His Presence* was then, and still is, palpably felt in Herakhan. In 1987 his two main disciples, Shastriji and Muniraj, were in charge of the proceedings.

The pilgrimage to a spiritual master, as a tool of personal evolution, is one of the fastest means of expanding one's mind, clearing one's head, and manifesting one's greatest potentials. Firstly, just disengaging from a pressured routine of daily life and retreating to a place of relaxation within oneself is the first boon of a pilgrimage. Secondly, to travel internationally and see another culture, another way of doing things, is a benefit that will change your whole world outlook. Thirdly, to associate with like-minded people—who are looking for something more from the "meaning of life" than work, raising a family, then dying—introduces the principle of "right association" and helps one to "adapt upward." Fourthly, to go to a "sacred site" on the planet expands one's consciousness to the edge of the Absolute. The sublimity of Herakhan is unsurpassed. It is a place on earth that automatically helps one to transcend the mundane and relate to the divine nature of everything. And lastly, to relate to a Being who has freed Himself/Herself from all mental and physical limitations blows your mind and lifts your soul beyond belief! The India Quest, for me, provided all of these benefits.

From 1984 to 1989 I was being prepared for reverence for the teacher, it seemed—with kundalini yoga through Yogi Bhajan, with Rebirthing, the India Quest, and my initial introduction to *A Course in Miracles* through Sondra Ray—for *something* the likes of which I could not quite fathom. In the winter of 1988-89 I blundered upon a cassette tape in a new age bookstore owned by one of my Rebirthing friend's in Exton, PA. The title was *"Bringing A Course in Miracles Into Application,"* by Tara Singh. Interesting, I thought, that a Sikh would be speaking on such a "Christian" scripture. But I knew it was exactly what I needed. All I remember from the recording was the stillness I felt within myself after about twenty minutes of listening. I felt the same stillness and silence in India when we met Sondra Ray's teachers, Shastriji & Muniraj, who were Babaji's main disciples.

Within the case of the cassette tape set was a pamphlet that described Tara Singh's work, his Foundation for Life Action, a federally approved educational foundation. The Foundation sponsored workshops and retreats, and ran a *"school at the branching in the road"* for the serious study of *A Course in Miracles*, in Los Angeles, CA. Tara Singh and a small group of people lived and worked at the Foundation, produced books, recordings of talks, and seminars on the subject of *A Course in Miracles*. From Easter of 1983 to Easter of 1984 this group had conducted a "One Year Non-Commercialized Retreat" for the sake of studying and bringing the principles set forth in *ACIM* into application. This recording, which practically fell into my lap, was a productive result of the one-year retreat. As I listened more to the quality of Mr. Singh's voice, to the peace imparted to me from his words, and from my sustained attention, I became very interested in meeting this man.

After a phone call to the Foundation number, I discovered Mr. Singh would be in my area, at Stony Point, NY, conducting a retreat over the Easter weekend of 1989. I registered immediately and called one of my fellow *ACIM* friends to come with me. My relationship with Tara Singh, from just a few hours of listening to him on the recording, was fast approaching a destiny the likes of which I had no idea would transform my life so completely.

By the time I arrived in Stony Point I no longer wore a beard and a turban that I had donned in my three years as a Sikh with Yogi Bhajan. But I was half expecting Tara Singh to exhibit some quality of the Sikh characteristic of getting to the point, without much ado—and he did. There is a "brotherhood" Sikhs share amongst themselves, and already I felt an affinity toward him from listening to the recordings, and also having studied his original religion of Sikhism. I was soon to discover, though, that Tara Singh transcended all organized religions and would liberate me from them too— but at the same time would take me deeper into the holiness of my own Self than I had ever been before.

The workshop unfolded with Mr. Singh giving two lectures a day—one in the late morning and one in the late afternoon—with meal breaks before and after. There was an atmosphere of relaxation. There was no hype whatsoever. Tara Singh sat silently on the stage for some minutes before beginning his talk. Then we were all engulfed by the stillness and silence imparted from his words, and the intensity of life force that was obviously behind them.

What happened to me during that weekend became the defining moment for me for the next seventeen years. I had the miracle of direct contact with an enlightened being who was my teacher. It was as if the stars lined up for this meeting to take place, and the orbits of my life had all prepared me for this one cosmic alignment. Tara Singh was in front of me as the one who could introduce me to the real use, significance, and application of *A Course in Miracles* in my life. He was the one assigned to me, to my process of awakening, to my soul contract with Divine Forces to fully wake up in this lifetime. He was the miracle of a *master* in my life, one assigned to me of actual flesh and blood who was directly interested in the evolution of my soul.

❖ *Chapter 1.* ❖

Miracle of Miracles

It was jacket weather. The cloudless sky was that clear, deep azure blue you only see on a cool, crisp autumn day. I was driving the car with Tara Singh through the streets of North Philadelphia to the *Miracle House*—a halfway house run by my friend Al Barnes, a fellow *A Course in Miracles* student. Tara Singh had encouraged us to dedicate some of our time to a "service project." *Big Al*, as we called him, was six-feet-five and a gentle giant. The *Miracle House* was his *laboratory* for service—and also mine. Big Al helped drug addicts get clean. I helped Big Al in whatever way I could. This led to me helping Al build some shower rooms in the back of the *Miracle House*, so homeless people would have a place to go to get cleaned up. I worked in the building trades at the time so this was only natural for me.

As he often did in the car, Tara Singh was giving a short talk on lofty subjects, at the same time observing and commenting on the sights and sounds whizzing by outside.

He noticed everything, including the gradual transition into the deteriorating neighborhood of the ghetto. All the while I was driving and *listening* in a state of *full attention*.

With Tara Singh, you had to be willing to have your mind and life fully examined. Self honesty, self inquiry, real soul searching reached such an intensity in his presence that even the most submerged secret, the most hidden concern or fear would surface into the light of full exposure. You could not hide anything. And you could not pretend to know something without having a direct realization of it. This was the forte of Tara Singh's teaching method. He had a way of *pulling the truth* out of you. It was not always comfortable, but it was always transformative and valuable for a person's evolution.

A crescendo in these exchanges increased to an energy of urgency in the very atmosphere. I felt like I was on the "hot seat" while driving the car. But usually a jewel of wisdom came at the end, which would be the catalyst for change. As we were getting closer to the *Miracle House*, Tara Singh was cornering me with a question, "What are you doing with your life?" When I told him all the things I was doing with my work, my house and studio, he pointed out to me that I was complacently stuck at the "survival level" of life, where most people find themselves, going on with my *routines*. I was essentially remaining the same, pursuing enlightenment but making sure not to find it. I was desperately clinging to the "known" of my world I made up, but having a nagging notion of its limitations—and falling far short of life's greater potentials.

After stating this sobering fact to my face, he ended the conversation with this jewel of wisdom:

"In order to go beyond the survival level, you need to make contact with miracles."

The words shot into my heart like an arrow of necessity, like an edict for change that would be a matter of life or death in the throws of my spiritual journey.

By then we arrived at the *Miracle House* and the devastation to my ego had been delivered. We climbed the stairs through a very dark and narrow stairwell to the second floor, and entered a living room filled with a half dozen wide-eyed men and women who were living in the house under Big Al's guidance, who were making an attempt to be productive again by remaining clean from their drug addictions.

There was not a whole lot to say. Some folks who had nearly given up on life, who came from little to no social privilege or education, whose natures were rather raw and visceral, were now meeting a man whose level of refinement had taken him to the highest heights of cultural, political, and spiritual echelons. Tara Singh had close associations with some of the most pre-eminent minds of the 20th century: the likes of Mrs. Eleanor Roosevelt, Supreme Court Justice, William O. Douglass, Mahatma Gandhi, first Prime Minister of India, Jawaharlal Nehru, the world teacher/philosopher Mr. J. Krishnamurti, and the scribe of *A Course in Miracles*, Dr. Helen Schucman.

24

Nevertheless we were there, and this meeting of unlikely acquaintances was taking place. I was in a state of silence brought about by my conversation with Tara Singh in the car. He spoke to this small group of recovering drug addicts in a simple way, suggesting that they find something they like to do and to give. There was little expectation that they would hear what he said, the gulf was so great—yet I could sense the compassion of their hearts coming together, even if their minds could not join him at the level he was speaking. They showed him a child-like respect, and thanked him for inspiring Big Al to start the *Miracle House.* After the conversation completed its cycle, we ushered Tara Singh to the soup kitchen on the first floor, then to the shower rooms we had built in the back of the house for the homeless people to come for a shower, completing our tour in the large hall where the daily meetings were held.

This field trip with Tara Singh ended a major piece of my sentimentality. I recalled a line from Henry David Thoreau— "The greatest service a man can render to his fellow men is to rise to the height of his own being." It was not through "philanthropy" that I would rise to this height, though my service project with Big Al had taught me many lessons about myself, and human nature. It was a contact with my true SELF IDENTITY that would liberate me from the "survival" level where the mass of humanity and I were stuck. And to make this contact I would not need another service project, another halfway house to preoccupy my "do-gooder" tendencies. I would need "miracles"—I would need an awareness that would transcend what I thought were my "best interests."

Miracles are not just supernatural acts that defy gravity and the time/space continuum. Miracles are "shifts in perception" that change a person's whole world-view—a person's whole self-view. They change one's way of "seeing" altogether. They turn the mind upside down and bring new possibilities for life into being. The main *Miracle with my Master* on that day in North Philadelphia was to see that *survival* was at the root of my mindset, and I needed to transcend that if I was going to awaken myself to my full potentials, my true life's purpose. Fortunately, the very miracle I needed I had received already from Tara Singh in the car that day. His willingness to confront me with the status quo of my life got me to see things differently. I had to rise above the conventional response to life, even the conventions of "helping others," in order to come face to face with my own inner poverty. On that day in North Philadelphia I was "disillusioned." I could no longer fool myself into thinking "good works" alone would liberate me from my own motives of survival and ego based preoccupations. I thought I was "doing good" when I was still caught in my self-imposed limitations. I came face to face with the *miracle* in *A Course in Miracles,* and the *miracle* from Tara Singh—a fact that most people's egos never want to see—*"I do not perceive my own best interests."* *

ACIM, Workbook for Students, Lesson #24

❖ *Chapter 2.* ❖

Sondra Ray & A Course in Miracles

In 1986 there was a great optimism in the air. The personal growth seminars were in their zenith, and people were searching for answers in places outside the conventional systems of education. I looked for meaning beyond my own very *unconventional* art school and University experience for a greater spiritual connection. This search had led me to study kundalini yoga with Yogi Bhajan, starting in 1984—and also to receive some sessions of Rebirthing/Breathwork at a center in Philadelphia. All of it was good, and mind expanding. My search came at a time when people were looking for answers not within the systems of study we pursued in college, but within the *inner system* between our head and our heart, between our sophisticated educations and our deeper yearnings to know something more satisfying, more loving and sublime. It was a different time and age of self-introspection. It unfolded in our lives as the *consciousness movement*. It was heralded as the *New Age*.

I had one foot in this *New Age*, but I was not quite prepared to receive the likes of Sondra Ray. She was a force of nature, a dynamo of energy and clarity and joy of a caliber I had never met. A major voice of the Rebirthing process and conscious relationships, Sondra Ray had written many books on the subjects of Rebirthing, how one's birth script affects relationships, loving relationships in general, and Indian spirituality. Her Loving Relationships Training®, the LRT®, was taught at that time all over the country in many major cities, and all over the world as well. It's main content was designed to clear a person of their conditioned family patterns that formed the basis of all their relationships. The LRT® made you more conscious of why your relationships were the way they were. It was a different kind of curriculum. The subject was life itself. I had never attended such a class.

Within the LRT® there were different sections on various Life subjects. But the main principle was this: "Thought always produces a result, so all of one's experiences in life are results of pre-existing thoughts that determine those results." Change your life by first changing your thoughts. No one is ever a victim, but rather the total "maker" of his own life and destiny. Even experiences that seem like "accidents" or events beyond one's control are still the effects of thoughts, be they ever submerged and subconscious. The purpose of the LRT® was to bring the subconscious to the conscious, and by doing so be free, or at least be aware, of self sabotaging *thoughts*.

The other principle of Sondra Ray's LRT® was this: "Love brings up everything unlike itself for the purpose of healing and release." So the main action of the Loving Relationships

Training® was to show a person how much they lived their life *NOT* in a state of love—and thereby begin to make the internal corrections and forgiveness necessary to clear the mind of debilitating and limiting thoughts and memories.

There was a section on God in the LRT®. We looked at all the negative thoughts and programming from our conventional religious indoctrinations—of guilt, fear, punishment, sin, obligation, sacrifice—and the belief of going to a heaven or a hell in the "afterlife." All these submerged beliefs were having their impact on our lives, whether we were aware of them or not. Sondra Ray had made it her mission to free us from these mistakes of false religious theology by which most of us had been programmed.

On the Sunday of the training, during this "God Section" of the LRT®, came a precious stone of wisdom from the queenly crown of Sondra Ray: "I want to introduce you to the most important book written in 2000 years. It is called *A Course in Miracles.*" This was my first real entrée into a *course of study* that would totally transform my life and my entire way of thinking. Sondra not only introduced thousands of people to this modern day scripture in the LRT®, she had also written a study manual to help a student best use *ACIM*, called *Drinking the Divine.*

She continued, "Jesus even said in the Bible, the power of life and death are in the tongue—so, what you say is what you get—and even what you think is what you get." Sondra Ray delivered this message to the participants with perfect certainty that it was the absolute truth. This kind of certainty was something at a higher level than any teaching I had learned in college. This was a *life teaching,* one that rose above the "how to's" and the "accumulated intellectualism" of the academic world from which I had come. Her statements entered the realm of a simple truth that had no opposite.

This was my first introduction into taking 100% responsibility for *all* of my life. If what I say is what I get, and what I think is what I say, then what I think is what I get. It made perfect sense to me. This irrefutable logic proved what Sondra Ray was presenting: "Thought is creative. Negative thoughts produce negative results, just as surely as positive thoughts produce positive results." This is basic metaphysics "101," and she delivered it with the simplicity and clarity that even an eight year old could grasp and understand.

Later I found it was also what Jesus was saying in *A Course in Miracles.* Yet, He was saying something even more lofty in His teaching. He was saying there are thoughts you think in separation from your Divinity, your Source, and Thoughts you think in union with your Source. And the thoughts you think with God are your only *real thoughts.* Either you think thoughts of death, or thoughts of life; either you think the thoughts of relative dualism, of opposites, and therefore with conflict—or the absolute eternal Thoughts of the Oneness of Creation and LIFE IMMORTAL—of LOVE ITSELF. These Thoughts lead a person to total inner peace. There is only one decision to make, and this is it. Which thought system are you going to use? The ego's or the Holy Spirit's are your only two options.

All this, somehow, Sondra Ray got across in one weekend seminar called the Loving Relationships Training®. She had a way of summarizing the essence of a thing into a few potent and mind provoking statements. Her words would sear into your mindset like a branding iron of truth, leaving their mark far after the trauma of facing all your garbage. All the "unlike itself" would come up, all the dark side of "not love," all the consequences that *free will* allowed us *make up* in order to cause ourselves our own suffering and pain.

My eyes were *opened* quite a lot by Sondra Ray. The Loving Relationships Training® and Rebirthing were two of the most powerful transformative tools I encountered in my search for greater truth after my graduation from the University. *A Course in Miracles* was at the head of these teachings, and Sondra Ray was one of the main harbingers of its utmost importance. She changed the course of my life, sending it in a wild new direction. It was a journey that part of me knew very well, that part of me had agreed to travel, even before taking a birth. It was a journey I would take toward my total liberation in this lifetime, even to the very ends of the earth to realize and fulfill. It was a *journey to the East* that would blow my mind and rearrange my whole destiny.

❖ Chapter 3. ❖

Journey to the East

The journey to India went in the direction of East, through
Europe, with a change of planes in Frankfort. There was a
layover, about six hours, so we went into the city to have a
good meal and to bide our time. Our flight to New Delhi
would leave in the late afternoon, and arrive in the middle of
the night in India. The whole trip would keep us on the road
for over 24 hours. For unseasoned travelers that was a long
journey, and we were certainly unseasoned. We arrived on the
other side of the globe feeling as though we had been through
a gauntlet of sleep deprivation mixed with a punishment of
sitting. When the taxi dropped us at the Centaur Hotel, not far
from the New Delhi International Airport, it appeared as an
oasis for burned out crusaders on a quest for anything
horizontal resembling a bed—much less a launch pad for a
pilgrimage to the "Mecca" of spiritual heights that would
transform our lives beyond the believable.

It was not until late morning the next day that we landed
in our bodies and gained full realization of where we were.

The atmosphere was pleasantly aromatic in ways that only India can be—with smells that were coaxing and indelible to our senses. The hotel was beautiful and dramatic. There was a central atrium of open space that went the full height of the building, capped with sky-lit domes, making the whole interior of the lobby seem palatial. We ventured down to the first floor on elevators with glass walls, so one could see the wide vistas and beautiful inlaid marble floors of the atrium from many moving levels. Soon we found the restaurant and began to bump into other India Questers with Sondra Ray's group. They were from all over the world, but many from Australia and New Zealand.

It was apparent the service in India was different. Labor was divided into the smallest increments of work tasks. One man took the order; another man brought the water to the table, another took the order to the kitchen—someone else brought the food and served it, and another would check in. The original waiter was never seen again. And the whole process took an hour or more. There was no such thing in India as *fast*—or *efficient*. To a Western mind this could be disconcerting. And the more disconcerted you became, the less efficiently things worked, until finally you realized that whatever you thought in India manifested with instantaneous force and confirmation. Being very careful what thoughts you dwelled on became a necessity. At that time Westerners still had a sense of "superiority" over the other races and cultures of the world. So it was easy to get upset in this culture where things did not work as well, or the people exhibited a slowness and unworldly naiveté. That was what happened with many

33

Western visitors who would not allow their *western mindsets* to fall apart. They got very irritated and missed the whole point of surrendering to something *uncontrollable.*

And that was one of the premises of the India Quest—to surrender to a Higher Power that was not of your own making. In fact, that Power was the force of Creation itself, the force of your own creation. It was a surrendering to LIFE in capital letters. It was a surrendering to God that had no belief system attached to It. It was a surrendering to the mystery of the Unknown that kept the universe going, but nevertheless could not be explained away with the intellect. The India Quest in 1987 for me was a tremendous leap of faith that I would discover something more meaningful than I had ever known before. It introduced me to a purpose for living that transcended my little world of "accumulated knowledge" and connected me with a movement of such magnificence that even the orbits of the planets would seem small in comparison. I went on the India Quest to have my mind blown away—and it was.

The group met for orientation that evening, and the next day was used to explore New Delhi on our own. Taking the three wheeled "took-took" taxi into Connaught Place was an adventure in itself, a kind of open-air carnival ride through a wide range of socio economic dioramas. In the center of New Delhi was a bustling chaos of traffic of all kinds, adding new meaning to my notion of a *busy city.* I knew what "busy city" meant in terms of New York and Chicago, or Philadelphia. They seemed mild in comparison. Yet an Asian *busy city* added another dimension to my urban experience—it felt rambunctious and raw, like an amusement park gone haywire, with rides spinning in every direction off the track. It was a hustle and bustle with no rhyme or reason. It was a pile of population unregulated. If a city encounter could have been compared to my first sex, it would have been *unprotected*.

These excursions under our belt, we all gathered early on the third day to leave New Delhi for "points north." It was about an eight hour bus ride that we endured on narrow dusty roads, often shared with brahma bulls and bullock carts, with lines of walking women in saris carrying loads of firewood, water pots, sheaves of grasses and everything domestically imaginable on their poised and stalwart heads. India was the 20th century and the 15th century superimposed on one another, all playing out simultaneously. From the vantage point of the bus window, I was glad to be a spectator, not a participant, in this drama of human survival that seemed incredibly raw and rudimentary to my western sense of facility and refinement. I had not known how *sheltered* my life in the West had been, even hailing from a lower middle class background, until looking this sight in the face—of how most of the world's population lives at the level of daily survival, scratching the surface of a laborious existence just to come up with the basic living needs. My eyes were widening into a broader scope of counting my blessings.

When the bus pulled into Haldwani, a bustling town on the northern edge of the province of Uttar Pradesh, we were all a bit haggard and jostled. It was an eight-hour bus ride over rough riding Indian roads, passing what seemed an endless string of bustling towns and villages along the way. We pulled into the Mountain View Hotel, and welcomed the rooms with cots and Indian bathrooms with cold running water. Buckets become essential in India. Water pails are the mainstay of domestic affairs from showering to cooking to necessities. In the hinder lands the first thing you buy is a bucket—if you are smart and thinking ahead.

After a meal in the town we all gathered for a meeting in the Hotel, where we would sing the Aarti together, a chant sung in Sanskrit to a simple tune played on a small, hand-pumped organ called a harmonium. The Aarti is sung all over India as a daily devotional prayer, but this particular version was sung in Herakhan by Babaji and his followers, and had special significance to the India Quest and Sondra Ray. The yogis in Herakhan were meditating in the cave where Babaji had manifested His body, and the words to this Aarti (which means offering of lights) appeared in the air in gold, as if descending from on high for their benefit to write down— which they gladly did. This hymn became the mainstay of worship for those close to Babaji, and it became the mainstay of worship for the India Quest as well. We would sing the Aarti twice a day, 7AM and 7PM, without exception. As we sang the Aarti that evening in our preparation for hiking into Herakhan the next day, we were met with the most incredible boon. Muniraj, Babaji's main disciple, appeared with dozens of sandalwood malas, strings of 108 beads, to give to each person in the group. As we sang the Aarti, each of us went up to Muniraj and he bestowed around our neck a blessing from Babaji, our first devotional tool—a sandalwood mala. This was a seemingly simple act with un-seemingly great significance.

36

One could feel the saintliness of Muniraj's touch and graceful movements. He was a man in total inner peace. We got our night of rest to wake early the next day, to be taken to the edge of town to a place called the "dam site." This was the trailhead to Herakhan, where we would embark on a five-hour journey up the river valley through the mountain ranges to Babaji's remote ashram. Fortunately we had a cadre of porters to carry all of our bags, so we only had to manage ourselves over trails and river fords on our hike through the Himalayan foothills. The trek was unspeakably beautiful, but there were times when we had to cross the river where rapids moved swiftly and nearly swept us away downstream. Fortunately the porters were also seasoned guides and trekkers, so with their help the whole group arrived safely—even the stragglers who took extra time to make it, going the *long way* over hill and dale.

I remember my first impression of the Herakhan gateway of gardens and buildings on the banks of the Ganga River—I thought I had arrived in Shangri La, a place of remarkable purity and beauty that transcended any place I had ever seen. It *was* a Shangri La of course, but I would grow to recognize that is was a Shangri La inside myself that I discovered. Herakhan is not primarily a place—it is a state of being. It is a place within yourself that hearkens to know who you are as God created you. It is a place of the heart that transcends the brain, and makes contact with the very holiness of existence. It imparts a very sacred quality that makes us human beings, capable of knowing a force of life that is immortal and never tastes the pangs of death. It is a state of absolute liberation from all that is not love and joy and happiness in ourselves. Herakhan may very well be the center of the universe, the seedbed of a compassion the likes of which are unsurpassed anywhere else on the planet. But it is most certainly the symbolic center of all human aspiration and purpose in which the flowering of the soul comes to completion. It is where the soul goes to evolve and to meld itself and be one with the universal forces of love and all of life. It is a state of mind within that realizes the universal nature of the Self, of the OM that is the first sound of original existence. Herakhan is the quintessential home of miracles.

This travel to the East was the great gift that Sondra Ray gave to me, and thousands of others, as even today she ferries people to Herakhan to the feet of the Master, to the feet of their true Self. This was the beginning of my real quest to know my Self. India is imbued with the search for truth, with the spiritual journey of a soul towards its total God-realization. It has its many distractions and problems like all other countries, but the essence of its highest aspiration and truth as a culture is this passion for the spirit, its passion for knowing God and truth directly. The yogis and the saints of India are Her national treasures, Her contributions to the overtures of humanity's greatest accomplishments. India has produced philosopher saints by the thousands. This travel to the East was my entrée into a quest for truth that was only a beginning of real purpose in my life. It gave me pause to reconsider my priorities. It launched me in the right direction. It gave me a real alternative to the conditioned lifestyle of survival that most people never wake up from in their dream world of conventional life. The India Quest of Sondra Ray brought me more inner transformation than 20 years of schooling. It was a great blessing that gave me a pure intention—to travel to a place within myself of eternal peace and joy.

❖ *Chapter 4.* ❖

An Easter Encounter

It was the end of winter in the Philadelphia, so we were tired of the dull gray color of everything. The first George Bush had just moved into the Oval Office. Cracks in the Iron Curtain were beginning to appear. Gorbachev was introducing more open policies in the Soviet Union. "Glasnost," he called them. So things were changing, things were moving forward, it seemed. Yet on the third day of spring the Exxon Valdez dumped 240,000 barrels of oil on the pristine Alaskan shoreline due to a foolhardy and drunken captain of the ship. The extent of the human drama seemed far-reaching, even into the wilderness of territories hitherto unpeopled. It was apparent there was not a spot on the planet unaffected by human consequences.

These were some of the events in 1989 that occupied the news. I had been studying *A Course in Miracles* for nearly four years and recently blundered into a recording by Tara Singh speaking about bringing the *Course* into application in my life.

It was not to be *learned*, he said, it was to be *lived*. And between learning and living *A Course in Miracles* there was a vast difference. It was apparent the world needed miracles, but what was a person to do to make them real in their life, to make them actual, not just some good idea memorized out of a book?

I sensed the urgency in this question, but certainly had no answer that was satisfactory. All that changed when I heard the voice of Tara Singh speaking on the nature of the human condition, which was determined by each person's attachment to thought, and to problems of thought. This attachment kept him unwilling to go for the solutions of a still mind, a mind at peace with itself and the universe around it. With Tara Singh the answers were not external. The real questions were basic to life, and everyone, regardless of nationality, race, culture, or creed, were subject to these basic life issues. He had discovered politics could not solve them; technology could not solve them; more intellectual learning could not solve them; religions and belief systems could not solve them. The issues of fear, of survival, of self-Identity, of meeting these basic needs of life, these physical, mental and spiritual imperatives, all from a common stalk—all these essential issues stemmed from a basic need to know who we are as God created us, who we are in the most *real sense*. We must be aware we are connected to the Divine Intelligence that rules and runs not only our own life, but the whole life of the Universe of galaxies, stars and planets, solar systems and literally, everything in the cosmos.

There was something in the quality of Tara Singh's voice that captivated me to hear more, to listen deeper, to pay more attention to the words he was saying. "Do you have the ears to hear?" he would ask. Ears to hear what, I wondered. "Are you able to listen, to really listen?" Again he would make the subject of his talk the very thing that you had to face in yourself by listening. "Why do you give so much meaning to your own opinions? Are they facts?" The lectures on the recordings brought my mind to a new understanding of attention. Tara Singh was speaking in statements of simple truths, simple facts, step by step, one by one, whose combined impact built to a level of undisputable clarity. Moving from one fact to the other, my mind would come to stillness, quietude and a silence the likes of which I did not know possible from listening to spoken words before. Later I would realize he was not speaking about more information. He was actually subtracting things from my mind, taking away the preoccupations of thought. By doing so, my whole being became immersed in a kind of attention that was more whole, more engaging of all my senses, and more *awakening* to all the systems of my awareness. It was nothing particular, having no pre-conceived direction, but in general using each particular statement to open and extend my mind into an overall awareness, a kind of silence, a kind of all pervasive observation that included everything.

Tara Singh could stop my own brain chatter and introduce me to a broader use of my mind that was not restricted to my personal sense of self. He introduced me to a Self all right, but it was the larger Self connected to universal intelligence, a Self healed and whole in the perfection of its holiness; a Self not restricted to limitations and the fears of survival, not limited by the particulars of my personal history and memory. This *Self* is shared by all human beings, irrespective of their race, nationality, socio-economic background, and particular personal experiences. The words spoken on that set of cassette tapes totally transformed my outlook on what it meant to be objective, to be wise and intelligent. I had not met anyone of this caliber in my life—of that I was certain. And I had been to two colleges, had my Masters degree in art and humanities, and had met many brilliant professors over that period of ten years. Tara Singh transcended them all. He was in a league all by himself, speaking from the certainty of an actual truth that existed beyond thought itself, beyond the constructs of intellectual "knowing". He was a force of life to be reckoned with—and something deep within my core told me I had to reckon with him.

I drove with a friend of mine, who had been studying *A Course in Miracles* with me for a few years, up the Palisades Parkway to Stony Point, New York. We went to attend a retreat with Tara Singh over the Easter weekend at the end of March in 1989. We stayed in a small retreat center there, simple in its accommodations, yet quite adequate in filling all the requirements for meeting a spiritual master. Tara Singh would speak in person on this most lofty spiritual self-help manual that was available in our modern day. A unique scripture, written in our English language, it came out of New York City in the 1970's through what seemed like the most unexpected people and setting. Scribed by Dr. Helen

43

Schucman, a clinical psychologist at Columbia University, *A Course in Miracles* contains the words of Jesus, the Christ Mind. It leads the student to discover his own Christ Mind within himself. Tara Singh, Stony Point, and *A Course in Miracles* all came together on that weekend of spring thaw to provide me with a remarkable opportunity to make contact with something authentic and intrinsic in myself. This weekend held out for me the opportunity for self-transformation right in my own backyard.

Tara Singh would have agreed with Sondra Ray—*ACIM* is the most important book written in 2000 years. And for the one who is serious about his or her enlightenment, it provides the necessary exercises to elevate a student to a whole new level of spiritual awareness hitherto unavailable through conventional religious means. In fact *A Course in Miracles* is for the working person in the world who has experienced a certain degree of religious disillusionment and is looking for another way to realize a spiritual and holy lifestyle. I knew this was true about the *Course* when I met Tara Singh, yet it was my relationship with him over the next seventeen years that would put the whole urgency of its message into total perspective, one that would affect my greater life destiny. This holy relationship with a Master made my encounters with *A Course in Miracles* actual to my life, not merely intellectual exercises.

The meeting room at Stony Point was spacious, with a view of the grounds behind us, and before us a low stage that rose a few steps above the audience. On the evening of arrival, after the dinner meal, we all gathered in anticipation of the first evening talk of the workshop. There was a chair on the stage, empty, beside a small side-table with a vase of flowers and a copy of *A Course in Miracles*. A glass of water was on the table too. We sat quietly awaiting Tara Singh's arrival on the stage, and this crescendo of quietude intensified the anticipation. I recall he was not exactly on time, perhaps still absent five or ten minutes after the posted hour of commencement on the schedule. Then he came with no introduction.

A man of medium height in his late sixties, perhaps early seventies, climbed the few steps to the stage and sat unannounced in the simple cushioned chair. He was poised, wearing a sharp pair of slacks, dress shoes, a shirt, tie and sport jacket.... quite distinguished in his appearance and Western in his overall attire. He sat erect and faced the audience, looking silently around at the participants, as though he was sizing up each person in the multitude of listeners, making some inner inventory that connected him personally with each one. When his gaze fell on me I felt penetrated—not in an intrusive way, but in a way that connected me to the powerful essence of his energy and life force. I saw this was a man of conviction, a person whose presence and words had no superfluous parts, and no motives that sought my approval.

Tara Singh closed his eyes and sat in the stillness and quiet of the moment. As we were there to hear him speak and absorb the energy he was transmitting, we all entered into this quietude that surrounded him and emanated from this Presence he naturally invoked. This silence went on for

45

minutes as we lost track of time and entered into another dimension of peace and quiet within ourselves. It was only after this Presence was palpably felt that Tara Singh began to speak, as though he was waiting for this energy to descend upon the room and envelope himself and the participants as a benediction to the seriousness of what he was to say. I was touched as the quality of my attention intensified, and he had not yet said a word!

"I have nothing to teach," he began to say with the authority of certainty. "You all know too much already." Wow, that was different, I thought. *A teacher who has nothing to teach*—I had never met such a teacher. I sat in a state of shock. "You have learned a lot of things," he continued. "You have learned how to be insecure, greedy, limited and afraid. You have learned how to be an American, a Democrat or a Republican. You have learned to speak Chinese, or English, or French, and to think your country is better than all the rest." He proceeded to speak undisputable facts about how the human brain operated. "A true teacher has nothing to teach, " he went on, "he comes to undo—to undo what you have already learned. He comes to free you of your conditioned thought. He comes to take away your opinions, belief systems and prejudices—and you would want to stone such a person." More and more stillness entered the room. You could hear a pin drop in the space between Tara Singh's statements. He was presenting facts that I did not necessarily want to hear, but nevertheless were exactly the statements I needed to hear. He was liberating me from my illusions, from my flimsy sentimental opinions about others, and myself from my thoughts of life and the meaning of life.

He went on to speak about a wide range of life subjects. He made it clear that there was nothing more to learn, that we had accumulated enough "knowledge" already. In fact, knowledge was the storehouse of memory, and within memory was the source of all of our problems, all of our conflicts, all of our troubles and unhappiness. We needed to come to a "still mind" free of the conditioning of thought. He asked us if it was possible for us to "rest the brain," to suspend the normal workings of thought long enough to make contact with a different energy, a different quality of attention and awareness that was not subject to our opinions about things, about ourselves, about our life. In short, Tara Singh was imparting the energy of the first ten lessons from the Workbook of *A Course in Miracles*: "Nothing I see means anything."—"I see only the past."—and, "My thoughts do not mean anything." In the space left behind his words there was a stillness and a deep quiet the likes of which I had never experienced or heard. He was shocking my thought into silence. It was exactly the quality of energy I had experienced in India in the presence of Muniraj, except Tara Singh was transmitting it through the speaking of *true words*, indisputable facts that were not subject to the debate of my opinions.

A revolution was going on in my mind. I was almost enthralled by the sound of Tara Singh's voice in that atmosphere of silence, which I came later to understand was brought about by attention. This was a full attention that was concerned only with the facts of "what is," not containing any

47

opinions, prejudices or any opposing views, but rather the truth of the psychological and everyday conditions in which we find ourselves. Tara Singh was naturally a great psychologist, though I found out later he had only a few years of formal schooling. He made fun in his talks of the limitations of learning. "C—a—t spells cat," he would say in his poke-fun comments on how we are conditioned and led by authorities and educational systems to not have our own mind. But this is not to be misconstrued, as Tara Singh had the utmost respect for higher education. But his point was that education in the West stops short in the most basic teachings that transform a person from the inside out. In the West, he would say, education is focused on acquiring skills. The traditional education in the East focused more on the type of human being you would awaken into; it was an education of values. Without undoing the internal impurities inside—like fear, anger, envy, attachment, dis-honesty, self-centeredness, etc.— then all of the skills in the world would not bring about a truly happy and productive individual, and therefore not bring about a truly happy and productive society. In a society of incessant "how to's" Tara Singh was asking the question of "why," "what for," and "to what end?"

The Easter weekend of 1989 was a turning point for me. I began to question everything in my life as a result of meeting Tara Singh. The stories he told about his own process of awakening were very interesting, and demonstrated that everyone goes through a process of waking up. For him, the *teachers* he met in his life were crucial to this process. And these teachers were not necessarily found in schools, they were

48

found in the arena of life itself—in the encounters he had with the wise ones whom life put in his path. They came without him seeking them, but nevertheless were essential in his discovering his true Self-Identity, function and mission. Because he met the wise, and received the lessons from those meetings and fully integrated them, he could recognize the qualities of real wisdom instantly. It was this ability to divide the absolute truth from the relative "truths" of conditioned belief that made him free of all self-deceptions. He possessed an objective mind that could cut through the subterfuge of any mental confusion, opinion, assumption, conclusion, or otherwise conditioned thought. Tara Singh was a man who simply could not be deceived or influenced by false points of view. He had a mind like a crystal clear diamond that could cut through even the densest slag of prevailing belief, motive or vested interest. He lived as a mystic, totally defenseless in a state of motiveless action. It was his mission not to merely share *A Course in Miracles,* but to rise to the actuality of miracles in his own life—and to extend these possibilities, realized in himself, to all who made contact with him through his books, recordings and workshops. He had a ministry, no doubt, but it had no pretense of a church or religion, or even an organization. For practical reasons he operated out of the Foundation for Life Action, later to become the Joseph Plan Foundation, but the real basis of his mission came from his acute conviction and understanding that his life was fully an extension of the will of his Creator. What is called "God's Plan for Salvation" in *ACIM* became integrally the whole purpose of Tara Singh's life and work. And at the root of this Plan was his conviction that "the human being comes first." His whole mission was an extension of *life for life*, holy relationships. Every student who passed through his door had the blessings of this conviction.

I was impressed at such a deep level I could not fathom the changes that would take place in me over the next seventeen years. I was touched by the stillness and peace surrounding Tara Singh, but I still had my own life to deal with, to transform. Though I knew what was being said was absolutely true, I also realized the internal undoing in myself would have to be my top priority in my life to bring the principles of *A Course in Miracles* and the words of Tara Singh into application. The Stony Point Easter retreat brought a new order to my life. The importance of stillness and quietude became readily apparent. Just devoting some of my time to meditation, to reading the lessons in an unpressured way, to being more disciplined with the application of the lessons, and also to take on to "love another more than myself," these were the benefits readily received from four days of being with the wisdom of Tara Singh. It was a *life for life* bond initiated on that Easter morning between this man and me. It was a call to rise within the light of holy relationship in which motives and ego desires were dissolved. I was stepping into that grace of holy relationship without fully knowing what it was. The all-pervasive extent I would be swept into this life action would demand of me total inner transformation. Tara Singh had planted the seeds that began to grow inexorably into the giant sequoia of the True Self within my whole heart and awareness. He had changed the whole direction of my destiny in a matter of a few hours of lectures on an early spring weekend amidst the thawing grounds of my frozen and conditioned mind. The flame of inner transformation had been lit within me, and there was no turning back now. The direction to go all the way toward total Self-realization in this lifetime was made clear to me, with Tara Singh as my newly found and providential guide.

❖ *Chapter 5.* ❖

40 Days in the Wilderness

New Mexico had always been one of my favorite places in the whole of the United States. It's state motto is "land of enchantment," written on its auto license plate. It is the land of pueblos, of Georgia O'Keefe, one of my favorite painters, and where D.H Lawrence spent a spell writing in Taos for a few years of his life. Taos is nearly just a crossroads, but there is something in the vibe of New Mexico that is spiritually charged, something unworldly that feels descended upon by a dimension inaccessible to realms in East Coast cities such as New York and Philadelphia. In 1989, it seemed to be a crossroads of another reality, a sacred space that was *unidentified*, flying into one's consciousness from other worlds, yet nevertheless an *object* of tremendous palpability. One could just sense that if aliens were going to land and be well received on planet earth, New Mexico would be an outpost of receptivity, a landing pad for the far reaching possibilities of a more universal life force. If choosing a place for a spiritual quest in America sought all the elements of wide-open dioramas, majestic mountains, picturesque vistas of wooded yet arid landscapes, New Mexico would be the place. It retained the energy of the indigenous people's sense of sacred space, and is a likely candidate to uplift you out of the doldrums of urban sympathies and condolences.

It was no accident I ended up there with Tara Singh for the *Forty Days in the Wilderness* retreat in Angel Fire, New Mexico, only two weeks after Easter of 1989. I was on fire myself, and I could not get enough of the Presence that surrounded him. His true words entered my heart like a stream of ever cleansing clarity spoken in every utterance of his masterful sessions. It was no accident that very remote but spacious lodge hotel in Angel Fire was the setting for this six-week retreat. I had to disengage from the home life of my busy world in Philadelphia, and make the space for six weeks off of work. This in itself took a lot of conviction and courage to move through my fears.

The ski resort of Angel Fire is situated just east of Taos in the Sangre de Christo Mountains, translated as the "blood of Christ" mountains. How appropriate a setting it was for the vortex of energy I found myself in—studying *A Course in Miracles*, the most current words of the Christ in print, with one of the pre-eminent voices of this modern day scripture in Tara Singh.

One would think it to be virtually impossible to disengage for six weeks from any routine, no matter how loose and open ended it was. I worked as an independent contractor at the time in the building trades, so I had dominion over my own schedule. But even then, I was still in the momentum of various contracts and projects that had to be accounted for and completed. Yet the space opened up like the parting of the Red Sea. I was able to leave my foreman in charge of most of the work—enough to satisfy my commitments to my customers and workers—and the rest could wait until my return in late May. I had the money at the time to take the time off, so life provided the space and the means for me to attend this unprecedented event in the Spring of 1989 in Angel Fire. The momentum of my business was transformed into the greater momentum of this spiritual necessity. It was a miracle of sorts not to be confined to the limitations of thought—"I don't have the time," or "I don't have the money," or "I don't have the will power to make this unorthodox decision." All these checks and balances I levied on myself were blown apart by my first meeting with Tara Singh. He established a different priority of urgency and importance. This priority was liberation from the limited, conditioned and conventional life of the "self I made," so I may discover my actual state of being as the "Self God created." The *40 Days in the Wilderness Retreat* was apparently God's answer to my prayers. It was a beginning of the certainty I had around Tara Singh that *A Course in Miracles* provided the most significant encounter I had in my life with the Christ Consciousness, and that a real flesh and blood teacher could transmit its truths, in actual form, in actual relationship to me, as its student. Tara Singh and *ACIM* became one in the same at that moment of certainty. Our relationship was to become the laboratory of application

54

that he had spoken of in those first audiotapes I had purchased just a few months before. He was becoming the very person I would take on to "love more than myself," to fulfill the assignment he had given at the Easter workshop just a few weeks before.

I arrived at Angel Fire Resort reeling from the whirlwind of decisions I had to make in order to create the time, money and logistics to get myself there. There was an aura of newness and adventure that permeated the atmosphere around Tara Singh, the resort hotel, and the staff of the Foundation who prepared for our auspicious retreat. A dozen or so people came from the Foundation in California to manage these preparations. They served to greet and register the people, arrange the rooming lists, set up the recording equipment, tend to hotel & retreat paperwork, bring in flowers for the conference hall, and set up a prayer room to house the Altar and the pictures of the Holy Beings brought from the Foundation's house in Los Angeles. I was happy to be situated in a spacious double room with a man from North Carolina who had been studying the *Course* for a number of years. One part of me was delighted to be there, yet another part was asking myself what had I just committed myself to, investing so much time and money on my spiritual awakening? Was I being practical? Was this what I needed? Soon these concerns dissolved into a deep gratitude.

It was wonderful to be free of all the daily jobs and routines. Tara Singh gave two talks a day—like he always did in the workshops. One began around 9:30 AM and went until lunchtime, and the other began around 4:00 PM and ended just before the dinner hour. At the *40 Days in the Wilderness Retreat* there was an around the clock prayer vigil. Because over 100 people were attending the event, the Foundation set up an Altar and a prayer room in which the silence of prayer was honored, and two people would sit in chairs before the Altar in silent prayer for one-hour slots, switching on each half hour. It took 48 people to complete the vigil for one day, and each person was assigned a time in which he would come to the prayer room to sit for his/her hour. Of course one's time may be at 4:00AM, but it did not matter. Everyone was happy to have a time sitting at the Altar in silence. On the Altar were a set of consecrated Altar pieces, (a polished brass cross and two lit candle sticks), *A Course in Miracles,* a Bible, and some simple vases of flowers. Hanging on the walls and behind the Altar were pictures of many Holy Beings. These were beings such as Jesus, Moses, Krishna, Buddha, Quan Yin, and other holy figures from more ancient times—as well as Ramakrishna, Krishnamurti, Ramana Maharshi, Mother Teresa, the teacher of the Dalai Lama, and Dr. Schucman from our own modern times. These were the main figures represented, but there were many more Holy Beings who were hanging on the walls. Their Presence resulted in a very strong frequency being built up in the room that brought a person's mind automatically to silence. As soon as one walked into the space, this frequency of silence in the atmosphere was palpable. It was a depth of peace and quiet that was undeniable. People could go in anytime, and there were chairs for those who were not officially sitting at the Altar. The chain of the prayer vigil was kept unbroken for the whole 40 days. Not for one instant was there an absent space at the Altar—everyone honored their time assigned no matter what the hour of the day or night, and the energy in the room was accumulative. By the end of the 40 days the prayer room was charged with a definite holiness that was otherworldly and inspiring, and we had all contributed to invoking this sacred Presence.

I was well rested after a few days. The silence and stillness that took place in the sessions were beginning to have their calming effects on my whole system. The pressures of daily life were absent. I began to really relax, perhaps in a deeper way than I had ever done before in my adult life—or perhaps in my whole life. The times before the sessions in the morning were glorious. It gave me the opportunity to go early and take my seat in the front rows, and be in the meditation of a deep inner quietude. People at the retreat honored this quietude, and even prepared themselves to receive the lecture in a reverential way. One became attuned to a different teacher/student relationship. It was a new kind of sacredness that was awakening inside myself, a new quality of attention to the content of my mind, to the words spoken by the wise, and by the absolute stillness and silence that accompanied the words of Tara Singh and *A Course in Miracles.* As a teacher who Dr. Schucman ordained to share the lessons contained in the *ACIM,* Tara Singh rose to this role and brought people to the *actual state of mind* that the lessons were describing. He did not indulge in what he called "learning the knowledge of the about," but rather insisted on bringing his audience to the real moment of reckoning. Either you were in the stillness and silence of the peace of God, which *A Course in Miracles* imparts, or you were not. Learning "about" what it was saying would just be more meaningless thought. Tara Singh was only concerned with transmitting the *actual state* of God's holy Presence, which he had mastered. His talks offered this.

I sat in the front row day after day and allowed my newfound teacher to take me into this Presence of silence. He would undo, for certain, the ego beliefs and assumptions family, society, educational systems, church and state had conditioned me into. He would leave no belief unchallenged. Even people who *loved* their pets more than their family members were challenged. People who thought they knew *A Course in Miracles* were challenged. People who were stuck in jobs they did not like, remaining at the survival level were challenged. People who wanted to control their children and others in their family were challenged. Couples who were not in harmony with one another were challenged. In fact none were left alone from the questioning process that Tara Singh brought to bear. He was pointing out very direct and disconcerting facts about how totally conditioned the human brain has become, even in a world that considers itself advanced and progressive. How so few have come to a direct relationship with the life force of the divine, but are dissipated by the conflicts that their own thoughts perpetuate. We have all fallen "victim" of our opinions and beliefs, Tara Singh would point out, and these are keeping us limited and divided as human beings. In turn we become fearful and conditioned in the larger society. Basically he was pointing out the hell we had made in our attempts to make ourselves separate and special.

During the times between the sessions I would walk along the remote roads amidst the clear mountain air, and feel the cool breezes of a coming spring blow over the sage brush and the groves of scrubby pines. Pondering the sessions and the words of Tara Singh became my real daily bread, and the times in the session room were the fruits of a real cornucopia. On the walks I could take it all in and meld the vastness of the internal space the lectures were creating inside me with the tremendously beautiful and open spaces of nature in the New Mexican landscape. I had the best of both worlds in which the glory and magnificence of the spirit transmitted from Tara Singh's words met the vastness and beauty of this natural and pristine wilderness. The *40 days in the Wilderness Retreat* was a blessing that money could not buy. It was my fantastic fate that I blundered into Tara Singh, and was given by life this remarkable opportunity to spend time in his wisdom and aura, in the quietude of my own Self, and in the magnificence of a beautiful natural setting with like minded people.

Between the two talks a day in which Tara Singh brought some aspect of *A Course in Miracles* into the light of application, and the time spent in the Prayer room with the silence and the Holy Beings, the *40 Days in the Wilderness Retreat* was by far one of the holiest events in my life I had experienced in my homeland. America had been given *A Course in Miracles*. America had produced a being in Dr. Schucman who could bring in this remarkable scripture. And India had sent a man from its heritage to be the voice to deliver its importance and absolute significance to the world. And there in New Mexico I found myself a part of this sacred occasion that Tara Singh and the people of his Foundation for Life Action were initiating. It was a blessing beyond my understanding, yet there I was a part of it. I was developing a bond with a man the likes of which I had never known, and even then did not fully understand the forces behind this bond. The words he spoke daily in the sessions entered my heart and performed alchemy on my soul. If ever there was a relationship that transcended my own thought, it had its seeds planted and nurtured during this 40 days in New Mexico in the spring of 1989. I had been to the sacred waters of the Ganges in India, to the holy fires of Babaji and the Divine Mother in Herakhan, to the silent communion with the saints of the Himalayas, Muniraj and Shastriji, to the depth of clearing and appreciation of my breath with Rebirthing—but to the space of the Holy Mind that transcended all thought and physicality, it was my holy relationship with my master, Tara Singh, that provided the miracles for this awakening to occur. At the *40 Days in the Wilderness Retreat* I woke up to something glorious in myself. Love was revealed to me to depths I could not have fathomed by just reading *A Course in Miracles* on my own.

❖ *Chapter 6.* ❖

The Holy Beings

Growing up in the Methodist Church in Mount Vernon, Ohio, I was accustomed to seeing pictures of Jesus in Sunday school, and in the illustrated Bibles and study books that we were given as children. Even in the sanctuary of our Gay Street United Methodist Church there were stained glass windows that depicted scenes from His life, and carvings of various religious symbols on the altar and the pulpit, as well as on the woodwork making up the choir loft behind the ministers' place that faced the congregation. As far as I was taught in Sunday school, Jesus was the "only Son of God" who came to redeem us by dying for our "sins," and then by resurrecting Himself on the third day after a very gruesome death and betrayal—therefore meriting worship on our part. And thus, He was the only one deserving of an image of Himself in our church. Mary was talked about, but as far as statues or paintings of Mary, they just did not exist in the protestant faith. Those were left for the Catholics in Mount Vernon to sort out, and even those were confined to one Catholic church building in our town. The protestant churches of many varieties were numerous, and equally iconoclastic. Methodists were not exactly as stark as Puritans, but we were certainly understated when it came to religious iconography. It was a perspective that was limiting, not to say downright exclusive of any sacred being who did not hail from the Main Street version of "old time religion"—which in this case was only one, Jesus Christ our Lord and Savior.

Practicing yoga and going to India changed the whole religious scene for me. I no longer saw "holiness" as an exclusive commodity of the Christian church. Though the whole point of studying *A Course in Miracles* was to get closer to Jesus and the true essence of His Being, my mind was opened to a more egalitarian view of the possibility of beings just as evolved and saintly as Him. This was no longer a matter of Jesus being the "only Son of God" for me. Having been to Babaji's ashram in the Himalayas and having a direct encounter with real live holy beings in my midst, my mindset was blown wide open. So meeting Tara Singh was just an extension of that openness.

When Tara Singh began his ministry of sharing *A Course in Miracles* under the auspices of the Foundation for Life Action in Los Angeles, he placed a picture of Jesus over the Altar in the session room. But soon the inkling came to him that there was something "off" in that gesture of paying special homage. "I do not want to be alone," was the communication from that Presence of the Christ energy. Jesus saw the false theology that put Him on a pedestal and discounted all the other

62

enlightened beings who had walked upon the planet since time immemorial. So Tara Singh took that intimation and transformed the session room into a Prayer Room. Not only did he have the best pictures of Jesus, the Christ, above the Holy Altar, but he also had a couple dozen other pictures of Holy Beings from all times and cultures surrounding the Altar on the walls around the room. It was a coming together of the Great Rays of Enlightenment who had ever incarnated to impart the light of truth, to bring the Light of God to these physical dimensions. One encountered a palpable wave of stillness and silence entering this small room. One felt a hush of heaven in the very atmosphere that was transformed by the Presence of so many of these Beings congregated in one place. It offered a slice of nirvana in the midst of the routines and pressures of modern life. It was a refuge of rest and beauty far beyond even the most tranquil places of nature you could ever imagine. It was Jerusalem and Mecca, the Ganges and Varanasi, Sinai and Kailash all consolidated into one small chamber of absolute peace and devotion.

The Prayer Room was peopled with Holy Beings miraculously maneuvered together, joining to impart a strong Life Force. And it was the power of one man, Tara Singh, who compelled them to gather and unite in one time and place. Seldom had such an integration of enlightened beings happened in history, as most religions are focused on one character as the object of worship. But these Beings were called together with the help of Tara Singh, the Christ Mind and *A Course in Miracles* to make manifest a truly egalitarian and holy action in America. And for the most part, this action went largely unnoticed. Certainly unnoticed by the mainstream of Americans, but even unnoticed in its full significance by some of the very people Tara Singh introduced to this miracle. As He would describe the mystery of the "loaves and the fishes" in the Bible—"People came to Jesus and ate the fish and the bread—and never came back." People came to the Prayer Room, partook of the profound peace, and never came back. But for me, I saw the remarkable nature of this action of the Holy Beings. I came back and back and back—it became my Foundation for awakening.

My first experience of this Prayer Room was at the *40 Days in the Wilderness Retreat*. The Foundation for Life Action, which produced the retreats all over the United States, brought the whole Prayer Room to the longer workshops for the purpose of the round-the-clock prayer vigil. I was fortunate to be in the midst of the Holy Beings soon after my meeting with Tara Singh. I recall when I first entered the room at the hotel there was a different quality of atmosphere I had never felt or seen. The people sitting in the room were silent and erect, having a presence commensurate with the presence emitted by the Holy Beings, whose pictures circumscribed the walls around us. It was a 360° surround of energy coming out of these pictures, nearly life sized, from the faces of these holy characters. All cultures and religious affiliations were represented. Jesus, of course, was there. The painting of him by Heinrich Hofmann, deemed by Tara Singh to be one of the most accurate, was always a prominent picture in the room. Also, Taraji's

teachers were there, Mr. J. Krishnamurti and Dr. Helen Schucman. The Dalai Lama's teacher, whom Tara Singh had cared for during a period when he lived in New York City, was always somewhere in the Prayer Room. A photo of a sculpture of the Buddha, the best I have ever seen, in profile, was present. This picture alone could bring the mind to stillness. A painting of Loa Tzu was representing the Toa, and China. There was a bearded Sufi Saint, and Rumi, and also the calligraphy representing Allah, because in the Muslim faith pictures of Mohammad are not depicted or allowed. There were many Holy Beings from India. Sri Ramakrishna and his consort Sarada Devi; Swami Vivekananda, Ramakrishna's main disciple who brought the energy of India to the West. Sri Ramana Maharshi, the sage of Arunachala was there. Mother Teresa and Mary had their place. The ancient Vedic literature provided sacred characters: Sri Shankara, Yudhisthira from the Mahabharata, Lord Rama from the Ramayana, and Baby Krishna in blue were all there. And from the Sikh religion of Tara Singh, Guru Nanak and Guru Gobind Singh were present. And a stunning picture of Michelangelo's Moses was unforgettable. Swami Ram Tirtha and a bust of Socrates—all traditions of Truth were represented by the highest beings of peace who ever walked the earth, all together in the Prayer Room. This was by far one of the holiest places I had ever been, and it seemed like it was not even a place at all. It was an energy field of invocation that brought another Presence to the very atmosphere. Stillness and silence were the principle qualities of this atmosphere, and they were so strong that thought *itself* could be dissolved within its force field. The

instant you sat down in the midst of these greatest saints and teachers, your mind came to a place of quietude and peace; problems dissolved and a tremendous gratitude swept over your mind.

The Holy Beings were not just mere images of people from the past who had done great things. They were not pictures of people to be put on a pedestal and worshipped by rote. The Holy Beings were and are living beings that even now can be invoked to awareness and asked to help us in our process of ascension and spiritual awakening. They are beings who have ascended through the many levels of human existence to arrive at the facts and reality of the true human state, the Self Identity created by God in the likeness of Love, Peace and Joy. This Self Identity is every human's inheritance. Because they have realized these higher states of being within themselves, they merit being the "guides" or the "leaders" who can bring humanity along to this Self Realization. And each of these beings expresses a particular function in this process. For the Buddha, his function may be different than Mother Teresa's. For Socrates, his mission would look totally different than Ramana Maharshi's. Jesus makes His mission known quite clearly in *A Course in Miracles*:

> "I am in charge of the process of Atonement, which I undertook to begin. When you offer a miracle to any of my brothers, you do it to yourself and me. The reason you come before me is that I do not need miracles for my own Atonement, but I stand at the end in case you fail temporarily. My part in the Atonement is the canceling out of all errors that you could not otherwise correct. When you have been restored to the recognition of your original state, you naturally become part of the Atonement yourself. As you share my unwillingness to

accept error in yourself and others, you must join the great crusade to correct it; listen to my voice, learn to undo error and act to correct it.... 'Heaven and earth shall pass away' means that they will not continue to exist as separate states. My word, which is the resurrection and the life, shall not pass away because life is eternal. You are the work of God, and his work is wholly lovable and wholly loving. This is how a man must think of himself in his heart, because this is what he is." (Text, Chapter 1, Heading 3, from ACIM)

The Holiness of these words spoken in the very first chapter of the Text defines the role of Jesus, not only in His lifetime two thousand years ago, but also in the present state of being in which he communicates through *A Course in Miracles*. He is in charge of the forgiveness process—the *process of Atonement*—mentioned here. Miracles are always actions in forgiveness. His function is being fulfilled every time forgiveness occurs in the mind of anyone. Ramana Maharshi, on the other hand, would have a different function, which was to impart the importance of silence.

"Sri Ramana Maharshi maintained that the purest form of his teachings was the powerful silence, which radiated from his presence and quieted the minds of those attuned to it. He gave verbal teachings only for the benefit of those who could not understand his silence. His verbal teachings were said to flow from his direct experience of Atman as the only existing reality.

When asked for advice, he recommended self inquiry as the fastest path to liberation. Though his primary teaching is associated with non-dualism, Advaita Vedanta, and Jnana Yoga, he recommended Bhakti to those he saw were fit for it, and gave his approval to a variety of paths and practices."   (Wikipedia)

The picture of Sri Bhagavan (as he was called by Tara Singh) was one of the prominent transmitters of silence in the pantheon of Holy Beings. His eyes were riveting. It was almost impossible for one to be agitated in his energy, because the force of his peace and silence took over. He was so certain of his function to be this harbinger of silence, that all who came into the aura of his influence would encounter a unique energy, a palpable feeling of unequivocal peace. The Prayer Room was the accumulation of these energies rolled into one tremendous force of sacred Presence. Probably never before had all these Holy Beings been brought together in one place. Their combined power entered into the hearts of those who stepped through the door of holiness they represented. At the *40 Days in the Wilderness Retreat,* and later at the Foundation for Life Action in Los Angeles, Tara Singh gave me the great miracle to get to know these Holy Beings. This meeting was intimate and close, helping me to rise to a new level of holiness in myself as a result of "right association". Right association is a principle of teaching in which you hang out with people who are more spiritually evolved than you, so in their presence they force you to "adapt upward." This was certainly the case of my relationship with Tara Singh and the Holy Beings. They were forcing me to adapt upward in their presence. It was this combined Presence called in by them that was doing the work for me. All I had to do was to *show up.*

71

❖ *Chapter 7.* ❖

A House in LA

It was just a house in LA. Nothing special. Granted, it was in a nice neighborhood, middle class, next to a rather upper middle class section, but by no means Beverly Hills. Close to the Miracle Mile of Wilshire Boulevard, near the La Brea Tar Pits and the Los Angeles County Art Museum, 902 Burnside Avenue had the unique position of being one of the holiest spots in America on the grounds of what appeared to be an average middle class home. There was a watered lawn in the front with various rose beds, tree lined streets, a modest walk of stepping stones up to a bougainvillea encircled front entrance. Towards the back of the house was a walled in garden and private yard, with a two-car driveway to a garage toward the back. The garage was used for book storage and the shipping department, but that was not apparent from the street. For all practical purposes, the Foundation for Life Action was a well camouflaged 401-3C non-profit foundation situated in the heart of middle class Los Angeles with no indication of its own remarkable importance.

My first trip to the Foundation did not come for some time after the *40 Days in the Wilderness Retreat.* In the year after my first meetings with Tara Singh my life unraveled. My small contracting business became even smaller as a result of something I heard from Tara Singh in one of his stories about his relationship with his teacher, Mr. J. Krishnamurti. At some point in his tutelage with Krishnamurti, Taraji was told to "go and earn some money." But the caveat at the end of the instructions was, "and never take advantage of another." Well, that was a new shot of truth to me. It seemed like business could not avoid taking advantage of another—or at least it struck me that way. Favorable balance of trade meant to produce things for a certain amount of cost, sell them at a higher cost, and in the process receive some advantage, mainly money—more than the other people employed in the process. I had men working for me at the time I met Tara Singh. But with this new perspective on my whole life picture, my insecurities and my self made advantages, my motives and my checks and controls on how I managed my livelihood and work, I could see that I was taking advantage of others. I was making money on the labors of other men's energy, and even though this is an accepted modus operandi of the business world, it could no longer be my modus operandi.

Tara Singh introduced us to the principle of Self-Reliance, and had us read about the lives of the founding fathers of this nation. The spiritual founding fathers in his eyes were not necessarily Washington and Jefferson, Adams and Franklin.

The founding fathers who represented the spiritual pinnacle of America's evolution and contribution to the world were Emerson and Thoreau, Whitman and Lincoln. These were the men of the Spirit who took our culture to its highest peaks of truth and virtue. They related us to the Cosmos, to the God given truths that a government could only hint to as self-evident. To these men freedom was a matter of spiritual liberation, and in that way they connected with the ancients of the East who placed liberation of the Self above all else. To them, realizing the freedom of the soul is man's greatest achievement, and this freedom transcended all political, national, and ecclesiastical systems. This freedom is bestowed from a benevolent Creator upon all creation, whether recognized by a government or not. It is bestowed on every human being on the planet who makes it a priority in life to discover it, and even to every human being unaware it exists. And the process of liberating the mind from the confines of conditioned thought became the work of the Foundation for Life Action. It obviously used the means of *A Course in Miracles* and *God's Plan for Salvation* contained within it, through the wisdom and attention of Tara Singh who had brought its principles into application. The house in LA contained this lofty mission, even though it looked like an average abode in the center of a moderately affluent Jewish neighborhood.

After the *40 Days* I spent a year simplifying my life. I no longer had "employees." I was an artist, a painter, and the sole proprietor of a small contracting business. But now I took up the tools to do the actual work and the craft of what I sold to my customers. Ultimately this shift gave me more freedom

74

than less, and I could earn money and be the master of my schedule without being the master of other men. I thought of what Lincoln had said in my readings of his speeches inspired by Tara Singh—"As I would not be a slave, I would not be a master." Yet for Lincoln, this statement represented a higher mastery over his consciousness and soul. It was his liberation from ever "taking advantage of another" that made him a true human being and leader meritorious of this country's highest accolades. During this year I revisited Thoreau and Emerson as well, and the poetry of Walt Whitman. "I celebrate my Self," Whitman wrote, and proceeded to describe that Self in an unending variety of ways, both noble and ignoble, that formulate the vast nature of what it means to be human.

When I entered the foyer of the Foundation for Life Action in Los Angeles I saw these four American founding fathers' pictures on the wall just inside the front door. There was a different atmosphere the instant I entered. I was swept over by quietude similar to what I experienced in Stony Point and New Mexico with Tara Singh. It had been almost a year after the *40 Days* in Angel Fire. I was on my own forty-day retreat this time, as I drove across the US in my Ford Van and camped along the way. The stop at the Foundation, in hopes of seeing Tara Singh, was spontaneous. I felt compelled to go there by some force of nature, by some powerful draw that intimated the necessity of seeing with my own eyes what the Foundation was, where Tara Singh lived, what kind of place produced such an extension of his wisdom.

To the right of the foyer was a large living room with a high cathedral ceiling. At the end of the room was a huge picture window looking out to the front yard and the foliage of trees and shrubbery providing privacy. For the most part this room was left empty for times when larger groups of guests came in the evenings for Tara Singh's public lectures. There were a few tables with computers on them, placed around the perimeter of the room. A few stacks of folding chairs leaned against the wall. A fireplace in the middle of the room was tiled with some interesting decorative southwestern designs. And around the walls were pictures of the Golden Temple, the Sikh's shrine in India, Machu Picchu, Quan Yin, Jesus walking on water, and a few other holy beings. There was spaciousness in the place. Even though I knew this was just a regular house, it was as though I passed into another wonderland of Elysian Fields when I entered the Foundation's door. The whole quality of my attention was "stepped up," intensified to an acute awareness that a holy purpose and extension of something unprecedented was very present and palpably real.

Immediately I was welcomed by the staff, and invited to sit in the Prayer Room. Here in its original place, the Prayer Room was highly charged with the stillness and silence that accompanied it to the retreats. The carpet inside was a deep cerulean blue, and around the perimeter, under the pictures of the Holy Beings, were meditation cushions for sitting, stacked two high. These were of various brilliant colors. I took my seat along the wall on one of these cushions and sank into the deep internal peace that this space imparted to anyone who entered. At one end of the room the Holy Altar was lit, with pictures of

76

Jesus, Krishnamurti, and Dr. Schucman above it. I looked around at the other Holy Beings as the Presence of silence and stillness intensified, and soon took over. I could hear the muffled activity outside the door, but within this space all the pressures of the external world disappeared. Perhaps this was my first experience of an authentic sanctuary. I felt its blessings envelop me, and my mind came to a profound peace that was even deeper than what I had already experienced at the *40 Days*.

After some time spent in the Prayer Room, I was invited to join the staff for lunch. Tara Singh was in retreat in Ojai, CA, where he maintained a small cottage to be in silence, to write, and to prepare for the workshops. Meals were eaten outside, under a long canvas canopy on an equally long veranda, where there was a table that could hold about 20 people. Jasmine vines climbed up the canopy supports, and the whole area filled with the sweet fragrance of this aromatic plant. Every day at the Foundation, breakfast, lunch and dinner were prepared and provided to the staff and to the guests, free of any charge. It was a place that fed the people, and this kitchen was as integral to the work as the Prayer Room, the workshops, the production of books and recordings, and the daily sessions with Tara Singh that composed the action of the Foundation. Feeding people, not only food for the body, but also food for the soul, was the Foundation's principle mission. In the kitchen, through which one had to pass to enter the back gardens and dining veranda, there was a handwritten sign above the door that said, "Man cannot live on bread alone, but on every word that proceedeth out of the mouth of God." It was a quote from the Bible, from Jesus. Boy, did that express my sentiment for being there, and for having the contact with Tara Singh and *A Course in Miracles.*

The lunch was spread out across the long counter top in the kitchen and was served buffet style. People filled their plates and proceeded to the table on the veranda to take their place. But before filling our plates, we all stood in a circle and said a short prayer of thanksgiving, spontaneously in our own words. Each person was given a chance to say something, if they wanted to. The ministry of the Foundation was one based on service and gratitude. Tara Singh called it the "Ministry of Gratefulness." He had been well trained by his teacher, Dr. Schucman, to express gratitude in his daily life. She had even insisted that he keep "gratefulness journals." The atmosphere at 902 Burnside Avenue in Los Angeles was one of this permeating gratitude. You could feel it in the very walls. Joy was emanating from the sweet fragrance of a holy presence that filled this sacred, yet seemingly unheralded place. It emanated from the hearts of the people who worked there. And it was transmitted by every word that "proceedeth out of the mouth of God" through God's servant Tara Singh, who had been entrusted with this mission to share *A Course in Miracles* in a most serious way.

Tara Singh was ordained by Dr. Schucman to conduct the workshops—one of the first who did so, before any others. He was guided to form the Foundation for Life Action in this house in LA. This modest middle class home became the "command central" for one of the holiest experiments in America. It was not a "commune," not an "organization," not a church or a religious institution, not an "ashram," and not even a "new age" center. It was a place that offered the opportunity to realize the truth of what ACIM referred to as a *Holy Relationship*. It became the home of an action of divine service of a man extending the will of God, without any motives on his own part. It was an extension of the peace and joy talked about in *A Course in Miracles*, but brought into application by the virtue and integrity of people touched by the light of true words, words flowing out of the mouth of God in *ACIM*, and out of its representative, Tara Singh.

❖ *Chapter 8.* ❖

Pocono Mountain

In the Pennsylvania Borsht Belt, as it was called by the Jewish community in Philadelphia, the Pocono Manor loomed large as a destination of choice. Situated in the heart of the Pocono Mountains in upstate Pennsylvania, it nestles itself amidst gently rolling mountains forested by deciduous woods of oak, maple and beech trees that go on as far as the eye can see. In the autumn months there is a spectacular explosion of color, and mostly for this reason Tara Singh chose this place as the venue for his fall, Yom Kippur retreat. Yom Kippur is a holiday in the Jewish calendar known as the "Day of Atonement," one of the holiest, in which one confesses all of his "sins," asks for forgiveness from God, and hopes to have his name inscribed again by God in the "Book of Life." The fact that forgiveness is also a key point in *A Course in Miracles* made this particular religious holiday notable in the mind of Tara Singh. So, for quite a number of years in the 1990's he would conduct a fall retreat at the Pocono Manor over this period that contained Yom Kippur in the calendar.

It would be for a week or ten days. Much in the genre of what he had already established as the structure of the workshops, the Yom Kippur Retreat provided similar benefits to the attendees. Tara Singh would give two talks a day— morning and late afternoon—and the rest of the time would be free to walk the grounds, spend in meditation, and also to participate in the round the clock Prayer Vigil. The Holy Beings were always brought to the longer retreats. The Prayer Vigil was conducted from start to finish without a break, without an intrusion into the peace and quiet that it certainly established. People looked forward to coming to these semi annual talks, spring and fall, just to step out of the pressures of everyday routines and to charge up their spiritual batteries in the relaxing atmosphere of the daily sessions, the Prayer Vigil, and the beautiful natural setting. For the first few years of my attendance at these events my wife at the time accompanied me. We drove up from Philadelphia where we lived to attend the Yom Kippur workshop in the Poconos. Through the painted oranges, crimsons and yellows of the autumn foliage, we wove our way through the mountains of unending color to the relaxation of this blessed week of leisure and contemplation. Tara Singh often referred to *divine leisure,* and certainly his retreats were an embodiment of that phrase.

Once settled, we got into the rhythm of the day. The Pocono Manor, situated on top of a mountain and amidst the dense Pennsylvania forests, had walking trails and narrow lanes that looped around the buildings and entrance to the estate, circling around spectacular vistas of multi colored mountains and expansive green fairways of the large golf course surrounding the Manor. It was a spectacular time of year to be walking in this cool atmosphere through a spectrum of color unsurpassed in the whole Appalachian Range. Mountains in the East are more like huge rolling hills, gentle in their ascendency. They are not the rugged and sharp forms found in the Western States. Rated as *old mountains,* these Poconos appeared soft and pristine, contributing to the motherly peace of mind that nature brought to the retreats of Tara Singh. The beauty of the natural setting was always integral to the profound beauty of what was shared in the sessions during these holiest of days.

The session room was encircled by windows through which one could engulf himself with the beautiful vistas into the forests of autumn colors. Before Tara Singh arrived to begin his talk, the sound of Indian classical music played over the loudspeakers. This music was of a different nature and caliber of anything composed in the West. The men and women of this tradition studied their craft with a master, much was passed on orally without notation. The sophistication of the sound and compositions were very subtle, and related more directly to nature than the classical music derived from a European heritage. This music induced meditation and lifted the listener into states of mind transcendent of thought, of likes and dislikes. The rhythms are more intricate in this music, and though much of the sounds are from fewer instruments playing at once, the profound nature of Indian classical music becomes apparent after only a little careful listening. Recordings of its essentially holy nature were introduced to us in the workshops. Tara Singh had collected these recordings over many years of connoisseurship. Ali Akbar Khan, the premier sarod player, was often played. I considered him as evolved as any guru. Zakir Hussein, purported as the best tabla drum player in the world, was also featured in these pre-talk concerts. A new passion came over us to listen to this music from the East. It had a different level of refinement that related us to our inner life of the spirit. These men and women who played were like musical yogis. They mastered their instruments and dedicated their spiritual lives to the attainment of enlightenment through the practice of playing divine sounds. I was in awe, often, that human hands could produce such sounds—they were so virtuoso in their skill. It was a blessing to walk into the room in the Pocono Manor and prepare ourselves in such a way to receive the lectures from Tara Singh. Already we were in the right attention, the right state of inner stillness and peace to have the ears to hear what he was to say.

There was a peace and stillness that surrounded the man. Tara Singh had spent three years in silence in Carmel, California, in the early 1970's. He lived alone, practiced yoga, read no book, had no phone, bought his own groceries in the supermarket, took long walks on the beach, drove a Volkswagen Beetle, and spoke not a sound to anyone. Having been with Krishnamurti for years as his student, he used this time to prove or disprove what Krishnamurti was encouraging everyone to do—to leave the world of thought, of relative knowledge, to make contact with a still mind that was more connected to universal intelligence than the memories we collect and accumulate in our brains. Tara Singh was to Krishnamurti what Thoreau was to Emerson—the real student who tested the "theory" put forth by his spiritual master by putting it into the application of everyday life. Carmel was Tara Singh's Walden Pond, excepting that Tara Singh did not feel compelled to write anything about his experiences here. In fact, it was his mission by taking these three years in silence to see if he could even transcend *experience* itself. The one experience he yearned to make contact with was to bring his mind to absolute silence. To have a mind totally free of judgment, of opinions, of the conditioning of memory, of accumulated knowledge—this was the experiment to which Tara Singh gave his whole heart, mind and being. This was the test of his twenty-five years with Krishnamurti. His three years in silence would prove if he could be one of the few who his teacher reservedly claimed in private, after all of his sixty years of giving talks around the world, would have the *ears to hear* what he had said.

Tara Singh had subjected himself to the rigors of having a spiritual master who would take him through all the many levels and scenarios of life necessary for him to outgrow, to transcend, the personal *self*—or ego—he made up. This is the job of a spiritual master: not ever to make the student dependent on him or her, but to hold up a mirror, a reflection of the person in their actual state of mind. If the student is full of insecurity, anger, fear, inconsistency and doubt, it is the job of the true teacher to point this out. Then to question why? — and to point out that he or she has a true Self, a lofty Self that exists beyond these problems. Problems are mostly conditions of thought, belief and memory that are learned and inherited. Because Tara Singh had confronted these demons of his thought and self-made personality—and undone them in his three years of silence—Krishnamurti was compelled at the end of his experiment with silence to give Tara Singh this confirmation: "Now that you have it, how would you like to express it?" Taraji told me later when recounting this story of meeting Krishnamurti at the end of his three years in silence, he did not fully know he "had it," nor have any idea how to express it.

Yet, when Tara Singh took his chair in the conference room in the Pocono Manor amidst the brilliant infusion of fall color all about us, he had absolute certainty what he had, and how he was going to express it. The years of tutelage with Krishnamurti and the years in silence in Carmel had prepared him for his real mission in life—which was his meeting with *A Course in Miracles* and its scribe, Dr. Helen Schucman, and the subsequent twenty-five years of sharing his and the *Course's* wisdom with serious students.

By the time I met Tara Singh in 1989 he had fully freed himself from the ego-self, and had a divine function ordained by the same Higher Forces that brought in *A Course in Miracles* to these dimensions in the first place. He could bring his mind to silence and stillness, and in so doing transmit that actual state of absolute peace to those who sat before him and listened. He most certainly had the "ears to hear" his teacher Krishnamurti, and he demanded the same from those who sat at the feet of universal wisdom at his retreats and workshops.

This was a serious affair to him and the staff of the Foundation for Life Action. *A Course in Miracles* represents another way, in terms of the holy words of Jesus, for us to transcend the judgments and contradictions of thought which plague us to be in conflict with our world, with our relationships and with our selves. It provides an actual means to come to a state of mind free of the opposites of thought, to a state of absolute inner peace. Tara Singh was entrusted to represent *A Course in Miracles* and bring a few serious students to the absolute state of peace and stillness this modern day scripture is meant to impart. The Pocono retreat was an extension of this sacred trust, and I was gratefully part of its action.

I sat in the room looking out at the trees, while listening to the lines spoken by my master, like jewels of verbal truth that uttered forth from the mouths of the sages of old. One could easily imagine what it was like for the young men of Athens to sit at the feet of Socrates in the Lyceum, listening to his true words spoken, feeding them not with the bread of physicality baked in the fires of a worldly sustenance, but cooked in the crucible of truth that made every word the bread that manifested forth from the mouth and ovens of God. Socrates brought his students to the Absolute state of Love, of wisdom, of truth, through the process of exposing all their self-deceptions and undoing them. Even to this day his methods of inquiry are equated with the principles of deductive reasoning that define the manners of scientific and philosophical logic. In Tara Singh these abilities of crystal clear thinking were revisited. He meant what he said and he said what he meant—and if the word in A Course in Miracles was "peace," then he considered it his responsibility as a teacher to impart that actual state of peace in the minds and hearts of his listeners. And he could do that, usually by such a rigorous set of questions and statements of self-inquiry, which made the lessons he discussed in *ACIM* came alive. He was able to transmit their truth with the certainty of a man in his God-lit Power.

The Yom Kippur retreat gave each person an opportunity to come to the peace and stillness within. We did not go to "learn" more data, to get the latest technique in a New Age repertoire towards self-improvement. We went to discover who we are as God created us, which *A Course in Miracles* so highly emphasizes. Fortunately for us, this man, Tara Singh, had realized his true Identity. He could bring us to the state of being we so longed to know, so longed to make contact with, amidst our urgent attempts to escape the avalanche of useless information inundating us for decades of learned education. We were all but buried in this avalanche, in the tomb of decaying memories of defeated aspirations. And in these crisp fall days on the top of Pocono Mountain, in the bright surround of the bursting explosion of autumnal colors, in an atmosphere prepared by the Indian music of an unworldly nature from the other side of the planet, this simple man from the Punjab, a most unlikely candidate to be ordained as the one to share the most important Christian message given in two thousand years, resurrected us out of this tomb and brought our minds to a new vitality. We entered into a silence and stillness the likes of which we had never known, into the light and peace and joy of our God created Self.

❖ *Chapter 9.* ❖

Lake Tahoe and Asilomar

California is the state of my birth. I was born in Hollywood on the eleventh day of the eleventh month in 1954. It was the day declared to be the end of all wars, thirty-six years prior to my birthday. Of course that was not true—there were plenty of wars, even bigger ones, after that day of declared armistice. And by then America was entering the Cold War with the Soviet Union—that "godless evil empire" of communists who were pointing their nuclear weapons right at our hospitals and schoolhouses from far across an ocean and continent. We were doing the same to them, of course. But California seemed to defy these concerns in my mind, and represented a new Eden somewhere out West, a place of unlimited possibilities and a sun filled land of golden fruits and cornucopias of burgeoning abundance that composed a pax Americana that would transform the whole planet into a heaven on earth. Was it not true, I thought, that in my birthplace any story you wanted to tell could be produced and projected on the silver screen, and transmitted almost instantly to every heart and mind in the country? The bigger than life "movies" became the defining cultural wherewithal of our progressive society. In America we could tell any story, and through our uncanny ability to act it out in larger than life terms, with larger than life Hollywood stars, give the impression that a world advancing toward a Utopia could actually exist. The 20th century was America's century, and California a part of the New World with its films and silicon valley that seemed to defy any limits of conventional reason. We were a "can do" culture, and the "just do it" jingles coming out of California made the attainment of unlimited possibilities an advertising reality in our minds. And Hollywood became the great icon of a nirvana attained.

I did not get to stay in Hollywood. My father became ill, and my parents, my sister and I moved back to live in Mount Vernon, Ohio—lock, stock and barrel. We moved in with my grandparents on mother's side of the family when I was less than two years old. Middle America of *small town USA* became my home, a far cry from Hollywood and Los Angeles. It was no *City of Angels* with possibilities of unlimited imagination, but rather the county seat named after George Washington's homestead, steeped and confined in the conventions of *Main Street*. The people there adhered to the hard work ethic of middle class virtue and self-sacrifice—which got the top billing on the marquis of daily life. My small town life was mainly a story of respectable survival with the confirmation of a weekly sermon from the minister, and a few songs sung from the hymnal in our local Methodist church.

Mount Vernon was a sleepy small town of about 15,000 people in my days of growing up there, situated on the banks of the Kokosing River. It had strong ties to the Grand Army of the Republic, the Cooper Bessemer iron foundry, spectacular Fourth of July festivities with an impressive parade and fireworks, and lazy summer nights spent watching the local soft ball teams bat it out under the lights. My childhood had many elements of happiness. We caught fireflies after dark, put them in a lidded jar with nail holes punched in the top, and watched them light up like a lantern next to our bedside. We roasted marshmallows over the charcoal grill, and played "kick the can" into the late hours of the night. Our schooling was above average, but without family money or social leverage, natural intelligence was not enough to get you into Ivy League. The closest real cultural highlight was Kenyon College, the alma mater of Paul Newman and the literary bastion of John Crowe Ransom's Kenyon Review. The most notable events I experienced around Kenyon were Jane Fonda and Dick Gregory speaking out against the Vietnam War; and Paul Newman came to dedicate a theatre in his name on the campus. He also provided the chance encounter for my mother to see him buying underwear in the local Ringwalt's Department Store on Mount Vernon's Main Street.

I almost got paperboy of the year for the State of Ohio when I was thirteen—(beat out by an Eagle Scout)—and did receive an artistic accolade for a couple of my pictures picked to be in a State of Ohio art competition for high school students while in my senior year. Before that, I went to the Rhode Island School of Design for a three-month art program in Providence during the summer before graduation. The work I did there got me the Kenyon College Faculty Prize granted to a promising student in Mount Vernon High who expressed exceptional "creative talents and abilities." This made me want to go to art school, which I did. Also, during these years I rode my bicycle often the fifteen miles to and from Kenyon for the exhilaration of coasting down the long Ohio rolling hills. From 8-18 I played baseball pretty well, batted 400 a couple of years in a row, and played the violin during those same years congruently, ending up doing a stint in the local county symphony in the first violin section. I remember playing Mozart and Mendelssohn. And before I left my town for the Cleveland Institute of Art, I was the class valedictorian even though I did not feel very smart.

My interest was toward art, and toward what Emerson referred to in his essay on Self-Reliance—*non-conformity*. Though I had not been back to California but once, when my sister Carol lived there a short while after college, it was still imprinted in my subconscious memory as a place of my significant origins. The events of life had taken me to Ohio for a sheltered upbringing, then to Cleveland for an art school education and a harsh urban awakening, then to Philadelphia for more art study in graduate school. This all led to the crux of a married life, including a spiritual life. But it was California that loomed large in the core of some birth memory, some place in the perpetual sun that stood for my true aspirations unabated.

In California lived the man who had taken my life and turned it upside down. Tara Singh was told by Dr. Schucman to, "Go to California, settle in Los Angeles. Activity is seething below the earth." These were his instructions from his teacher of *A Course in Miracles,* and he followed them. *ACIM* and what it meant to lead a spiritual life became his main subjects to teach under the auspices of a school, which trained students in its principles and application. This led him to settle near the Miracle Mile section of Wilshire Boulevard, where he and a small group of students formed the Foundation for Life Action. The Foundation would become one of the principle disseminators of *ACIM* in America. In addition to the students who lived and worked at 902 Burnside Avenue, Tara Singh inspired students all over the country to study the book with conviction, and to attend seminars and workshops he gave on the *Course* throughout the year.

In the Spring the Foundation for Life Action produced a retreat to celebrate Easter Week. These Easter retreats gave people the chance to step out of their every day pressures and join Tara Singh in the honoring of this holy day. Easter offered a rebirth of the human being to know their true Self. My master used the contemplative dynamism of self-inquiry to pull out our impurities—usually at one of the most beautiful natural settings in California. A hotel in Lake Tahoe, in the early 1990's, became the venue for the Easter retreat. Later in the decade, Asilomar Conference Center in Pacific Grove, near Carmel where he had spent his years in silence, was the place of choice. Both settings were remarkably beautiful. They were havens for the soul to be restored to sanity by the clean air, spectacular nature, and the relaxing rhythm of Tara Singh's lectures on *A Course in Miracles.*

It was a financial stretch to manage the regular attendance of these semi annual retreats, but I considered them to be an essential component in my life. Most people do "vacations" to escape from the routines of boredom and the pressures of a career; these retreats established a different lifestyle in me in which pressure and boredom were eliminated altogether. Lake Tahoe was expansive. The Ponderosa pines around the hotel were so still and majestic. There was a different atmosphere that had an aroma that seemed to cleanse your whole system, and integrate body, mind and spirit in ways that city life could not do. Stepping out of pressures and routines of daily living became one of the major lessons insisted upon by Tara Singh, and he offered many opportunities for his students to do that. These California Easter retreats were a few of them.

The meeting room in the Lake Tahoe venue was spacious. Built with high ceilings and brilliant views of the pines, it provided the perfect setting for Tara Singh to bring the participants to the space of stillness and silence. Around the room were the pictures of the Holy Beings. One felt surrounded by the energy of the Masters when sitting in the hall hearing the very poignant words of the speaker. He would take us through the various steps of letting go. Taraji was adept at moving from one fact to another, without missing a beat in his lecture, to bring our minds to a different state of inner peace. He did so by the process of undoing our thought, by using stories and insights from his many years on the spiritual quest, as well as the lessons from A Course in Miracles, which were designed to do the same thing. The undoing of

93

thought was his principle tool for invoking the Presence of stillness and silence. He took all of our belief systems and questioned them, exposed our habitual behaviors and inconsistencies, and essentially wiped our mental slate clean of all our doubt and concerns. He took us to a place in the mind beyond all words.

Even people who study the *Course* for years may never get to this place of the mind beyond the words. When lesson #10 says, "My thoughts do not mean anything," many gloss over this statement. They perhaps do not even receive its true significance, reading on without making contact with the miracle the *Course* is capable of imparting. In the strong Presence around Tara Singh, brought about by his insistence upon application of the lessons, the miracle of a peace of mind beyond the words, the actual state of peace, was always imparted. What would be the point, otherwise? This was his gift from all the years with Krishnamurti and Dr. Schucman— and from his three years in silence—he could transmit the living Presence of awareness beyond thought. This awareness was from a still mind that could see with crystal clarity the truth of the statement, "My thoughts do not mean anything," and have the sacred energy to drop them. What was then left over would be an incredible stillness and silence that was so palpable, everything was enveloped in a kind of intensified beauty that was integrated and whole. It was as if everything miraculously reconnected into a unified field of energetic oneness. Of course the oneness was always there, but through listening to Tara Singh's words, the undeniable contact with it was fully restored.

Asilomar Conference Center is situated in Pacific Grove, on the Monterrey Peninsula. Founded in 1913 and designed by acclaimed architect Julia Morgan in the Arts & Crafts style. It is composed of beautifully constructed buildings and lodgings on one of the most spectacular shorelines in the US. Its grounds are 107 acres of dunes crisscrossed with carefully placed trails and boardwalks that lead to pristine and uncluttered beaches. Being there, for the annual Easter retreat, felt like a heaven on earth. The simple but elegantly designed cabins were equipped with fireplaces that could be lit for a cozy atmosphere. The climate was mild but cool, and the vistas of the Pacific Ocean were breath taking. Again, in the spirit of finding the best possible setting for his work, Tara Singh insisted that the people attending his retreats would have a memorable experience of nature as well as a relaxed atmosphere to bring their minds and bodies to a state of absolute rest.

People from all over the United States, from Puerto Rico, and even from Europe attended the retreats at Asilomar and the Poconos. These were times given to us, it seemed, from a Divine Intelligence that had our best interests in mind. Not only were the retreats better than a vacation in terms of being spiritually uplifting, they provided a rhythm in our lives that kept everything in balance during the rest of the year. Perhaps in ancient times the celebrations of fall harvest and new spring were essential gatherings of thanksgiving that kept the social fabric and an individual's inner well being intact. Between these times of attending the retreats, I noticed I became more certain, more peaceful, and happier. The retreats provided me with respite from activity, and helped me establish a new order in my life.

Tara Singh had a plan, which was not merely of his making. This extended as his mission with *A Course in Miracles* to bring everyone he met to a new level of inner awareness. And in so doing this plan became intensely holy. For all the participants who received its blessings, it seemed part of the Will of God in actual, not theoretical terms. By being part of this plan our entire lives were lifted into new heights of our Sacred Being. Angel Fire, Pocono Mountain, Lake Tahoe, and eventually Asilomar near Monterrey became the places of pilgrimage as great in value as Jerusalem or the Holy Ganges. They became the catalysts for discovering a *peace within* that had no place at all, but strongly established inside of us as a result of meeting Tara Singh and spending these weeks in the stillness and silence he imparted.

❖ *Chapter 10.* ❖

Memorable Walks

When I first became interested in classic American literature during my junior and senior year of high school, one of the first real contacts I made was with the writings of Henry David Thoreau. His book on his experiment at Walden Pond really sang to me. In it he described where he lived from the summer of 1845 to the summer of 1847, in a small cabin he constructed himself, outside of Concord, Massachusetts. I connected with his voice, and I thought his powers of observation of the nature of the woods, the wildlife and the seasons, coupled with his observations of human nature, were acutely accurate in stating the truth like it was. I discovered that a truth existed outside of time. Thoreau had lived and written a century before me, yet what he was saying had the freshness and power of wisdom spoken in this very instant. I discovered how the power of true words could inspire and transform my life, change my view of the world around me for the better, in the living moment of reading them in the present. His words were intensely alive as though we were sitting together having a conversation, and I was hearing sonorous utterances of great inspiration.

Thoreau was freed from the fetters of convention and conformity. He represented a voice all his own, with insights of self-discovery that he made during these two years of dynamic contemplation. He was not a pacifist in the sense of removing himself from society and hiding out in his cabin on the lake, as a hermit in some fantasy of grand escape. But rather, he was a scientist of human thought and behavior who got to the root of what was keeping a man from really being true to himself in this life. Like Gandhi, whom he inspired nearly a hundred years later, he was a pacifist of action. He was civilly disobedient when disobedience put him in touch with higher laws of the conscience and spirit. He was a pacifist of the well-examined life and mind, using this time alone to get clear on the status quo of human conditions, and the alternatives for a life free of the accepted confinements of the day. He would not accept the notion that people had to be enslaved to their jobs, their mortgages, and their own conditioned thought in order to survive. He questioned the boundaries of this conditioning and elaborated on the freedoms that were inherent to a life that related to cosmic laws, higher laws of nature that transcended those made by men. Thoreau championed the freedom found in nature, and the freedom of the human spirit that was an integral component of that natural liberty. To him freedom was an inalienable right not established by church or state, but by the

Creative Forces that spawned not only humanity, but a whole immense and infinitely diverse natural universe. These forces of life were benevolently on freedom's side, and conducive to human freedom as its highest expression.

So it was of no surprise when Tara Singh mentioned Henry David Thoreau as one of the founding fathers of the American spirit with whom he had made contact in his early days in America. In the 1950's Tara Singh lived for a time in New York City, making his way in the New World, freshly arrived from New Delhi, having been mentored by such giants of humanism as Gandhi, Jawaharlal Nehru, Gyani Kartar Singh, the leader of the Sikhs, and other eminent figures in the newly independent Indian government circles. Yet in New York City, for a foreign person not quite integrated yet into this culture, the vibration of America in the busiest city in the world was one of severe loneliness. Apart from his homeland, he felt the pangs of this loneliness and wanted to make contact with someone interesting and great, but could not. He walked and walked the streets of New York, and wrote later, "if my feet had eyes, they would have left a trail of tears." The loneliness was excruciating—until one day he went into a bookstore and began to make contact with the real voices of America. Henry David Thoreau was one of them.

He read Thoreau's essay on Walking, and then his whole life changed. What had been an exercise in loneliness now became an adventure of exploration and elation. Walking became an art, and the neighborhoods of New York City the frontiers of new discovery. Walking became an integral part of his day, and the means of lifting his spirits out of the doldrums of loneliness. It was not long before he felt comfortable in this new land, and made contact with eminent people who represented the highest in America, such as Eleanor Roosevelt, Supreme Court justice William O. Douglass, and others at the highest level. Walking was never better described by Thoreau in his essay, which transformed Tara Singh's life in New York:

"I have met with but one or two persons in the course of my life who understood the art of Walking, that is, of taking walks, who had a genius, so to speak, for *sauntering*; which word is beautifully derived "from idle people who roved about the country, in the middle ages, and asked charity, under pretense of going "*à la sainte terre*"—to the holy land, till the children exclaimed, "There goes a *sainte-terrer*", a saunterer—a holy-lander. They who never go to the holy land in their walks, as they pretend, are indeed mere idlers and vagabonds, but they who do go there are saunterers in the good sense, such as I mean. Some, however, would derive the word from *sans terre*, without land or a home, which, therefore, in the good sense, will mean, having no particular home, but equally at home everywhere. For this is the secret of successful sauntering. He who sits still in a house all the time may be the greatest vagrant of all, but the saunterer, in the good sense, is no more vagrant than the meandering river, which is all the while sedulously seeking the shortest course to the sea. But I prefer the first, which indeed is the most probable derivation. For every walk is a sort of crusade,

100

preached by some Peter the Hermit in us, to go forth and reconquer this holy land from the hands of the Infidels."

Henry David Thoreau — from the essay, *Walking*

Thereby Tara Singh become a *saunterer* of life, and a fine artist of the *walk*. In my long tutelage with him over a seventeen-year period, there were numerous memorable walks we took together. These became the benchmarks of my life lessons that came forth from these *crusades*, these forays to the holy land, to the *sainte terre* of our relationship. In these memorable walks we crossed directly over the sacred grounds of the heart toward our highest destination, which not only established our teacher/student relationship, but later our friendship in the holiest terms possible.

The first time I was invited to spend a couple weeks at Tara Singh's school in Los Angeles, to my surprise, I witnessed the leisure that was an integral part of the workshops and retreats was the day-to-day norm at the Foundation for Life Action. Tara Singh gave two sessions, early morning and early evening, in the Prayer Room, with the rest of the day devoted to the work of the Foundation. Yet, there was absolutely no pressure imposed on anyone who lived and worked there. Everyone was *self reliant*, as it were, to be productive and creative without the need for a boss—or even for Tara Singh to be the overseer of his or her actions. The level of relaxation that the people brought to everything impressed me deeply.

So it was natural for Tara Singh to take a walk at about ten o'clock. He did this religiously during his time at the

Foundation and in Ojai. After the early morning session, after breakfast, and after opening the day's correspondence, he would take a walk, most often with a guest or someone at the Foundation. The neighborhood was conducive to this. The streets were tree lined and quiet. The houses were sharp and upscale. The routes led past well-manicured residences, and easily ended up at the park grounds around the La Brea Tar Pits Museum and the Los Angeles County Art Museum. So on my first walk with Tara Singh, there is where we headed.

The lawns were expansive on these museum grounds. Maintained well, the grass was thick and the earth well watered and cushioned. There was a set of trees and shrubs at the entrance to the park, and Tara Singh would take off his shoes and socks, and hide them in the shrubs, while liberating his feet to feel the soft earth and damp grass under his bare soles. This was a joy to be free and in touch with the actual vibration of the earth. He pointed out that we were disconnected from the earth by rubber-soled shoes, and that the actual current of the earth could not flow into us as it should, with this kind of footwear. It affected our health adversely, not receiving this energy. So barefoot walks were a way of restoring this earthly connection that was so vital to human life. Walks on the ground with no shoes were a way of connecting energy to the body, and even to the mind that was now in touch with its natural habitat and support. When is the last time you walked barefoot on the grass? A good question I asked myself. It had been decades.

After this walk I got rid of most of my rubber soled shoes. I seldom wore sneakers again. Leather soled shoes became preferred, and I was instantly more conscious of this electromagnetic connection with the earth that was so basic and important to life. Tara Singh and I walked together through the wet grass, past the tar pits, around the back of the Art Museum, circling through the Museum grounds, past the Nancy Graves and Alexander Calder sculptures, along Wilshire Boulevard, down the walkway that led past the main tar pit where mastodon remains were found, and then finally back to our hidden shoes. This walk was perhaps the first real walk I had in my life. My awareness of the surroundings was heightened to the degree I could see what I was seeing, smell what I was smelling, and feel what I was feeling, all simultaneously without effort. There was no motive in it. I was not going from point "a" past point "b" to get to point "c" — and then to present a travelogue about it. I was truly sauntering with Tara Singh, and time seemed to stand still. We were in a dialogue of the present, with an acute observation of what was directly in front of us. I was alert to be attentive to what he was saying, but doubly alert to be present to everything we were seeing and experiencing in that very moment of the holy instant.

After a week at the Foundation, the rhythm of my days were in tune with that of Tara Singh's. It was a glorious time to spend at the Foundation, helping with the work, taking our daily walks. When Taraji left with one of the staff to spend time in his cottage in Ojai, I was sadly disappointed. Yet, the boon was given to me to move my things into his room on the second floor, out of the small sleeping shed I was staying in situated in the back yard. For the rest of my stay I got to sleep

103

in his bed and be in the aura of his room. It felt like a blessing beyond blessings. In his room were hung many pictures of art from the art museums in New York. There was a Kandinsky print that was explosive; a reproduction of the Henri Rousseau painting of the Lion visiting the Sleeping Man in the Desert, and a Gauguin figure of a woman from Tahiti. In this room at the Foundation I found the compassion of Tara Singh so freely given to me, I was astounded at the manifestation of the Holy Relationship referred to in the Course. I was experiencing an example of it, in flesh and blood confirmation. This man fed me, counseled me, housed me, enlightened me, walked with me—and now gave me his own bed. I had never met this kind of Love, I had never been with this kind of energy of true caring. I could see his life was an extension of *A Course in Miracles*. Not only was he teaching it to his students, he was living it in the very heart of his being, in every second of the day, in every action of his life.

When the time grew short for my stay at the Foundation, one of the staff drove me to Ojai to meet Tara Singh on the day before my departure. This was a ride of a couple of hours to the small town in the mountains where Tara Singh had his cottage. Just down the road from the Krishnamurti Library, the cottage was situated in the back of a larger property, surrounded by orange groves for as far as the eye could see. They produced a fragrance so powerful that it filled the whole town with a sweet perfume. By the cottage were persimmon trees, full of bright red-orange fruit. It seemed like the whole place was an Eden of natural abundance. The Shangri La that I had left when I was one year old was now coming back to me.

Tara Singh was my teacher, my master, into whom I had blundered, and he was bringing me back to my real Identity, my real birthplace in the sun filled lands of California, in the brilliance of a hospitality unbeknownst to me ever before.

That evening we drove to the Oak Grove before my return to Los Angeles to catch my flight the next day. My second memorable walk had an even deeper significance. Krishnamurti was Tara Singh's spiritual mentor, guide and teacher for many years. Ojai was his main home while in the USA, as he travelled all over the world giving his talks, imparting his wisdom in India, Australia, and Europe. In Ojai, in the Oak Grove, thousands would come to hear him deliver his teachings to the public. It was like the Deer Park in Sarnath where the Buddha taught the dharma—holy ground indeed. Krishnamurti's presence could be felt on these grounds preserved by the school he left behind to continue his work after passing in 1986.

Tara Singh and I got out of the car and walked through the gate to the Oak Grove. I could hear the sound of the wind passing through the limbs of the majestic trees. We walked with shoes on this time, but with a silence and reverence that surpassed mere respect. I could feel the sacred homage Tara Singh paid to his teacher, without him uttering a word. We walked to the place where Krishnamurti sat while delivering his talks. I could feel the intensity of the silence building around us. As we moved through the oaks, I could almost see the thousands gathered to hear the true words spoken, so eloquently and honestly by a master. This was a pilgrimage of quiet beauty. I could not speak. Tara Singh did not speak. For awhile we sat on a bench in the shade of the oaks, as the sun went lower in the sky behind the purple mountains. The birds flocked to their evening nests in the Oak Grove. I was in touch with a wave of gratitude that my good fortune had brought me to—this place of intensely sacred ground. It was sacred not only because such a great soul had delivered discourses on the nature of life and truth, the likes of which were some of the wisest the 20th century had known, but that in this holy instant I was present with my own master, my own spiritual mentor in the juncture of my life that was transforming me. It was sacred because I recognized I was within a course of events that were leading me into the truly miraculous. This was a memorable walk indelibly recorded in my mind as one of these miraculous events that were happening in my life as a result of meeting Tara Singh. He had gripped my heart, and stolen me for a walk to the holy land, to the *sainte terre* of my soul, and hearkened the sound of true love that served ever as the guiding voice toward which my journey was directed. In Ojai, that evening, the stillness and peace of his presence enveloped me in a walk that would never end. To this day he keeps my course true, sauntering toward the sacred ground of our complete liberation.

❖ *Chapter 11.* ❖

The Ears to Hear

In the ancient epic, the Mahabharata, there were five saintly brothers, the Pandavas, who formed the protagonists of the story. The oldest, Yudhisthira, was known for his piousness and adherence to the Dharma, or the code of virtuous conduct. Taraji told the story of Yudhisthira, of his good qualities, and of his ability to apply the truth in all situations. As a boy in school, an incident occurred that demonstrated the depth of his character, and also demonstrated what Tara Singh would call, "having the ears to hear." For him, intellectual "knowing" had very little meaning. A truth must be applied in order for it to be true for that person. Taraji used Yudhisthira as an example of this application. He was such a person, who applied the wise words to his life, and thus, had "the ears to hear."

When Yudhisthira was in school learning to read in one of the school primers, he seemed to be floundering in his studies, while all the others boys were keeping up, moving forward, and advancing at a pace the teacher deemed acceptable. When the other boys were fifty pages ahead, and Yudhisthira was still on page one, the teacher scolded him on his dull and slow nature. "You are such a dunce," the teacher shouted in his chastisement, "why are you so far behind?" Yudhisthira took a moment to answer. "Dear teacher," he said politely and with no tone of apology or guilt in his voice, "on page one of the primer, does it not say to never tell a lie?" The instructor gave an affirmative nod. "Well," said Yudhisthira, "I still tell lies, so I cannot go on yet to the next page."

This was "having the ears to hear," according to Tara Singh. It was not enough to read the lofty words of *A Course in Miracles*. If you were not applying them, what difference did it make? This was the issue 2500 years ago with Yudhisthira, 2000 years ago with Jesus, and now with the words of *A Course in Miracles*. Who really "has the ears to hear?" Over and over Tara Singh would stress this one point. Of course he would also say that we are "intentionally dull", and do not really want to go all the way to enlightenment. We have too much "unwillingness," he would say, which is the status quo of our thinking. Lofty words all sound very good, but we are much too complacent in accepting an intellectual understanding of the words, and do not insist, like Yudhisthira, on coming to the actual state of what they are here to impart.

I got it. Something in me, at least, had the *ears to hear* how false my *wanting to know God* was. It was a pretense, a wish, an unfulfilled desire, perhaps—but not an unequivocal fact. This changed the whole playing field, and rendered me speechless.

Gradually, all my *searching* was coming to an end. Closer and closer to the present, the words of Tara Singh brought me to the actual state of inner peace imparted in the lessons and statements found in *ACIM*. But this stillness and silence in the present was an atmosphere of attention Tara Singh had taken many years, even decades, to nurture and be able to harness. Some 30 years with Krishnamurti—then years with Dr. Schucman in his preparation to share *A Course in Miracles* with the public—all had brought Tara Singh to the state of mind in which he could speak with certainty, by virtue of "having the ears to hear."

After the three years in silence, there was an inner guidance in Tara Singh to travel to the East Coast. Having avoided books for these years, one day quite unexpectedly he opened a book by Edgar Cayce, the great American psychic, and read Cayce advising people to "drink water before having a meal." He thought, "This sounds like Ayurveda, the ancient Indian system of health and wellness." So he decided to travel toward Virginia Beach, where Cayce had his posthumous organization. He travelled across the country with a couple of his students. They camped in parks, because the shock of being back in the commercially stimulating world was too much for Tara Singh in the heightened state of awareness. In one park near Virginia Beach, he was approached by a man with a cassette recording. The voice on the tape was that of Paul Solomon, another prominent psychic living in Virginia Beach. On the recording the voice said to Tara Singh, "You have been brought half-way around the world to be here," meaning, to be with Paul Solomon's organization. So that was what he did for a few years after his silence, giving classes on *Bhakti yoga*, which is the yoga of devotion. Until one day he blundered into a copy of *A Course in Miracles*. When he opened it up to the first page and read, *"Nothing real can be threatened; nothing unreal exists. Herein lies the peace of God,"* he was stunned. Never had he heard such powerful words spoken in the English language.

Soon he attended a lecture given by Judy Skutch, one of the publishers of *ACIM*. During the lecture in which she discussed the content of the book, she referred to "the lady" who wrote it down. The more he listened, the more he got interested in this "lady." What kind of a being must she be to write down such words, with such authority and certainty, he thought. After the lecture he went up to Judy Skutch and asked if he could meet "this lady." With considerable back and forth, and some insistence on Tara Singh's part, they arranged for Tara Singh to come to New York and meet Dr. Helen Schucman at Judy's apartment.

Dr. Schucman was an objective person, a serious person, and did not "suffer fools" or waste time with the non-serious. At the time Tara Singh met her in New York, he was wearing Indian clothes—and she said, "Are you a holy man?" in an air of quizzical skepticism. He responded with something like this: "In ancient times there were wise teachers who spoke to their students. If a student was inattentive, and answered a question wrongly after the answer had been given to him on many previous occasions, the teacher would pick up a rock from the pile next to him and hurl it at the student, giving him a shock. I was the student who picked up the rocks, and kept them neatly in the pile."

Two beings met at a level beyond our thinking. This was the woman through whom Jesus chose to deliver his message for these times in the form of an unprecedented *course* on self-healing and enlightenment—according to some his *second coming* that he spoke of 2000 years prior. And, this was the man who was sitting in silence during the time *ACIM* was coming through—preparing himself to be the messenger for this work, and the one who would bring it into application. It was a meeting of destiny. It was as significant as *ACIM* itself. He asked her upon leaving if he could contact her the next day by phone, and she said, "Yes."

Tara Singh was on fire. He knew he had just met a being on the caliber of Krishnamurti, of impeccable qualities and with something as significant to give to humanity. He was determined to establish a contact and relationship with her. He called her the next day, asking for another meeting at her apartment. "No," she said. "I have too much to do today. This evening I have an event and I don't have time to see you—but you can call another time if you want to." Tara Singh was walking the streets of New York, calling the number from a pay phone, not even knowing where Dr. Schucman lived. In about an hour he called the number again. "I have to see you today," he insisted. "No, the answer is no. I just have too much to do—but call another time, " as she stuck with her previous decision. But here is where the real determination of Tara Singh came into focus. To him "no" was not an option, and he would question why life would bring him all the way to New

York City to meet Dr. Schucman if the door would then be closed? He called back again. This time Dr. Schucman was not so polite. "You are a pest, didn't you hear what I said? I cannot see you today, and that is it!" CLICK. Now to any other man, this would be enough to feel about two inches tall, while shaking in his boots. By now Tara Singh had walked miles, and had no idea where this journey was taking him.

Yet, to the great men of India—Gandhi, Nehru and Gyani Kartar Singh—who had mentored him, the word "impossible" did not apply to Tara Singh. He wandered for another half an hour or so, and called for the fourth time. "I just have to see you, please, just one more time. I have a burning question, I have to, please." It was as if his whole will came to the crescendo of an intense necessity of throwing himself at the feet of truth, and insisting for the mercy of the heavens to grant him this one essential boon in life. After a long pause, Dr. Schucman said, "Yes, OK, but you may stay only five minutes." And to his amazement, when she gave him her address, he was only a block away. Wandering the streets for hours, unbeknownst to him, life had brought him practically to her door.

He stopped to buy her flowers at one of the shops. In India one never goes to the teacher empty handed. He rang the bell and she answered. There was a foyer with a couple well-made chairs. She showed him into the foyer and sat down. When he handed her the flowers, she threw them into the waste basket and said, "I don't like flowers." More silence rushed into the room, charging the atmosphere with incomparable stillness and beauty. He sat down, and time stood still. His mind went blank like it had with Krishnamurti. The length of time he was there, most likely 20 minutes, seemed like 20 years. Not a word was spoken, but both beings knew that destiny had brought them together for this meeting at an impersonal level. After awhile Tara Singh knew he had stayed long enough. As he rose up, so did Dr. Schucman to see him to the door. "May I call you tomorrow," Tara Singh asked. "Yes," she said. And as he was about to step out, Dr. Schucman, with the back of her hand, caressed Tara Singh on the cheek with no words. He said it was as if the hand of Christ had just touched him and blessed him forever.

Having the ears to hear was Tara Singh's main gift. He could take any encounter and extract the nourishing marrow out of its very bones. He could see the essence of a thing instantly, without the experience of study. He had a sixth sense with which he could cut through the false and go right for the truth of any situation. As he described Dr. Schucman as one of the greatest beings America had produced, he also saw her glory at a much higher level:

The Higher Forces that brought the *Course* into being said of her, "She is not Mary, but she is at the same level of evolution. Mary gave birth to Jesus's body. Dr. Schucman gave birth to Jesus's mind."

And to Tara Singh who had the eyes to see who Holy Helen really was, that was an absolute fact.

So, for two-and-a-half years, Tara Singh called Dr. Schucman at the same time every day. The woman who wanted no attention called to herself in this mission of bringing *A Course in Miracles* into the world, who "had no students," all of a sudden, had a student. And this was not just any student, but one who had the "ears to hear." A Holy Relationship was established unexpectedly between these two people. Tara Singh was religious about calling her at the appointed hour. During his two-and-a-half year tutelage with her he never missed a call. What must that discipline have been, for both, to stick with it and see it through to the end? Tara Singh kept up this relationship until Dr. Schucman passed in 1981. But before she left, she said to him of his role with *ACIM*, "I leave you the Course, and it is for the rest of your life."

❖ *Chapter 12.* ❖

New Order in Life

Most of our houses in America are filled with things we do not even need. So much superfluous stuff abounds in our lives and in our minds, that the very nature of our everyday existence is clogged with the unessential. The TV is in the center of our living rooms, and we are programmed, as it were, by the programming that flashes across the screen. We work jobs to support the price tag of all of this complexity, which arose as a distraction from not liking the job in the first place. Acquiring more things also applies more pressure to support and assure the survival of this little Camelot we have made. At the same time, we have lost sight of the life of simplicity that affords us the deeper peace and fulfillment of a more divine leisure, with an enlightened and conscious purpose.

I was like most. I had a house or two, a couple of cars, a mortgage, and a small business to pay the bills. I even had a studio, my artistic work, and a spiritual teacher who I deemed wise and who enriched my life. But something always seemed like a struggle to maintain the small fiefdom of my estate I called my own. I remembered seeing the man on the TV talent show who spun the plates on the sticks, keeping all of the dozen or so plates spinning simultaneously. He would scurry frantically around the plates, giving each a spin, to keep them all going. But at no instant could he rest for fear that all the plates would lose steam and come crashing down. That was what my life felt like at times, especially after meeting Tara Singh. I knew the seeds of happiness were in what I had, mostly what I had inside of myself, but I also knew there were things I could clear out of my life that would bring that happiness closer to my immediate awareness. Tara Singh encouraged us to simplify our lives. I discovered a new order; peace is in the space, not in the accumulation of stuff.

I began to simplify, getting rid of things I did not need. I was inspired by Tara Singh's descriptions of his silent years. He had one fork, one knife, one plate—one pencil, and he always knew where each thing was. Nothing was ever wasted, and nothing he did not need ever distracted him. And he never felt deprived of anything. At the same time he had tremendous space to be himself, without the fears and concerns of survival. The days were glorious. He basked in the space of ultimate simplicity in which pressure was non-existent. Not one time did the fear of the future or the regrets of the past touch him. He remained in the holy instant of the present, clear that his purpose was to be in the absolute silence and stillness of his true mind that Krishnamurti stressed was so essential. Only in this mind could one know those higher states of awareness—of love, of virtue, of the real sanity of true reason.

Order in Life begins with an internal order, and that can only be realized by paying close attention to the quality of one's own thought. Meditation could simply be described as the observation of one's own thought. And gradually as one observes thoughts, like the beads on a rosary, one notices the space between the beads. As the intensity of the attention grows, the space between the thoughts widens. Gradually one notices the space more than the thoughts, until one is more with the space than with the thoughts. In this space of silence is the real peace of God realized. This is the real order in life, when the mind is enveloped by this peace, and reactions, opinions, judgments and motives cease. Then one receives the glory of silence into their life.

Tara Singh wrote in *The Voice that Precedes Thought:*

**"THE PURPOSE OF EVERYTHING
IS TO BRING THE MIND TO STILLNESS.**

Spend time each day in quiet.

Put aside the preoccupations of the day.

**You are much more with nature
when you are quiet inside.**

The still mind is ever present,

117

thus transforming energies of Heaven
accompany you wherever you go.

A Silent mind is the Mind of God —
free of all mortal fear, belief, and knowings.

Why do you evade stillness?

NO KNOWING CAN BE WORDED.
KNOWING IS A STATE OF STILLNESS.

ONLY IN STILLNESS IS ONE WHOLE."   P.125

The real order in a person's life begins when stillness and silence are valued more than thought. Thought divides and separates us from wholeness, from each other, from even our Self within. The whole purpose of meditation, of the miracle, of *A Course in Miracles,* is to silence our thought and give us a real, actual contact with the *force of life* in the present, independent of thought. This present is still and silent, pristine as the rising morning mist off the glass-like surface of a calm autumnal lake.

I began to take Tara Singh's advice and spend part of my day in silence. I even set aside a prayer room in my house, and made a simple altar there, and put some of the pictures of the Holy Beings around the room. It became the refuge from all the activity of the rest of the day, the place I could go morning and evening to step out of the pressures and tensions of work. And then I found that the stillness and silence I discovered in myself, easily in this room set aside for this purpose, I could take into the rest of my day and extend into my work and encounters with others. Not only was this order in life cleansing me inside, but it was also positively affecting the nature of all my relationships.

What I had resisted in my daily work, I had no more resistance. My work became *a worship*. I built kitchens and bathrooms for my clients, and it became as much an art form as my paintings and drawings. Everything took on an inner beauty of an intensity I did not notice before. My powers of observation, which had always been fairly developed, became even more developed. And all of this was an involuntary transformation happening within, as a result of my relationship with Tara Singh and with the teaching of life he imparted. The order in life that was already present, already permeating all of creation, rushed forth into my awareness. I was no longer *absent* from the peace that was always present. As a result, the superfluous things in my world dropped away, and the unnecessary had less pull toward me. As a result, I had more energy, more space. I got rid of a lot of things I did not want or need. My life became more simplified, and I was grateful for this transformation. I had time to read and revisit the classics. I read *Walden* again, the words of Thoreau that had so stunningly touched me in my teens. But now I was a man, and could appreciate the maturity in myself, and in the life teachings that Tara Singh had given me commensurate with Thoreau's:

"I went to the woods because I wished to live deliberately, to front only the essential facts of life, and see if I could not learn what it had to teach, and not, when I came to die, discover that I had not lived. I did not wish to live what was not life, living is so dear; nor did I wish to practice resignation, unless it was quite necessary. I wanted to live deep and suck all the marrow out of life, to live so sturdily and Spartan-like as to put to rout all that was not life, to cut a broad swath and shave close, to drive life into a corner, and reduce it to its lowest terms, and, if it proved to be mean, why then to get the whole and genuine meanness of it, and publish its meanness to the world; or if it were sublime, to know it by experience, and be able to give a true account of it in my next excursion."   Henry David Thoreau — Walden P.114

My time with Tara Singh was delightfully my "time in the woods." It was a retreat from the confines and expectations of the routines of daily living, into which I had fallen. These were gradually eroding me away, keeping me from realizing my highest spiritual potential. If I stayed in these routines out of some false sense of duty, I would end up like Thoreau says, *"....when I came to die, discover that I had not really lived."*

Order in life is an insistence one makes to live their life to the fullest they possibly can, beyond the boundaries of family patterns and conditioning, societal conventions, and personal beliefs in limitations. Order in life is *liberation* from the past that has held us in the vice of unrealized goals, and unfulfilled expectations. Order in life is a meeting with the present that is so vital, so charged with hope and gratitude that everything is provided in this very instant to know a state of grace and perfect happiness. It is a meeting with the truth of our own divine nature. Mostly, this realization is known in stillness and silence, beyond the words of thought. It was Tara Singh who introduced me to that state of being. He brought order to my life, and silence and stillness to my mind—and affirmed the fact of what ACIM so clearly states:

"Spirit is in a state of grace forever.
Your reality is only spirit.
Therefore you are in a state of grace forever."
ACIM — Text p.10

And truly from Tara Singh, I felt the hand of grace upon my soul, and the Peace of God imparted to me from the pure determination and intent of his compassion.

❖ *Chapter 13.* ❖

The Work of Service

From a video on Mother Teresa that was played at one of the retreats, I discerned there was a mission somewhere in New York City, in the Bronx. I called information and was able to track it down to a couple of numbers—*Sisters of Charity, Missionaries of Charity*—or something like that. When I inquired, I found the place that was in the video, the Missionaries of Charity, Mother Teresa's Mission in the Bronx, was not far from Yankee Stadium. I talked with one of the Sisters who had a heavy Indian accent. "When could I come and offer my services?" I asked. She said, "This Saturday at 7AM sharp, you can come help in the soup kitchen. Don't be late." That was it. For me to be there at 7AM I would have to leave Philadelphia at 4AM. I Thought, "OK. I could do that." So one wintry day in 1995 I rousted myself out of bed, revved up my Ford Van, and headed out to the Big Apple—on a mission.

The New Jersey Turnpike at that time of day was not crowded. Usually it is solid traffic from Philadelphia to New York. But it was fairly smooth sailing on this day, not many cars that early in the morning. Soon I crossed over the George Washington Bridge, through Manhattan and over the Harlem River, down the Major Deegan Expressway and off at the Yankee Stadium exit, just minutes after the sunrise was coming over the Bronx hills of endless high rises. It was not far to the Mission, and when I arrived I parked the van and sat silently in the driver's seat awhile, collecting my resolve to be there on time. I saw a chain link fence with a gate, and a handwritten sign wired to the chain links—*Missionaries of Charity*. There was a doorway and a button for a bell to the gate. I rang the bell shortly before 7AM. A Sister in a white sari with three blue stripes running down the edge opened the gate, welcomed me, and showed me to the kitchen area.

They were obviously getting ready to serve a large crowd. There were enough seats for over a hundred people to sit comfortably in chairs around more than a dozen long tables. The Sister put me to work immediately, helping to break some bread into manageable sizes to serve the people. I slipped right into the volunteer crew, obviously filled with people who often came to serve. After preparing the bread, we began to set the tables with napkins, plastic bowls and plastic spoons. After we had the room looking quite impeccable and ready to receive the people, the dining hall was filled with the waiting crowds off the streets—mostly men, mostly black and Hispanic men. There were a few mothers with babies in strollers. When people sat down, and after the sisters recited a prayer, we commenced serving the multitude of homeless and poor. Many were disgruntled and demanding. They were not particularly grateful—perhaps even the opposite. So I noticed how I felt about this, knowing that whatever reward I was to receive was going to come from within myself, not from some external "pat on the back." Not even the sisters got into sentimentality, or overtly gracious thanks. They had a job to do. They were happy for the volunteer's help in doing it, yet they were not going to fluff you up with any praise to get you to come back again.

The whole job, start to finish, was over by eleven AM— food preparation, service, clean up, and starting the preparation for the next day. I was there for roughly four hours of work, all done quite efficiently and reverently, without much ado. Then the Sisters disappeared. Not one "Thank You," or "see you next week," and certainly no "can you do this or that for us." I looked around, and saw the faucet on the kitchen sink was leaking. It was an old stainless steel sink with a shelf-back faucet—with an extra long spout for getting large pots underneath. I could see a new faucet was what was needed. That would be what I would contribute on my next visit—I thought.

A week later I left on Saturday morning, 4AM like before, but this time with my plumbing tools, a new faucet for the sink, and some deep satisfaction in myself that I was contributing something that I wanted to give to help the situation. I headed for Yankee Stadium again, and to the Missionaries of Charity in the Bronx. I travelled the same route, and the same Sister let me into the complex when I arrived. As I passed through the hallways to the soup kitchen, there was a drawing of a simple hand, like a child's version of tracing around a hand on a piece of paper. And at the end of each finger and thumb were written these five words: "You"— "do"—"it"—"to"—"me." It referred to a passage in the Bible where Jesus tells his disciples, "What you do to the least of my brothers, you do it to me." And this was the Mission of Mother Teresa—to render service to the "poorest of the poor" and to see the face of Christ in them. Well, that she did—that she did. And she trained her thousands of Sisters, the Missionaries of Charity, to do the same. All that they gave to the poorest of the poor, they gave with this line in mind: "You"—"do"—"it"— "to"—"me." The Sisters were impeccable people. They lived a lifestyle of selfless service, and felt the privilege of serving Jesus in all that they did. Theirs was a balance of prayer and action. They lived for God, but they lived for God in service to their brothers and sisters. The two were not separate. Without the *action* of service, the faith and prayer would be just meaningless concepts to them. This is why, probably, Tara Singh encouraged all of us to discover the *joy of service* in getting acquainted with people like Mother Teresa and her Sisters. He was a *man of action*, and he recognized others who were of similar convictions.

Now I was in my element, really giving something that I wanted to do, knew how to do, and found very fulfilling. After the work of the soup kitchen was over, I took out the new faucet and showed it to the sisters. "You need this, Sister. This old one is shot and not worth trying to repair. I will just replace it with this new one." They were overjoyed. I went to the van to get my tools to do the job. Within the hour I had the old faucet off and the new one nicely in place. What a difference to not have the perennially dripping faucet for the clean up duties. Efficient spiritual action is also aligned with efficient physical order and action. Tara Singh taught us to see something through to the end, and if we were going to give of ourselves, to really give from the heart. Then, he insisted, we always complete that which we truly were inspired to do. I must say, installing this faucet for the Missionaries of Charity, and ultimately for the poor people they served, was one of the most joyous jobs I had done in this field. And I needed no pay, no thanks, no pat on the back, and no reimbursement for my expenses. It was a pure act of giving that was introducing me to what Tara Singh referred to as the *Joy of Service*.

As I was installing the faucet, one of the Sisters asked me where I was from. I said, "Philadelphia." She replied, "Didn't you know there is a Mother Teresa Mission in Norristown, PA?" I said, "No—I didn't." Norristown was only a half an hour drive from my home in Philadelphia. I did not need to drive all the way up to the Bronx to find a place to serve. So, to my surprise, life made it easier for me to devote some of my time to the work of service. I started to go to this Mission in Norristown once a week, giving my time and energy to whatever they needed there. At first it was just work in the soup kitchen, then gradually some shuttling of food goods from Philadelphia and Norristown to the Bronx. Then I would install tile flooring in the Norristown soup kitchen, until finally the Sisters asked me to do some construction project on the third floor of their building—to build a series of shower

126

rooms. They were very much needed for the ladies with young children who stayed there in the Mission, whom the Sisters accommodated until they could find more permanent housing.

The sisters were trained "never to take advantage of another," just like Tara Singh had taught us. So on these larger projects that would take weeks, the Sisters were happy to pay me for my time, which I gladly accepted, for a much-reduced rate. This pay allowed me to devote more of my time to service, and also to stay afloat financially while I was doing it.

For a number of years I worked at this Mother Teresa Mission alongside some of my other A Course in Miracles friends who had also attended the Tara Singh retreats with me. Kiki Vekkos, Alexander Barnes, Clarke Van Sant, Sue Sipos, and Paul Meistering and I would often go on Wednesdays to do what was needed. It became a way we could contribute something together in the spirit of service, to which Tara Singh emphasized and encouraged us to do. It was not long after he stressed this Divine Service that the Foundation for Life Action changed its name to the Joseph Plan Foundation. Joseph was the prophet in the Bible whose brothers sold him into slavery, then he found himself in jail interpreting the Pharaoh's dreams about the seven fat cows, then the seven lean cows. The "lean" cows represented a famine, and the Pharoah appointed Joseph to be his main minister. During the "fat" years Joseph stored much food and grain throughout the land. When the famine came, there was plenty due to Joseph's foresightedness.

Taraji took this story to be indicative of what was needed in the last years of the 20th century and the new millennium, in which conservation of resources would be absolutely essential to the survival of the modern economic system, and ultimately the people. He predicted there would be financial crisis and worldwide "scarcity" brought about by the economic policies of fear and greed. But to cope with this, he stressed each individual must discover this principle: "Having something of your own to give" is how he would put it. Without this intrinsic work to extend something of value to humanity, one would stay stuck at the self-centered and survival level of human existence—which, according to Tara Singh, was no real existence at all. And this level would become increasingly tough to navigate in a highly competitive and ultra modern world.

The computer would take over the human being, and represent a *higher intelligence* than the level of his own being. He would become stripped of his freedom of thought, and become more and more conditioned by the pressures of jobs, economics, education of skills—all this to fit into an ever increasing system of artificiality and market driven motives. Power would be concentrated in the hands of the few, and people would not even have their own minds to make a life of having something of their own to give, to extend. The down side of affluence without true wisdom would end up being self-destructive to mankind in general, and to the individual in particular. All in all, the *Joy of Service* was a way of reversing this trend. It was a way for the individual to discover within himself the greater potentials that he came to these planes to give and express. And through giving one would find their true fulfillment in Life, not through any other way. Having something to give was so intrinsic to a human being, yet something we had grossly forgotten in this commercialized and calculated world, that we had to actively reverse this trend. We had to let go of the "getting" of self-centeredness by devoting some of our time to selfless service. Tara Singh inspired us to do that, and this was a great lesson in finding what we had *to give*, rather than *to want*. In the giving we would find our true Self, not in the un-fulfillment of seeking goals and pursuing the stimulation of unessential outlets and distractions.

Service became something that the Joseph Plan Foundation and *A Course in Miracles* extended. The overriding theme of the workshops became "what do you have to give?" People were challenged to find in themselves the surplus they could extend to their brothers and sisters, to those whom the *Course* says, "temporarily have less." Tara Singh encouraged us to band together in groups of five or more to do something of service. We were fortunate. As I previously mentioned, one of our friends, Alexander Barnes, who was part of our small group of people who studied *A Course in Miracles* and attended the retreats, was also a drug and alcohol counselor in North Philadelphia. His life mission became one of helping others "kick the habit" and get clean. We all helped Alexander start a half-way house for recovering addicts, and even did our own mobile soup kitchen off the back of Alexander's pick-up truck once a week in the worst area of North Philadelphia. We took the lessons we learned at Mother Teresa's Mission and just applied them to the mobile soup kitchen project. For a couple of years we kept this up. The Miracle House became a place for addicts to get what they needed, for a few to live, and for many to attend the daily meetings of Narcotics Anonymous in the downstairs hall of the building. We even built some shower rooms where homeless people could come to get cleaned up if they wanted to. All in all, the years I spent doing this "work of service" prepared me for the later times in which I would devote my self to world service with Sondra Ray and Liberation Breathing®.

❖ *Chapter 14.* ❖

The Foundation

The Foundation for Life Action, and subsequently the Joseph Plan Foundation that it morphed into, were federally approved, 501 3-C, non-profit educational foundations. Tara Singh and his close students set them up to be the clearinghouse for the work, for the school to teach students of *A Course in Miracles*. This involved a wide range of actions: from an actual school where people came to study with Tara Singh; to a publishing house for the books and tapes that came out of the lectures of this school; to the production of a rigorous schedule of seminars and workshops that Tara Singh offered around the country on *A Course in Miracles*; to a kitchen that fed the people; to the place where people like myself, who had attended the workshops and retreats, could come for a respite from their routines of daily life in order to be part of the Foundation's work and extension. In its zenith in the middle 1980's and early 1990's the Foundation, as it was called for short, was a bustling place of serious business. I say business in a non-commercialized sense. It possessed a most impeccable nature that worked efficiently as a well-tuned organization at a whole new level of humanism and dedicated service. The Foundation's philosophy was simply, "The human being comes first." It proved over and over again that the *life for life* relationships that Tara Singh developed with his students and friends were at the forefront of the whole Foundation's reason for being.

When questioned once in an interview about the Foundation, the interviewer asked, "Is it an organization?" In his usual confronting nature of self-inquiry, Tara Singh said, "Well, the military is organized." Then he proceeded to point out the many pitfalls of an organization, of its practices and rules that conform its members; of its not living up to the expectations of its original intentions, though those intentions may be of the loftiest kind; of its dependence on outside support from donations to keep itself running; of its aspirations toward a cause, that are often left grossly unrealized in its members. No, the Foundation was not an organization. So what was the Foundation, then? It was a school, an educational foundation, but what was it teaching? The *School at the Branching of the Road* was often used to describe the Foundation, but what exactly was that? The principle is best described in this section in the Text of *A Course in Miracles*. It expresses the intensity of a decision the Foundation required of all those who passed through its doors

"IV. The Branching of the Road

When you come to the place where the branch in the road is quite apparent, you cannot go ahead. You must go either one way or the other. For now if you go straight ahead, the way you went before you reached the branch, you will go nowhere. The whole purpose of coming this far was to decide which branch you will take now. The way you came no longer matters. It can no longer serve. No one who reaches this far can make the wrong decision, although he can delay. And there is no part of the journey that seems more hopeless and futile than standing where the road branches, and not deciding on which way to go....

And so you and your brother stand, here in this holy place, before the veil of sin that hangs between you and the face of Christ. Let it be lifted! Raise it together with your brother, for it is but a veil that stands between you. Either you or your brother alone will see it as a solid block, nor realize how thin the drapery that separates you now. Yet it is almost over in your awareness, and peace has reached you even here, before the veil. Think what will happen after. The love of Christ will light your face, and shine from it into a darkened world that needs the light. And from this holy place He will return with you, not leaving it nor you. You will become His messengers, returning Him unto Himself."

ACIM TEXT, CHAPTER 22, Section IV

I endeavor to give my own impressions of the Foundation as one who was a witness to its action, yet not so close as to be a member of its staff, or an agent of its practical extensions at its headquarters in Los Angeles. I was a student of Tara Singh's, and a guest at the Foundation. For a period of time, I was on its board of directors. I always paid my way to the workshops and retreats, as well on my trips with Tara Singh in my later years with him. Tara Singh treated me like an honored guest in his house, which was also the Foundation's house. And I treated him as well in my own home. I did not receive any pay for any service I did for the Foundation, for Tara Singh, or for the retreats I attended. In fact I spent tens of thousands of dollars to attend the workshops, to travel with Tara Singh, and to be at the Foundation on occasion. And I never regretted spending a penny of that expenditure. The principle meaning and reason of the Foundation for me was to discover the joys of service, to question myself through the wisdom given by Tara Singh in the seminars, books and recordings, but also, most importantly, to discover the real meaning and necessity of the Holy Relationship to which *A Course in Miracles* gives so much importance. In the end, I say with utmost respect and reverence, I came to consider Tara Singh my closest FRIEND—in the Capital sense of the word, and the Foundation the place in which this Holy Relationship could flower. It was truly the school *at the branching of the road* where I was given the great opportunity to see the Christ in another, namely Tara Singh, and know for certain this vision was the most significant perception, and blessing, of my life. With Taraji, he taught every relationship in your life is holy.

Like all mystery schools, you cannot adequately define its full purpose and action. What some people needed to receive in this incarnation, they received through the grace of God in abundance from the Foundation and Tara Singh's work there. I was no different. The Foundation represented *the branching of the road* for me, as well as for everyone else who stepped into the mighty vortex of Tara Singh's energy and integrity. The Foundation was a place where "thoughts had no meaning," and only the actuality of your status quo in life, and who you are as God created you deserved its attention. All of that which was not of your divine nature came to surface at the Foundation, and you had to be ready to deal with it in the most serious and utmost way. If for one instant you took for granted the incredible uniqueness of this gift, of this blessing of Life to provide a space in which true Love could flower, and self correction could take place, you could be assured that the forces of life would take you out in some fashion, and your welcome there outlived. When entering the Foundation, you entered through the doors of a genuine hospitality the likes of which were all but unknown in America. It possessed a vibration from another dimension, one in which the Holy Relationship was a *fact*, not an idea. And Tara Singh was the holder of this space that allowed only this to take place. Casualness was absent, as was sentimentality, and ideas were things long outgrown. One came with the nakedness of their own soul fully exposed when they came to the Foundation. It was a place of great purity, but it was also the crucible in which all your own impurities were intensified and burned away.

135

The Foundation was a place where all the self-imposed limitations I had placed on myself could be removed. It was here, at *the branching of the road,* that I came to put aside my childish ways and grow up into a mature spiritual being in actual realization. Tara Singh was the voice of reason, the voice of the Christ Mind who represented *A Course in Miracles,* and because he was taught and ordained by Dr. Schucman to do this work, he came with the *power* of the Holy Spirit behind him to impart the actual energy of ascension the *Course* was written to impart. Like Yudhisthira from the ancient Indian times, Tara Singh not only had "the ears to hear," he had the Voice to speak authoritatively on *A Course in Miracles* and harness the very same divine force of life that brought it into being. He was a man of conviction who did not compromise. Either the students would endeavor to *live* by the principles set forth in the Lessons of *ACIM,* or they would not be at the Foundation. It was that simple. It was not a place of mere *intellectual learning.* In fact, Taraji considered that a meaningless indulgence. He called it "educated ignorance," because if failed to open a person's heart up to love. One was either willing to put themselves through the test of application, or they had no business being in the benevolent grace of the Foundation's Holy atmosphere. And to him, application meant to rise to that level of integrity inside yourself that would demand of you to come to the Christ Self—that is your true Identity. There would be no compromise in this. Either you considered this your loftiest aspiration, or you did not belong at the Foundation.

"Above all else I want to see things differently." is Lesson # 28 in *ACIM*. Being at the Foundation made that perfectly clear. Well, "above all else" meant you had to place your awakening process on the front line of your deepest desire; to be liberated from all falseness and fear, all motives and ego goals, to discover the intrinsic nature and what you came to this life to give. These were the guiding functions of the Foundation for Life Action, and for the work of Tara Singh in the world. And by virtue of being at the Foundation, they became my functions in life as well.

Of course the Prayer Room was the heart, soul and battery of the work at 902 Burnside Avenue. I described it in the chapter on the Holy Beings, but I did not stress the importance of this place in the overall function of Tara Singh's work. Twice a day he would give sessions in the Prayer Room— around 7AM and 5PM. These sessions would go for about an hour, every day that he was there, without fail. Most of them were recorded. They were given in front of a lit Altar, with the energy of all the Holy Beings behind them. *"Truth will correct all errors in my mind."* is Lesson # 107 in *ACIM*. This lesson represented the energy of Tara Singh's lectures. He took you though a series of facts that would undo your errors of thought, undo your tendencies of destructive behavior, even undo the subconscious memories you were carrying, unbeknownst to yourself, that were sabotaging areas of your life. Most often what he would say was confronting and poignant, and required real self-inquiry to keep up with it. But this was the whole purpose of being there. I considered it such a blessing to be in this intimate setting receiving Tara Singh's wisdom, not edited or held back in any way, that I saw it as an opportunity to be confronted and transformed. The issue would always be one of application of the truth of the lesson, and the letting go of the ego patterns that blocked or prevented that application. This was the main function of the mystery school that Tara Singh offered—to free you from the little self you made, in exchange for the real SELF you are, as God created you. He was unwavering in this goal, which included the ending of your thought. Many people could not go this far. The stillness and silence that surrounded Tara Singh's teachings were palpably felt and irrefutably presented, but people would come right up against their inner "unwillingness" to go any further, and to completely let go of thought, in this case their ego's thoughts about themselves. Tara Singh would bring everyone to this *branching of the road*, but the decision to take the step would be totally your own responsibility. Some people would go as far as they could, then stop short and go home, back into their old life and all the problems inherent in that old life. Others would go a little further, and their lives at home would be transformed by a new order, and new quietude. And a few would be totally turned around in their views, and receive the boon of the Self that Tara Singh had to offer with its blessings of stillness and silence. But no one was ever "finished." Tara Singh made it clear that "inner correction," with love, was a life long process.

The Foundation offered a rest from the routines of the personal life, and introduced another energy of service and true caring for the human being. The whole purpose of this *Life Action* was to bring a person to a totally different sensibility and refinement—also, to a self-honesty that was hitherto undiscovered. Tara Singh could absolutely deliver that. To me, my relationship with him, my relationship with *ACIM*, my relationship with the Christ Mind, and my relationship with the Foundation were ALL ONE in the same —one of a Holy Relationship.

❖ *Chapter 15.* ❖

My First Trip

My first trip with Tara Singh was to Mexico City. He called me out of the blue, which in 1999 was quite a surprise. Seldom had he called me personally. Usually it was a member of his staff who called with some logistical question about a workshop, either one I was attending or one I was helping to organize. This was such a surprise I hardly knew what to say. "Why don't you come out to Los Angeles, spend a few days, then we will take a holiday to Mexico." Wow, this was so totally new to me, for a teacher to invite me on a trip with him, alone, I could hardly believe it.

I had to rearrange some things, but it was doable. I flew to the Foundation in the late summer and stayed in Los Angeles a few days before Tara Singh and I embarked on an adventure to Mexico City. One of the few times he travelled to a place without having a workshop or a connection at the other end, this trip to Mexico represented a different action for him and me. Though he knew I had been his student for more that ten years now, there was a newness in our travels of an unprecedented nature. I was not quite sure what to expect. I was not quite sure what the mission was, except to get closer and see what it was like to live together in such close proximity.

As we flew into Mexico City I remember the green trees—forests and forests of them. Somehow I expected to see a dry and arid climate, nothing green at all. We landed and I was a bit nervous to collect our things and go through the customs, find a taxi and get to our hotel. But I got over my initial shyness and reservations as I moved our things, and us, through the customs and got us to the taxi area. Soon, in the early evening, we arrived at our hotel, checked in safely, and were taken up the small elevator to our room. It had one double bed and a couch. I opted for the couch in order to give Tara Singh the bed. After having a shower, we dressed and went outside to find a restaurant. We were impressed by the cosmopolitan nature of the city, and noticed how the mistaken notion of Mexico gives Americans the wrong impression of some backward country, languishing in poverty and sending its masses of downtrodden north to the American promised land of milk and honey. From the moment we arrived we realized there was something wrong with this picture. Mexico had its proud and long cultural heritage. The notion that all of Mexico was Tijuana, impoverished, backward and troubled was just not true. In fact the Mexicans had something of great commodity that we lacked—a sense of divine leisure. As we walked the wide avenues of Mexico City and stopped in the open air cafes for dinner, it felt more like a European city of high culture than a backward, "south of the border" banana republic.

141

Tara Singh was an acute observer of facts. He noticed everything down to how the waiter walked and poised himself; the grace or lack of grace in which he executed his service; the neatness of his dress; how attentive he was to our dining needs. We enjoyed ourselves with a Mexican beer—a Dos Equis—and the meal was one of total relaxation. No pressure to be anywhere. The conversation was mostly about how grossly wrong people's impressions of Mexico were in the North. We had a false sense of superiority, when there were cultural qualities of this country that far exceeded our own. Perhaps it was the remnant of the ancient Aztec and Mayan cultures that gave it a richness of heritage as well—a well developed indigenous pride. The fact that these native Indian people had cities built of stone, and were not of the nomadic varieties of the northern tribes, and possessed a system of writing, all contributed to a richness of culture that was somehow retained in the juxtaposition of the conqueror with the conquered.

After the meal we strolled leisurely back to our hotel down the wide avenues on the tiled walkways, with their colonnade of shade trees. It was warm, but not unbearably hot. Some fruit for our room was easily obtained from a stand on the street next to the hotel. We looked forward to a good rest, and the unknown adventure the next day would hold. I had my Lonely Planet guidebook for Mexico, so we were well informed of the highlights to see in Mexico City for the next few days. When we returned to the room we settled in. I was on the couch, but it seemed like a palace to me, because I was with my teacher for the first time so close, sleeping in the same room.

Stillness pervaded the room when we awoke. After having our showers we prepared some of the mangoes we had bought the night before, and had a simple breakfast in the room. I read over some of the highlights in the tourist guide for Mexico City. The Museum of Anthropology was purported to be one of the best in the world. After a morning of getting our bearings, we headed out in a taxi for this museum, in a chartreuse green Volkswagen Beetle, and arrived there in the late morning. We walked the grounds, took some photographs in front of a huge Aztec figure, the God of Rain, and entered the majestic façade of the museum's modern architecture. The ancient artifacts from the former Indian cultures were preserved and presented in the most stunning fashion. All around us were the highest contributions of a whole people who came and went, left their artistic marks, and disappeared as the Spanish ascended the throne of cultural dominance. We walked through the front of the museum that entered into a vast courtyard. By then we were hot from the taxi ride and the walk through the grounds, so we headed down the stairs to a cool café, shaded in the lower verandas, and sat in a pleasant outdoor space at a table under an umbrella. The cool beverages were a delight. We sat and talked, always about something poignant concerning the state of affairs in the world, the nature of the times, the status quo of my situation, or something else that was a fact. If I had a problem, Tara Singh would want to know all about it, to get to the bottom of it and dissolve it.

After our brunch we ascended to the main level and left the museum, hardly having seen a quarter of its exhibits. It never occurred to me that our time together had nothing to do with "sightseeing" until that moment. We were in the flow of a different energy that had no motives, no projected plans, and not one expectation. I was discovering what it was like to *live in the present*, without a past or a future. Tara Singh lived constantly in this presence, and those who were in his vortex of influence were taken into that moment outside of time and space. In his short walk through the museum, he took in the whole thing, fully comprehended and absorbed it, not missing one iota of what it had to offer. He did not need to stay any longer, after our conversation. It was time to move on to the next thing, the next action of life.

After seeing another art museum, which was full of murals of Siqueiros and Rivera, Tara Singh and I visited one of the most celebrated shrines in Mexico, the Basilica of Our Lady of Guadalupe. The famous icon, which is a painting that miraculously appeared, is described here:

> "Two accounts, published in the 1640s, one in Spanish, one in Nahuatl, tell how, while walking from his village to Mexico City in the early morning of December 9, 1531 (then the Feast of the Immaculate Conception in the Spanish Empire), the peasant Juan Diego saw on the slopes of the Hill of Tepeyac a vision of a girl of fifteen or sixteen years of age, surrounded by light. Speaking to him in Nahuatl, the local language, she asked that a church be built at that site, in her honor; from her

words, Juan Diego recognized the Lady as the Virgin Mary. Diego told his story to the Spanish Archbishop, Fray Juan de Zumárraga, who instructed him to return to Tepeyac Hill, and ask the lady for a miraculous sign to prove her identity. The Virgin told Juan Diego to gather flowers from the top of Tepeyac Hill. Although December was very late in the growing season for flowers to bloom, Juan Diego found at the usually barren hilltop Castilian roses, not native to Mexico, which the Virgin arranged in his peasant tilma cloak. When Juan Diego opened the cloak before Bishop Zumárraga on December 12, the flowers fell to the floor, and in their place was the image of the Virgin of Guadalupe, miraculously imprinted on the fabric."
(Wikipedia- Our Lady of Guadalupe)

As with many icons of this kind of miraculous formation, taking the story on faith is almost required. There was a silent energy in the Basilica due to the reverence paid by thousands of pilgrims who have come to pay their respects over the years. Tara Singh and I also went into the church to see for ourselves the holy nature of the place. It was impressive. The energy had been built around the Virgin by centuries of worship. We basked in the silence and stillness as we meandered past the painting:

Whether one believes the miraculous story of the painting's origins or not, it does not matter. For me, I was happy to be on a pilgrimage with my teacher. More than anything it was the time together that was the real holiness to experience, in which our wills seemed to be joined into one Life Action. Ten years of attending the workshops of Tara Singh were beginning to flower in my life, into a real live flesh and blood relationship.

The next day we found a travel agency not far from our

hotel. We planned a trip to Teotihuacan, and then to the artist's community of San Miguel de Allende. At first it seemed like there was much more to see in Mexico City, but the movement of the trip had its own energy and dynamics, and I was learning to flow with a plan that was not of my own making. We took a tour bus to Teotihuacan. The ancient pyramids and grounds were very expansive, taking the eye far into the distance, down vistas and thoroughfares that could only be seen as majestic. The Pyramid of the Sun dominated the landscape, and the Pyramid of the Moon served to complement its flank. All the smaller pyramids formed sentries along the avenues. We were in a state of wonder. What must these times have been like? What were the people's ideas of the Divine? Surely the elements were important, and the astrological studies of the heavens. Was there human sacrifice? What were the relationships these people had with each other, with Higher Forces, with themselves?

We had some picnic lunch of Wasa Crackers and smoked salmon. The day was coming to a close, and we boarded the bus to return to our hotel in Mexico City. More than seeing the sights of this spectacular archeological preservation, the trip to Teotihuacan marked the beginning of a new journey for me, one in which the limitations of time and space ceased to exist between myself, and the experience I was having right before me. Every moment became one of wonder and gratitude, of newness and appreciation. And in the presence of Tara Singh, this newness was constantly unfolding and expressing itself, much to my benefit.

147

The next day we were to travel the 270 kilometers to San Miguel de Allende by private car. The same young woman who conducted the tour to the pyramids was our driver, and was scheduled to pick us up at nine o'clock in the morning. I was up and packed, early in the morning, as I wanted to get myself ready and out of the way for Tara Sigh to have his space and time to shower and get ready. I was waiting in meditation for the driver to come, when, out of the blue, Tara Singh laid his first correction upon me. It was like a chastisement I least expected. "You live constantly under pressure, and you do this to yourself. I am on a holiday, and I will not be pressured. This has gone to your head, and you don't know what divine leisure is. You have no clue about it. You have become arrogant, and have no idea how to treat another human being." Wow! I was devastated. I did not even realize that I was pressuring anyone, thinking that to be on time for our driver was more important. I was certainly humbled and silenced, and all I could do was let the timing unfold, and not be concerned about the driver waiting outside for us to appear in front of the hotel. There was a lesson in this, but I would have to do some deep soul searching to find where I was "off." This was my first lesson of the day—and there would be more. Needless to say, this correction made me more alert. Being with Tara Singh became a continuous dance of attention.

As we drove through the city streets to points north, we passed many small markets. Colorful wares for sale hung in the small shops, and at some point we stopped near one of these markets to walk through the bazaar. An open-air

148

veranda offered a view of the marketplace, and also a café for our midday meal. Afterwards, we travelled through the countryside and fields of farmland, fertile and green, on the way to San Miguel. At some point the trip seemed long, and we yearned to arrive. In the early evening we pulled into a hotel on the outskirts of town. "We are not staying here," Tara Singh made it very clear, "we want to stay in the center of the town." But this was the place the tour company provided. Their pictures of San Miguel did not indicate the hotel was outside the town. I went into the hotel to negotiate a refund. They would not budge. But Taraji was insistent with the driver, "Take us to a hotel in the town." This was processing my "don't rock the boat" mentality. I felt uncomfortable asking the driver to take us somewhere else. Also, I did not want to lose the money we had already paid to the tour company for the hotel—but I could see there was no way out. Tara Singh had a plan that was better than mine, no matter what it looked like at the time.

We were taken to the very center of San Miguel de Allende, to the town square, and there we found an old world Spanish hotel built around a courtyard, overlooking the square. It was beautiful. We booked in, and dismissed our driver until the next day when we would meet for lunch. That evening we strolled the town, found a restaurant on the square, and enjoyed our leisurely meal in the thick of this Mexican cultural highlight. A colorful band played in the large gazebo across the central park, as people circumambulated around the square. As it was the custom, the young girls walked around the square one way, the boys the other way, in hopes of an eye-to-eye meeting. Their parents sat on the benches throughout the square as chaperones. It was a festive sight. We marveled at the community togetherness, and the sense of absolute relaxation and joy emanating from the people. It was then clear to me why Tara Singh insisted on being in the center of town. Staying on the outskirts, we would have missed the whole essence of this experience.

Our time in San Miguel was in this essence of divine leisure. We wandered the streets without direction. We would buy some fruit in a Mercado and sit on a park bench to share it. The shops were full of artistic things that were enjoyable to see. The streets in the middle of town did not permit cars, so the strolls seemed out of a different era. We could appreciate the beauty of a pedestrian scale of things. One would be hard pressed to find this level of tranquility in an American community centered around the automobile. The atmosphere was clear, and an azure firmament made a dome of delight over our blessed togetherness. By the time we returned to Mexico City a few days later we were in a different consciousness altogether. There was silence in our steps, and gratitude ever flowing from the common choreography of our daily movements. My first trip with Tara Singh was coming to a close. Yet, something happened to me I had not quite fathomed at the time. The beginning of a real Holy Relationship was taking shape.

❖ *Chapter 16.* ❖

India with Tara Singh

The Preparation

Some events are beyond our control. Y2K was a buzz in the air and as it turned out, nothing happened. There was no worldwide computer glitch, and January 1ˢ of 2000 came and went quietly as we were ushered into the forerunner year of a new millennium. And the movements of a great Mother Nature occur with a force, also, it seems, beyond our control. There was an early January snowstorm in Philadelphia on the day I was to fly out of JFK airport in New York City to meet up with Tara Singh in Paris. I had to postpone my embarkation and call the Foundation to get word to Taraji and another close student traveling with him, John McClure, both already in Paris, of my late arrival. Life and luck helped me to reschedule my flight the same time the next day. The next morning dawned a clear blue sky and my limo left from the Hilton Hotel on cleared roads to JFK with me in it, on the first leg of a journey to India to be with my spiritual mentor and friend. A stopover in France was part of the plan, because John spoke fluent French and we wanted to see the best sights in Paris.

I arrived the next day after an all night flight and had to find my way to a small hotel in Montmartre. On the train alone a feeling of absolute solitude came over me. Tara Singh had written me a letter preparing me for the trip we were to take together on our way to Ramana Maharshi's ashram in Southern India. "This is a very sacred journey," he was sure to point out, "and it is not touristing." I thought about this line a lot as I was traveling on the train to meet him in some unknown Paris neighborhood on a metro line I had not yet found. John had given me rudimentary directions—I came to a station hub that connected with the Montmartre line. I was in a world all my own, inexorably moving toward one of the most significant rendezvous of my life. When I emerged from the underground the light was brilliant. The corner cafes were numerously scattered at every intersection. Walking by a few of them, I soon arrived at the hotel. I checked in using some high school French, then crammed into the dinky elevator with my luggage and pushed the button to the third floor to meet my friends. As I emerged into the narrow wallpapered hallway I could see the door ajar a few meters away—which donned the room number I was given. I entered and there he was, sitting silently on the side of the bed. Our eyes met, and Taraji rose to give me a huge embrace. "You have made it." His words were a balm to my heart, and the aloneness I felt on the plane and in the Metro totally disappeared. "Do you need a rest?" he said with the care of a motherly love. I nearly cried I was so happy to see him. And—I was absolutely exhausted. I brought in my bags and collapsed on the bed, and within minutes I was out.

When I awoke it was a bright and chilly Parisian afternoon. The three of us went into the streets to search out a place to have a meal. There was a quality of freedom and adventure—the "three musketeers" is a term Taraji used to describe us. We were in the vortex of his energy, John and I, and speaking for myself I was on cloud nine. Soon, we were dining in a cozy café, the kind you can only find in Paris. The atmosphere was very high. John spoke fluent French, having a mother of French heritage. Taraji interviewed him on Paris, and his knowledge of the highlights. The Pere Lachaise Cemetery was well worth seeing, and we were just a few blocks away from it. The burial places of many famous artists and writers were there: *Gertrude Stein – American author; Oscar Wilde – Irish novelist, poet and playwright; Honoré de Balzac – French novelist of the 19th century; Eugène Delacroix – French Romantic artist; Max Ernst – German artist; Théodore Géricault – French Romantic painter; Jean Auguste Dominique Ingres – French painter*—to name a few. After the meal we strolled through the lanes and arboretum, past the tombs of the giants of art and literature. The remnants of immortality in the works left behind gave witness to the genius of these otherwise mortal men and women of arts and letters. In the flow of their worldly life would the uniqueness of their vision give rise to notice from generations then and now. In Pere Lachaise was the dust of past beings entombed, yet, in their art forms were they revitalized as immortal creators of a truth and beauty unsurpassed and elevated.

The next day we travelled across town to visit Notre Dame Cathedral and the Louvre. I was keen to see the Winged Victory of Samothrace, of which Tara Singh had a large photograph in the front room of the Foundation. The sculpture sat in a rotunda all by itself, majestic and pure, rising up at the head of the sweeping Daru staircase, sitting atop its ship like base. It was obvious to me the reason it was such a favorite of Taraji. He had a picture of it at the Foundation. The lines were so uplifting, and the whole aspirations of mankind to know a spiritual nature were imbued in its stone form.

As we came up the stairwell from the galleries below, we were stunned by its presence. I shed a tear from the beauty alone, and the palpable aura of authenticity it emanated. So long ago the anonymous artist set chisel to stone with a vision of spiritual necessity. What he produced was a meeting of heaven and earth. What must have rushed through the heart and mind of this creator? What spiritual connection must he have already had to be capable of such a creation?

Soon our time in Paris came to an end, and we boarded our plane to Mumbai. The long flight in store was timed to arrive in the wee hours of the morning. Upon arrival, we took the taxi to the Taj Mahal Hotel, where Taraji had stayed many years before. Nearby was a more reasonably priced hotel that we picked for a few days stay, the Hotel Godwin. It had a restaurant on top of the building, with an outdoor veranda. We were given a suite on the upper floors, with a view of the city that was breathtaking. One of the advantages of being so near the Taj Mahal hotel was being able to dine in the restaurant there. It was a sure bet the food would be good and clean, and we would not need to worry about picking up any food-born illness. So we ate our meals in this majestic hotel, overlooking the bay, while discussing our day trip to Elephanta Island, the main point of interest we would see while staying in Mumbai. Elephanta is situated in the Mumbai Harbor, and is host to one of the best examples of a rock cut temple sculpted directly into the mountain. This temple contains the famous Head of Lord Shiva in three views, or Trimurti, that was also pictured in the Prayer Room at the Foundation in Los Angeles. The head itself, over three meters high, is one of the most imposing sculptures I have ever seen.

"The three heads are said to represent three essential aspects of Shiva—creation, protection, and destruction. The right half-face shows him as a young person with

sensuous lips, embodying life and its vitality. In his hand he holds an object resembling a rosebud, depicting the promise of life and creativity. This face is closest to that of Brahma, the creator, or Uma or Vamadeva, the feminine side of Shiva and creator of joy and beauty. The left half-face is that of a moustached young man, displaying anger. This is Shiva as the terrifying Aghora or Bhairava, the one whose anger can engulf the entire world in flames, leaving only ashes behind. This is also known as Rudra-Shiva, the Destroyer. The central face, benign and meditative, resembles the preserver Vishnu. This is Tatpurusha, 'master of positive and negative principles of existence and preserver of their harmony', or Shiva as the yogi." (Wikipedia : Elephanta)

As far as I was concerned, just seeing this and the Winged Victory were enough to merit the whole trip. As we strolled through the caves Tara Singh became increasingly silent. The atmosphere surrounding the sculptures became charged with the energy of sacred ecstasy. The beings of Shiva depicted in the cave temple came alive, and a meditative quality of bliss was imparted to us. At one point we saw a figure of a baby, or a cherub in a trance, and Tara Singh startled me by pointing out in surprise, "SEE, SEE! He is in a state of absolute ecstasy! He is in a trance! The true nature of human beings is to be like a child in a perpetual divine trance!" It was true, when I looked at the sculpted figure on the wall there was a feeling of pure joy and bliss emanating from the very stone. Again, heaven and earth came to meet in the creations of these anonymous artist saints who many centuries before had carved these holy figures at the juncture of spirit and matter, into the mountain of living stone.

The next morning we arose early in the Godwin Hotel. It was the day we were to fly to Chennai, the place from where we would embark to go to Thiruvannamalai in Tamil Nadu, the town where Ramana Maharshi's ashram sat at the foot of the mountain, Aurnachala. This was the principle destination of our whole pilgrimage to India. The morning was still, on a Sunday—and I could sense the stillness outside as well. Traffic was not yet buzzing on the streets. We awoke and sat on the bed for a while in meditation, as Tara Singh prepared us for the next leg of our spiritual journey to the feet of the Master, and began with a few comments about the seriousness of our journey. As usual his words took my mind to another place of stillness within. It was as if a blanket of absolute peace spread over our room and the whole city as a result of what he was saying. He spoke of Ramana Maharshi, the Sage of Arunachala, and of the mountain on which he lived in silence for over seventeen years. He spoke of the great opportunity we were having to receive this darshan, holy vision, of such a spiritual Master so directly. He spoke of Sri Bhagavan's true connection to the Higher Self. He spoke of the necessity of relating to a spiritual Master of this Self, not the self of the personality we made up. He spoke of this absolute Self that connects us to the forces of universal intelligence and the wholeness of life. John and I listened attentively as the

Presence filled the room, and us, and we got closer to that Self who we really are, our true Identity.

As Tara Singh wove his sentences into the grace of an eloquent discourse on the Self, we were taken more and more into the actual state of this sacred awareness. And this awareness spread its gentle blanket of peace further and further outward, over the rooftops of Mumbai, through the treetops that lined the street below, and across the vast body of water in the distant harbor. It took our minds into a different dimension, one of joy and happiness that did not have a particular cause or object, no specific reason for elation. It was just a deep sense of inner calm, a blessing of inner awareness free of thought. Tara Singh was expressing and transmitting his gift of silence and stillness that was so essential to his ministry with *A Course in Miracles*. He was a living expression of the Holy Spirit's Mind in action, and it was his job, as given him by Dr. Schucman and Krishnamurti, to impart its blessings of deep peace to all those students who came into his vortex of influence. The unforgettable nature of this *blanket of peace* swept over me, and all of Mumbai for that matter, on that first day of the real pilgrimage to the feet of a true Master. It was indelibly imprinted on my soul. It was a gift the nature of which I had not received at this level of awareness ever before. It was a peace so profound that words fall strikingly short of any effective description of it.

As the three of us sat on the edge of the bed, we ended the session with this prayer from Lesson #157 of *ACIM*:

"Into Christ's Presence will we enter now, serenely unaware of everything except His shining face and perfect Love. The vision of His face will stay with you, but there will be an instant, which transcends all vision, even this, the holiest. This you will never teach, for you attained it not through learning. Yet the vision speaks of your remembrance of what you knew that instant, and will surely know again."

I often think back to that holy instant with Tara Singh in the Hotel Godwin in Mumbai, on that early January morning of our departure to Chennai. It was a moment outside of time, as he would have called it, and an experience that transcended anything I ever learned. As the prayer makes clear, it was a vision of Christ that I had in Tara Singh, in the great Master to whom he was taking me, and in my friend John who was accompanying me. But also, it was an instant that went even beyond this, the holiest of visions. It transcended experience and all memory itself, and left an impression of absolute Beauty and Wholeness that remain to this day beyond all others in my recollections. And I endeavor to have the trust and the faith for this instant as the lesson says, I "will surely know again."

The Clearing

We caught the night flight to Chennai and arrived late. We were tired, and Tara Singh was having some trouble with his legs. He felt a weakness in walking, and I was concerned that we get some adequate rest, and not be too long in finding a hotel with clean rooms and good amenities. There was a man at the airport selling his hotel with a sign. It looked good to me, and it included a free taxi ride to its door. Tired and exhausted from the travel, I took the offer, and we all ended up on a taxi ride that was longer than advertised. Again I was at the disadvantage of the unknown, and my premature decision got the better of me. We unloaded at the hotel, which was adequate and bright, newly constructed and with clean and spacious rooms. But when we awoke the next morning we discovered we were far from anything. Again I had chosen a hotel that was out in the middle of nowhere, in a field, miles from the center of town. Tara Singh was critical of me for such an under sight. He said we were not of the same mind, and this was the first time I had "acted on my own," without his input and guidance. It was true. I was more concerned with getting us a quick bed, than a hotel in the right section of town. The mistake I made in San Miguel was looming larger than ever in this hasty decision, and I had to field Tara Singh's admonishment.

We made the best of it. That morning we called the people in charge at Ramana Maharshi's ashram informing them of our location. They were sending a car to pick us up at the hotel, a five-hour drive away. It would arrive sometime in the early afternoon to take us south to Thiruvannamalai. Meanwhile we caught a taxi into town to see some of the sights, especially the Government Museum that housed some of the best antiquities of Indian culture. This museum contained prime examples of India's immense ancient artistic heritage of sculptures that

161

formed the basis of its spiritual life. The sculptures were considered holy objects of worship in the days of their making. They had a presence infused with the pujas and attendance they had received in their original sacred settings. Although they were now isolated in an academic museum context, they

still possessed a quality of startling sacred presence that was certainly noticeable. As we meandered through the museum, one sculpture after another struck its holy pose into our awareness, and brought our minds to a deep appreciation of this ancient and vibrant culture. They became alive with the grace of creation. I pictured an age of enlightenment in which the artists and craftsmen were charged with the inspiration of Gods, and the people received these creations with the reverence of authentic worship and celebration. After a few hours in the museum, we headed back to the hotel to wait for our car from the ashram. The taxi took us through the narrow streets of Chennai, past a procession of a holy festival dedicated to Lord Shiva, complete with elephants and colorful costumes donned by the participants. Life abounded in the streets, and we were in awe of the spectacles of holy adoration we were seeing around every corner.

When we returned to the hotel we sat in the lobby, awaiting the arrival of the car. The inner courtyard towered to the top of the hotel, creating an atrium of light and space that opened to the skylights ten stories above. We basked in the light and rested on the lobby couches provided for the guests, anticipating the car's impending rendezvous with us in this outpost near Chennai. Tara Singh began to share in an inquisitive way, as he often did in a new setting. "Did you ever stop to think that the ashram is going out of its way to send a car to pick us up?" He put this question to John and me. "They are sending a car, a whole five hours drive, all the way up here to pick us up. Did you ever stop and think why?"

There was a stillness that came over the setting, over us, over the conversation and the inquiry.

And then he looked me squarely in the eye and said, "They would never send a car for you. Did you ever think about that? They are sending a car for me, but they would never send one for you." The atmosphere could be cut with a knife, it was that charged with an energy and presence of attention. I felt as if I was just bitten by a cobra. Stunned, I had nothing to say. Tara Singh had brought my mind to total silence and humility, and I could not move. My thought was shocked into absolute stillness. He continued, "In fact, you and John should find your own way to the ashram. They are sending the car for me, but certainly not for you. You should start looking for your own way down there." Now we were not only stunned, we were thrown an interesting challenge, perhaps one of the biggest challenges of my life. We had no idea where we were, no idea where the ashram at Thiruvannamalai was, how we were to get to our final destination. I had never felt so abandoned in my life, left to deal with my own faculties and insecurities this challenge brought to the surface.

John and I went over to the desk and began to inquire about a bus or a train. The man gave us the prices for a taxi to the train, and for the tickets to Ramana Maharshi's ashram. I went back to Tara Singh to inform him of the plan to take the train. "How much will you pay?" he asked with the acute inquisitiveness of a stern schoolmaster. When I told him, he reacted with a disapproving outburst, "That is too much money. You are always wasting money. Go back there and negotiate the price." Again I was out of my comfort zone further than I had ever been. I felt like I was on the edge of the world ready to fall off into the monstrous mouth of the unknown, without any sympathy from the familiar to save me. When I returned to the desk I began to barter, but the man would not have any of it. He would not budge. I had to get firm, and I could feel my fear and anger rising inside. I kept reiterating that I would pay less for the package, and not a penny more. Usually this would cause a shift, and the price would be negotiable. But in this case the man held fast to his original price. I could not accept it, yet I could not go back to Tara Singh empty handed. I felt between a rock and a hard place, with no place to budge. But the man would not waive any part of the fees. In a state of humiliation, I went back to Tara Singh with the news. "This is the best I could do. I am sorry, but we will have to take this offer, or go into town and find some other way to get there. I am willing to do either. What do you suggest?"

At that moment a white sedan pulled up outside the hotel, and a man dressed in the traditional Southern Indian cotton clothes from the ashram came up to us inquiring about the party of Tara Singh. "Let's go!" said Taraji. The nightmare of my predicament suddenly vanished as a matter of an incredible and benevolent awakening. John and I carried the bags to the back of the car, and the man from Ramana Maharshi's place loaded them into the trunk and onto the roof rack as we three entered the car from all sides. Soon we were off on our five-hour journey to the south as if this incident had never happened. We were going to meet the sacred presence of the Master of Silence, Ramana Maharshi. We were going to the environs of Thiruvannamalai at the foot of the hill of Arunachala—more of a small mountain—that drew the attention of this great Sage for most of his enlightened life.

We drove around the city of Chennai on an outer belt roadway, and soon found ourselves traveling through the gentle flat fields of crops that spread as far as the eye could see. There were people in the fields farming by hand, and bullocks pulling the plows and equipment of an era of farming long since past in the western world. There was silence in the car. None of us spoke a word, and the driver, though English was his second language, remained in a trance of silence along with us. As we sped down the road, I was in a kind of bittersweet appreciation for all that had unfolded in the fist half of the day. The shock was still strong, and the silence of my thoughts was palpably noticed. I could see the stillness in every motion, and hear the silence in every sound. It was as if I was seeing with new eyes, and hearing with new ears. The old "me" was dying, and the new impersonal Self was emerging into my consciousness. I felt a "clearing" was taking place, and the climax of this clearing had happened in the realization that it was Tara Singh alone who was responsible for this great opportunity being given to me; it came in the form of this pilgrimage to one of the most sacred spots on earth, to be in the energy field of an authentic Master in Ramana Maharshi. Once, when Tara Singh asked his teacher Krishnamurti about the authenticity of the Sage of Arunachala, he said, "Yes, beyond the words!" So this was my first exposure to the world of Tara Singh in his homeland. When he had said this was "not

166

touristing," he was deadly serious in the matter of fact before us. And this day was showing the seriousness of a true pilgrimage. In order for a person to make a real contact with the Master, he must approach the meeting naked, in a state of stillness and silence, without any ego motives. Tara Singh was making sure my ego was being brushed away, so that when we arrived at Ramanashrama I would be clear enough to receive all of the energy, "beyond the words," that Ramana Maharshi had to offer.

We drove for a few hous until the man at the wheel pulled over to a roadside café. It was a pee break, and a chance to stretch our legs. We relieved ourselves and got a Coca Cola, then returned to the car for the remaining leg of the journey. The terrain was changing, and we began to enter a more mountainous region. But the mountains rose up like lone sentinels on a spreading flat plain.... scattered in measured increments over the fertile fields that separated and surrounded each mountainous cone which rose up from the tranquil pastoral floor. The sun was setting in the west as we traveled toward Thiruvannamalai. I noticed the day was slowly fading into dusk. The stillness and silence I felt was intensifying, the closer we got to Ramana Maharshi's vortex of influence. And before the sun had disappeared completely, we could recognize Arunachala rising up in the distance, beckoning us forward into the heart of the matter, into the newness of a pristine and holy place that was awaiting us. Other than a few words to procure our Coca Cola, not one word had been uttered from the driver or between us the whole five hour journey on the road. We approached the ashram with the reverence of a true pilgrimage. Truly this was not "touristing," and the clearing that Taraji had offered to John and I was the most important preparation we could have received in order to grasp the authenticity of holiness this place and the Sage of Arunachala had to offer.

"Moments Outside of Time"

Tara Singh called these encounters with the sacred— "Moments outside of time." Truly they were. As we drove through the entry gate to the ashram time stopped. We emerged from the car into another realm of deeper and deeper silence. Tara Singh knew exactly where to go, heading to the meditation room, which had been the sleeping quarters of Ramana Maharshi. We passed by the offices, the temple, through gardens, and arrived at small, unassuming building into which we entered. About a dozen or so people were already sitting in silence on matts placed on the floor. They sat in front of a bed that had on it an upright picture of the Sage lounging and smiling on that very bed, taken decades ago. We found matts for ourselves, and sat in silence. It did not take long to bring the energy of stillness and peace into our very being. Immediately our minds were erased, and the inner calm intensified. Of course we lost track of time, and eventually the driver had to come and get us to take us to our room in the rear of the ashram. It was down a quiet footpath, past a grove of huge banyan trees and amidst a very active colony of monkeys. We entered the suite of rooms, Tara Singh in one by himself, John and I in the other, making certain all our bags were accounted for. The driver left us to our rest once we were situated. By then we were exhausted from the activity of the day. The hard ashram bed, which amounted to a thin mattress on a board, on a simple metal frame, seemed more appealing than the most opulent accommodations of five stars. As soon as we got on our nightclothes, we passed out immediately into a deep sleep.

The next day the bells awoke us early in the morning, before dawn. We were surprised by a knock on the door. One of the ashram residents, a young man in his late twenties, had brought us two full pails of hot water. The bathrooms had obvious plumbing, and even western style toilets, but not hot running water. So each day this young man would bring us our morning bath water in pails. We became so grateful for this simple act of service to us. With a plastic dipper, we would ladle the water over our heads and appreciate a different lifestyle of total simplicity.

When we were all dressed and ready for the day, we gathered in Taraji's room for a session. He spoke of the gratitude he felt to be at Ramanasrama, where he had come many years ago, having been drawn here from a strong inner intimation. He even had the same room where he had stayed before, very private and quiet, set back from the busy activity of the daily ashram routines. We were fortunate to be living in the VIP suite. Others had to stay in dormitory type settings with many people sleeping in one room. But we were given these special privileges because Tara Singh had a long-standing relationship with the two brothers who ran the ashram, Sri Ramanam and Sri Muni. He had even sorted out some difficulties they were having in a transitional period, and they respected his insights as though the Sage, their uncle, was "speaking through him." Additionally, Tara Singh had contributed money to the ashram to install granite flooring in the main temple, much needed over what was there before. So they treated Tara Singh with the utmost respect.

The morning talk was on the nature of this place and the people who ran it. There was an order in the ashram that kept everything impeccable. The aspects of daily schedule—the cleanliness, the duties that were performed in the kitchen, offices, temples and grounds—were all well tuned and given in the spirit of service. The actions of the ashram were kept simple, but thousands of people a day were fed and spiritually uplifted. No one was preached at or made to feel "converted," even though there were many Westerners present. The ashram provided a wellspring of inspiration.

Taraji told us of his first trip many years ago to make contact with Sri Bhagavan. He was in Madras at the time, having attended a series of Krishnamurti lectures. He received an inner intimation about "Arunachala," the mountain that had been the home of the Sage for so long. At first, he did not have a clear understanding of this intimation from within, but he kept inquiring with the local people. After a while he realized that it was a place, and that this Sage of Arunachala was calling him. So he took a train and a taxi to the ashram, arriving after dark in the middle of the night. At the gate he was told there was no room, no space for another guest. Then he questioned himself, "Why would life bring me here if there was no space?" The man at the gate soon returned, "Come in, you can have the VIP suite." This result came from the certainty of Tara Singh to be divinely guided.

Ramana Maharshi lived into the 1950's, but his presence was strongly felt at the ashram where he had lived, fifty years later. Like many wise beings in India, the remembrance of their life and work continue on, well after their passing. The spiritual silence and presence of these beings is still available to receive by anyone who truly wishes to make the contact. As we walked the grounds later in the morning we ended up in the temple area where the people were singing bhajans, sacred hymns. Most of the worship in India is a celebration of life. No one preaches or gives sermons to the masses. The Indian way is to pay homage to the Gods and to the Sages. In fact, the highest homages are paid to a spiritual renunciant such as Ramana Maharshi. Even Indira Gandhi had dedicated a *murti*, a living statue, of the Sage in the rear of the temple, recognizing him as a living treasure of the Indian culture.

The highlight of our stay at the ashram was a walk around the mountain. It was a common practice in the time of Sri Baghavan to circumambulate Aurnachala, about a nine-mile hike, in the very early hours of the day. So on the second day we rose about 4AM to begin our walk. Commonly people walk barefoot along the road that runs around the mountain, so we began our trek with no shoes, as many Indians do. But these folks are used to the barefoot lifestyle day to day. By the time we completed the trek four hours later we were in need of a balm for our tired soles. Back in our room we rubbed lotion and oils into our raw sores, but with the gratitude that we had completed our pilgrimage of first precedent. Resting in our room, we noticed the colony of monkeys outside our door. A mother monkey with her baby sat on our veranda. Another monkey slipped into our room before we could notice and stole a bag of almonds, quickly high tailing it up into the banyan tree. There he sat on a prominent branch munching on his booty. Of course he did not share with the others in his tribe. He was so proud of his caper.

We met later in the day with the head of the ashram, Sri Ramanam. Tara Singh and he had a long history of mutual respect. He explained the workings of the ashram, and all that went into feeding the people. Thousands came to the ashram daily, and thousands were fed, not only the food from the kitchens, but food of the spirit that Ramana Maharshi imparted. On many levels this was a place where seekers could come to rest and sink into the deep spiritual reality that India so widely offers. As we sat in the office and listened to the very factual accounts of the actions of the ashram, I could not help but notice Tara Singh coming alive as a native son of this incredible culture, whose final stage in the development of a person's evolution in this life would most prevalently be spiritual enlightenment. The ashram, like thousands of spiritual centers around India, offers the common person an option of retreat from the world of commerce and striving, for a chance to connect to the peace and silence within. This type of place is the backbone of a way of life risen up over the millenniums, and I was a witness to its order and total giving nature. We have nothing like this in the west, I thought, that is of our own cultural making. Yes, we have a few copies of the Indian model, but nothing so authentic as our own to offer.

Tara Singh On Arunachala

After tending to our sore feet, we went up the mountain-side in the early evening of the fourth day. It was nearing dusk, and the atmosphere was clear, and the shadows were long. We passed a group of school children laughing and making a ruckus. About half way up the mountain was a cave in which Ramana Maharshi had lived for seventeen years in silence. By now the ashram had built a shrine around it, and it was well maintained as a place of pilgrimage. Many sages in India had this practice. Yogis would find these perfect shelters in the sides of mountains and use them for prolonged periods of meditation. In the Maharshi's time on the mountain, this would have been a remote and isolated place, far from the activity of human endeavors. He would have been able to go for weeks without seeing a soul. When he would need food, he would go down the mountain and receive it in the temples at Thiruvannamalai.

Our journey up the mountain was to visit the cave where Ramana Maharshi lived for 17 years in meditation. We spent some time in the cave and entered into a deep state of silence. It was a moment outside of time and space. There was such a profound peace in the cave we did not want to get up. But the dusk would soon be turning to night, so we began our descent in the hope that we would make it back to the ashram before nightfall. There was a slight anxiety in the air, so Tara Singh sped up the pace to make use of the remaining light on our decent. As we entered the back gate of the ashram, the night was almost upon us. Returning to our rooms, the peace we had felt in the cave was still ringing in our ears. We sat in the silence, and soon entered a rest so deep that I cannot remember ever having such a night of complete satisfaction and perfect sleep.

The ashram lifestyle is very structured: rise early in the morning; go to the temple or Ramana's room for meditation; sing songs (bhajans) in the temple; participate in pujas (worship) done to the murti (a living statue) of the saint; breakfast; more singing in the temples; work in the kitchen; lunch; afternoon ashram duties; rest; more songs in the temple; dinner; meditation in the quiet room; then early to bed. Each day has the same structure—maybe slight variations when there are special festivities, but mostly the same rhythm. It is designed to "reset" the inner clock, and get a person into harmony with nature, and the natural cycles of day and night. The program is also meant to "scramble" the brain routines and attachments so that a person can let go more, and rest the brain from "working so hard." All these elements of ashram life are designed to get a person in touch with their God created Self. Living in the ashram so near to the saint who has realized this state of Being in himself makes it easier for a person to realize his/her own true Self.

The days spent at Ramanasrama were glorious. We visited the ancient sacred Temple at Thiruvannamalai and witnessed a different golden age of India in which culture, nature, and worship for the Divine were all one. The inner complex of buildings with their carvings of the Gods in stone, were beautiful and moving. I could sense the energy coming from them, reminding me of the times in which they were constructed—how idyllic they must have been. No violence, no cars, no rampant commercialism, no slaughter of animals was to be found anywhere. The people were in harmony with each other, with the elements of nature, and with Divine Forces that were behind their cosmic existence. We walked the grounds and saw sculpted figures on the temple sides engaged in divine celebration. The pools for bathing were still being used by the people, even more than a thousand years after their making. Everything in the temple surroundings was designed to lift the participant into his sacred Self, and unify him in this physical existence with his own God nature, his own spiritual precedent. The lands of India have been imbued with this purpose of God-realization. It has been this culture's most lofty and fervent desire for its people to achieve liberation from all forms of mental and physical limitations, all beliefs that would keep a person bound to the cause and effects of thought. This is what Ramana Maharshi achieved and why he was so revered: he had freed himself from even the notion of "death" and made contact with his Immortal Identity in the Christ Self. By Christ I do not just mean Jesus, but that quality of Being that is totally immersed in Divine Love, Divine Truth and Compassion.

After the temple tour we returned to our rooms in the ashram. The monkeys were all around our building, hanging out in the huge banyan trees that grew very near our building complex. The mother monkey and her child sat again on our veranda, looking for a handout. But this time we were keen to their antics and carefully kept our doors closed. We took our rest with the certainty that the clever and fast males would not rob us again. After our nap, during the quiet afternoons, we would have tea in the dining hall. Chai, as it is called in India, is a tea mixed with buffalo milk and sugar, with some additional spices thrown in—quite delicious, but very hot, as they bring the brew to a boil. So the custom is to have two stainless steel cups, and to pour the chai back and forth between the two cups. People get quite gracious in this act of pouring, back and forth, from one cup to the other in their attempt to cool down the tea. So we gladly participated in this afternoon ritual of camaraderie, pouring our hot chai back and forth, from one cup into the other in our quest for the perfect temperature. As I cannot emphasize enough, our days at the ashram were leisurely and glorious, in which the mind and body come into total harmony and peace within.

In the afternoons we strolled around the ashram. We bought many books in the ashram shop to take back to the Foundation in Los Angeles, and met in the office of the ashram's director, Sri Ramanam, the brother in charge who was Tara Singh's friend. We attended a celebration one evening honoring Ramana Maharshi's birthday. To our surprise the pundit musician was playing the saxophone in the classical Indian style. The music lifted us to heights of beauty unsurpassed. We were almost in a trance when Tara Singh went up to pay homage to this musical master. We laid money at his feet, as no one ever formally charges a fee for these concerts. The audience responds from the heart for the great gift of holy music given forth from these musician *saints*. Into the wee hours we listened, and when we retired we were in another state of being, elevated and pure.

The last full day spent at the ashram was the Maharshi's birthday, and huge celebrations were given in the temple. The Brahmans performed pujas all day to their Master. They built elaborate floral altarpieces and did ceremonies with the elements—air, earth, fire, water and space—and recited ancient Sanskrit chants. We were enthralled watching them. At some point we circumambulated around the central altar area. It felt good to walk around the center, just as we had "walked around" the mountain of Arunachala. This circumambulation is very common in temples and holy sites in India, and considered a great act of reverence. It gets a person high just doing it. It takes them "out" of their ego and brings them closer to his God created Self. Through the grace of Ramana Maharshi, especially culminating on this special birthday celebration, he gave us the highest possible experience of himself that we could have in the week we lived in his home—near the holy hill of Arunachala.

When our days there came to an end, we dolefully packed our bags, gave gifts and tips to our new friends in the ashram, said our sad goodbyes to Sri Ramanam and his brother Sri Muni, and loaded the car for our long five-hour journey back to Chennai to catch our plane. We were en route to Paris, where John and Taraji would have a day layover. I was to catch my flight at the airport in Paris back to Philadelphia. Our flights were long. But by now the whole India quest with Tara Singh was circulating in my blood and emanating an immense gratitude. He took me to the heights of his land, his world, and I would never be the same. I experienced the silence of my own Self, and the ego was, for me, not so in charge of my soul any more. As I left Taraji and John at Charles De Gaulle Airport, my tears of joy within spoke of a profound appreciation the likes of which I had never known. We hugged one last time as I realized I was immersed in my own "Moments outside of time."

❖ *Chapter 17.* ❖

Meeting the Family

For Tara Singh and me, the trip to India sealed our relationship and brought us closer together. I was clear that he was my teacher, and hesitated to call him a friend out of the sheer respect of not intruding too closely into his personal world. Even Taraji himself warned me about "familiarity," and that it was not necessarily a good thing when it came to a teacher/student relationship. I wanted to get close, but at the same time I wanted to honor the proper reverence for the teacher and not get too "chummy." In fact Tara Singh was not at all a casual person. Though he could be charming and funny at times, extremely intimate and in your face at other times, and insisted that life was to be lived to its fullest and be enjoyed, his function as the teacher was always first and foremost in his mind—and I recognized that function was my principle reason for being with him. This relationship was never to be taken lightly, nor taken for granted, nor brought down to a casual or personal level.

So when Taraji asked me to travel with him to England and Ireland to visit his family members in the late summer of the year 2000, I was surprised, delighted and also challenged. I was in the middle of a large contract, and would have to divide the production into two parts, and then get my client's approval for a hiatus in the middle of the project. Nothing was ever easy with Tara Singh, who represented higher Life Forces. I would always have to rearrange myself to fit into those Forces, by which I often felt pushed into a corner to decide. This instance really pushed me into a corner. I had never stopped a contract midstream and made a client wait for my spiritual evolution, which obviously had a higher priority than completing a construction project. To my surprise, when I formulated this proposal to my customers, laid out the importance of my whole relationship with Tara Singh, and explained who he was to me, they gladly said, "Yes, by all means take advantage of this rare opportunity." So from that perspective, the way was cleared. And, because the contract was already lucrative, I also had the money to make the trip.

We left in the late summer months to go to England first, to visit Tara Singh's two sisters and their families who lived in Nottingham in the Midlands of the country, and then over to Belfast, Northern Ireland, to visit his son, daughter and wife. The purpose of the trip was to "bring their hearts to gladness," especially with his immediate family in Ireland. We arrived at Heathrow Airport and were met by his two brothers-in-laws with open arms. They had driven down all the way down from Nottingham, a few hours away, to pick us up. Driving up the M1 through the heart of England, I was bleary eyed from the long flight from Los Angeles, where I had met Tara Singh to begin our journey together. We arrived in Leicester first, where his youngest sister lived. We would stay there a couple nights, then moving on to his other sister's house in Nottingham.

In the traditional Sikh way there was a warm welcome. Many dishes of finger food were brought into the living room where we sat and caught up on the family news. The men drank whisky. Tara Singh sometimes conversed in Punjabi with his brothers and sisters. One brother was a retired college professor—the other a taxi driver with his own business. The taxi driver still wore a traditional beard and Sikh turban. He was married to the youngest sister, and possessed an air of nobility. He practiced yoga every day, and though in his late sixties, looked to be a man in his forties. There was a brightness in his eyes. He had an inner peace that the professor did not have, a simplicity that transcended thought. The hospitality was all consuming. We were given gifts and introduced to Tara Singh's nephews who also lived on the same street. The extended family all stayed together in the neighborhood. This was the traditional Sikh way. One of the nephew's wife had a father who was ailing, and we took a drive to see him. The house was full of people, and more gifts were given to us, because Tara Singh was being honored as the head of his family, and his niece was intent on paying him homage in this role. Of course I was included in this honoring, because I was his friend and traveling companion. The Sikh

182

way was being given to me. It was one of brotherhood. The brotherhood extended past time, space and boundaries. Even though they had not seen their brother in years, the sisters of Tara Singh paid their respects as if to a royal guest. And this was something I had never witnessed in my conventional American upbringing.

After a couple days in Leicester, we travelled to Nottingham to see Taraji's other sister, who was married to the college professor. This setting was more subdued. His sister here was older, and her husband was an intellectual. Their hospitality was more refined. His brother-in-law taught in the local college, in the education and child psychology department. He was a good conversationalist, and also a professed amateur painter. All around the living room were a ring of small oil paintings on canvas boards of still life subjects, all resting on a plate shelf that surrounded the perimeter of the room, a couple feet from the ceiling. They reminded me of the work of the Italian painter, Giorgio Morandi, with their simple bottles and bowls arranged on stark table settings. He and I discussed painting, and as with most amateurs he had a self-effacing modesty about his work. His small delightful paintings really were better than he thought they were, but I could feel the holding back, the intellectual boundary across which he could not place himself.

Tara Singh's sisters were both quiet people, refined people. They served us our meals in a proper English manner, as we sat at the dinner table and had long conversations about the present family situations, about their life in England, and their children and grandchildren. The older sister had one son, and he recently found out his wife had cancer, and was most likely not going to live much longer. This would be a tragedy for their two young daughters. We met their whole family at their parent's house. I took some very compelling photographs of the children in the back yard amidst its spreading English garden. One could feel the tension in the air as a result of this *not-to-be-spoken-about* bad news. The young mother did not look sick, but apparently her health crisis was serious. The children were happily engaged with me, a novel guest with a camera, so most of the time was spent in an upbeat manner.

After a while I was called from my photographic session with the girls in the back yard garden. Both brothers and Tara Singh were beckoning me to the local pub for an afternoon round of Guinness pints. This was a ritual of brotherhood, almost, and it was clear that the men had their "time together" without the women folk. This was a recognized tradition in the Sikh culture, and there I was immersed in it. Much to my delight, I might add. We had our men's talk, and were joined by other relatives from more distant branches of the family while in the pub. All this was a part of Tara Singh's homecoming. It had been a couple decades since he had seen his sisters' families, and they were making up for lost time with their warmth and hospitality.

The college professor was an exercise buff, and knew the best park in which to have our brisk morning walk near the Trent River recreational area. We drove one morning in his Mercedes Benz to the track that looped around the complex. It was a loop of a couple of miles, passing by a kayak course, flat water rowing course, a clubhouse and groves of English oaks.

184

The cool English morning air was invigorating. We made our way around the loop, stopped in the clubhouse for a morning tea and essentials, and after a couple of hours we returned the short distance home. Tara Singh's brother in law was proud of his home and environment. He had his life in order and this was a most important aspect of his demeanor. The external order was of paramount importance to him. He was a man of materialism, practical, succinct, and a little pedantic in his delivery—yet always very sincere and well meaning. Yet he did not see that this punctilious manner of speaking and relating as a professor was standing in the way of discovering something much deeper in the meaning of his life. He knew he had a tremendous spiritual heritage, yet he rather counteracted this life of spiritual precedent with the pragmatic stiff upper lip of an English air of skeptical positivism. As for Tara Singh's sisters, they appeared next to saintly.

The days spent in England were the springboard for a tougher leg of the journey. Meeting the son, daughter and wife of Tara Singh was a much more challenging affair. Firstly, though, I must mention that in the Indian culture it is customary for some, once they have raised their family and their children are grown, to renounce the "worldly life" for a "spiritual life." This can often mean leaving the comforts of a domestic setting for a life "on the road" of wherever that life takes them. Tara Singh had made this "break" with his immediate family, and this visit was in honor of them, yet in no way apologetic in the sense that any breech or error in his relationship with them was in need of correction. It was

185

natural at his stage in life to make his will "one with God;" this was the goal of the yogi, and it was Tara Singh's goal.

We flew to Belfast from Birmingham, England, the largest city in the Midlands. Tara Singh's son was there at the airport to meet us, dressed in a dark suit, white shirt and tie. He embraced his father, said his hello to me, and helped us with our bags as we headed for the parking lot and his small car. I could tell there was delight, mixed with apprehension, typical of a middle-aged man relating to his aging father. We drove to his house through the countryside, and arrived in a suburb of Belfast that was neat and clean with small white two story houses, fronted with pleasantly well-manicured gardens on a quiet neighborhood street. We pulled into the driveway and unloaded our bags through the side door. There was an air of something off, I could tell, because Tara Singh was very quiet. He inquired about his wife and daughter. They were not there to greet him. I could feel something brewing, something not flowing in this reunion, but I could not anticipate what was in store. As we sat in the front room while his son was preparing a tea, we looked at a picture of his son's guru, the Hare Krishna potentate, Swami Prabhupada, made so famous by his worldwide movement in the 1960's and 70's. This kind of movement did not impress Tara Singh. In fact, he felt it was just another belief system that people flocked to, to avoid having their own mind, their own self-reliance. He did not comment, but I could tell this was a point on which he did not agree with his son.

Suddenly, as if a wave of necessity came over him, Tara Singh said to me, "We must leave here. We cannot stay here.

They are not even here to properly greet us," meaning his wife and daughter. When his son returned with the tray of tea servings he reiterated this declaration. His son was stunned. I could not fathom this kind of action, but I accepted it and helped load our bags back into the car. I had to think quickly on my feet. What were we to do? We had another four days in Ireland. Where were we to go? What were we to do? I was in a crisis of practicality, let alone the crisis that was happening in Taraji's family. "Take us to the hotel we passed along the way coming to your place," I said to him. That seemed like the first step. Get a place. Shocked, but not argumentative, his son drove us to the hotel. There we booked a room with no idea what the next few days would hold. We said our goodbyes, and that was it. His son drove off without much more ado. Now we were on our own. We headed toward our quarters. There was a silence in the room when we were settled in. My head was still reeling from the 180° turn around, but I was getting used to this kind of life lesson in my travels with my Master. I thought of the lesson in ACIM very early on, "I do not understand anything I see." Lesson #4, and trying like mad to bring it into application in this situation.

We had a short rest, and then it occurred to me we had some friends who had attended many retreats who lived near Dublin in the Republic of Ireland. So we called the friend who was the wife of one of the Irish Members of Parliament. Fortunately we got right through. So delighted to hear from us, we arranged to drive the next day to meet her. The hotel shuttle dropped us to the airport where we could rent a car. Now on the road again, we felt free and alive, with no cares, and no regrets. The drive through the Irish countryside was idyllic. Within a number of hours we were at the home of Derry McDermott, our dearest friend and fellow student of Tara Singh and *A Course in Miracles*. She had planned a dinner for us that evening, and had booked us into a hotel nearby. Catching up on the news, and dialoguing with Derry's husband, the Irish MP, was a lively evening. We planned an outing the next day, and a meet up with another of our Irish friends, Theresa.

More of the spectacular Irish scenery was in the hills and mountains south of Dublin. The four of us drove through the sparsely populated landscape, enjoying our spontaneous reunion, and appreciating each other's company in the homeland of our dearest friends. We stopped to have a lunch in a roadside inn, dating back to the 1600's. Such a history was to be seen and felt, in a land that had been exploited by the British for so long, now standing on its own in all its independent glory. My heritage came from Cork, a county just south of where we were. I felt at home in Ireland. I felt the poets of old stirring in my blood. I felt the desire to know God—an inheritance from the country whose monks saved the writings of the Western classical world in the dark times after the fall of the Roman Empire. I felt the gratitude of being with my teacher and friends, and the lesson I was getting in letting go and moving on. I felt a sense of courage in being able to cope with a difficult situation and come out OK. I felt for an instant that perfect happiness was not only possible, but was also my natural birthright.

We stayed a couple of days in Clondalkin, outside of Dublin city with our friends, but then soon it was time to head back up north to catch our flight the next afternoon. Driving north to Belfast, Tara Singh began to speak of his wife and daughter. "I came all this way to see them—we must see them. We have to go back to my son's." This came as a surprise. I had no way of knowing where he lived. We did not have the address, though I had a very rudimentary idea of the area of his house. When we got closer to Belfast I looked for landmarks I remembered. One led to another. I recognized this building, then another road, another turn. Within a short period we were in front of his son's residence. It was an absolute miracle I could have found it so easily. It was as if the car was driving itself and knew where to go.

We had stopped in the center of town nearby and bought some flowers. When we arrived at his doorstep his son was just as stunned to see us then, as he was when we announced our departure. Tara Singh embraced him, and asked to be taken into town to meet his daughter. We got into the car and headed into the center of Belfast. His daughter was kind of a champion of the homeless. She dressed herself in orange clothing, as Sadhus often do in India, and she made it her mission to give spiritual solace and service to the indigents on the Belfast streets. Her mother lived nearby in a flat. Taraji walked swiftly to greet her. Some yards away I could hear their exchange, "I am disappointed you were not there to greet us, " he said to her. She said something I could not quite hear, but basically it was an emotional standoff. Eventually they hugged though, and we got around to agreeing that we would all go back to her brother's house, and pick up their mother, Tara Singh's wife, on the way.

The drive back was a little more relaxed, but still on edge for me. Taraji's daughter was known to be psychic, and I could feel myself being "scrutinized" by her in all respects. Who was this man with her father, coming so far, and with no former acquaintance? We stopped the car on the corner in a rather tough part of town, while the daughter got out to fetch her mother. A small, thin woman in her 70's, dressed in a wool sweater and simple dress entered the back seat. There was not much life in her. She talked about the bad news on the "telly." She seemed listless and without joy. We drove through the back streets of Belfast, toward the suburban refuge of her son. Within a half an hour, we had arrived. The family was together, and that was a miracle. They began to prepare a meal in the kitchen, as we all anticipated a new found family harmony. Taraji and his wife spoke in Punjabi, while their children chopped vegetables and reminisced about times gone by when the family was back in the village in India. Taraji asked about the family home that had been in his lineage for generations. His daughter had been back, and dedicated its use to a local school. The meal was served and the mood lightened. Life was beginning to come back in the faces of his loved ones. There was a joy returning, ever so slightly. We enjoyed this time together at the meal, and afterward we moved to the living room to have after dinner tea. Of course we had to stare at the life-sized picture of the guru, but Taraji did not seem to pay much attention to it anymore. His son mentioned being in the realm of Krishna Consciousness, or some such party line about his "faith." But even that went unchallenged by Tara Singh. I think it was enough for him to be together with them, and to "Let all things be exactly as they are." Lesson #268 from ACIM.

We had a good rest that night. And the next morning we were all together for a breakfast and a photo shoot. At that time I travelled with my Nikon camera, so a picture of the family together was an auspicious thing to capture on film. Against the tall deep-green hedge in the back yard I snapped a photo of the family. Taraji looked amused in a quizzical way; his wife looked more alive than the day before, even slightly proud; his son was smiling, but still a bit shell shocked; and his daughter looked bereft of happiness, somewhat down trodden and sad, as though she was bearing the burden of the world. Of course this was just a split second in the shutter of an eye of the camera, but when I got back to the States and processed the photos, the psychic status quo of the whole family could be read in the facial expressions of this moment "in time." It was a moment in time, yes, but for me just as potent a lesson as those moments free and clear of time, that I had experienced with Tara Singh in numerous places and settings around the world. The family mind is very strong, and one of the very obstacles that a person must liberate himself from in order to move up the ladder of his own holy awakening. This was the lesson I learned by meeting Tara Singh's family. Each member had constructed a personal heaven or hell, according to their propensity, but each had made so clearly a personal self that defined their life. The ones calling themselves holy were perhaps the least liberated from

191

this family mind; the one calling himself a "taxi driver" was perhaps, ironically, the most liberated and free, by virtue of his natural gratitude and happiness within.

All of us headed toward the airport in the late morning, and arrived well ahead of our departure back to England. Sitting in the airport café we were joined by the whole family. Even Tara Singh's grandson, whom we had seen briefly the day before downtown, joined us in the gathering. The final gift Taraji brought for them had been distributed now. He had brought each member of his family an ounce of gold. They were of course delighted to receive it. Each had his coin, and the joy of receiving money was shining on their faces. But this was more than a gift of mere money. Gold is a symbol of a heartfelt union when given properly. It is an element of purity, the value of which is eternal. Empires come and go; currencies are printed and then fail; but gold is always constant, never affected by the tarnishing of time. In this giving of gold, Tara Singh's family was left to receive this "Moment outside of time," and it would be up to them what they would do with it.

We returned to Nottingham in England, after seeing the Irish contingent, and stayed a few more days with the college professor and his wife. There was calmness in the atmosphere now, especially after the tumultuous events in Belfast. Some mention was made of Tara Singh's son's x-wife. Something was intimated to him to go and see her in Birmingham. So we did on the next day. She was gracious. She lived in a small flat, and had become a social worker in the health system of Birmingham, dealing with women who had experienced domestic violence. She had a noble air, a factual personality, but gentleness within. She told her story to Tara Singh. Why she had left his son. Why she was on her own now. Why there had been no communication with him or the rest of the family. There had been great difficulty between her and her husband. She spoke of her attempts to make it work, but to no avail. She broke down and cried. It was an impossible situation of family violence and abuse. She could not go on in misery. So she moved to England and began picking up the pieces of her life. One of her sons came with her; the other stayed in Belfast. She now had some semblance of stability in her life. Tara Singh listened, but did not judge. I could tell he was taking in her pain and transmuting it. He had known her father well, who was a noble man. She was refined and of high birth. He hugged her, and I could tell it was his way of apologizing for his son's violence and infractions toward her. It was a tender moment of compassion. No one was judged wrongly, but everyone was lifted up by the stillness of the Presence Tara Singh invoked. He was a Master of bringing in the healing energy that was needed to diffuse a difficult situation, pouring balm on a tremendous hurt, or bring calm to a potentially charged up turn of events.

The next day, we left England for Los Angeles. I had been privy to the meetings with Tara Singh's family. He had come to "make their hearts glad," and to the best of his ability, he had. What he brought with him was "gold of the heart." He distributed it among his family members equally and with due respect and appreciation for all of their roles in his life. Yet, underneath this external "completion" and expression of his gratitude toward them, I could see a greater message in the fact that he was internally completing things as well. It was as if he was saying goodbye for good, for the good of his own evolution. The family mind is something that we must all transcend and go beyond, if we are serious about full enlightenment in this lifetime. The dramas of the family occur at the personality level, at the ego level. Forgiveness is most needed there. It is our real "work to do." Yet in the completion of this work of forgiveness, there is a real chance for us to make contact with the Self God created, beyond the confines of the family mind. My trip with Tara Singh to England and Ireland was to make this lesson clear to me. Even saints and great men have families, and these various family members, though contributing to the life of the great man or woman, do not necessarily go the route toward enlightenment in the footsteps that lead toward greatness. In fact they can appear to go in an opposite direction, at the same time the man or woman of greatness is going toward his/her own internal and independent light within.

❖ *Chapter 18.* ❖

Raising the Dead

It was post 9/11. An energy of edginess pervaded America. George W. Bush was well entrenched in office, thoroughly engaged in the "war on terror." Tara Singh and I were scheduled to travel to Florida and Puerto Rico for a series of workshops in November of 2001. I flew to Los Angeles from Philadelphia to begin our journey, with the anticipation that Puerto Rico would offer new gifts of hospitality. Taraji spoke highly of the people in Puerto Rico, and of the culture that could relax and enjoy life in a leisurely way. I was well primed in my expectations of the ease and joy we would have there.

The seminar in Florida went well, and we had a couple days before leaving for Puerto Rico. It was around the time of my birthday. We received the unfortunate news that a plane had crashed in New York City, on November 12th, killing all 260 passengers. There was suspicion of terrorism. Tara Singh was uneasy. "We have to go back to Los Angeles," was his directive. But this would mean cancelling Puerto Rico, I thought. It was a lot of work down the drain, as they had labored for months to arrange our workshop and visit. Nevertheless, we headed for the airport that day with the intention to return immediately to California. Luckily our organizer in Florida, who worked for the airlines for years, knew exactly where to go to change our tickets. She made the change within minutes, and we all gathered in an airport café to wait for our flight and to complete with the people in Florida. Melanie Coulter, a close student from Iowa, and our organizer, Maria Ramirez, Tara Singh and I sat at the table. There was an incredible sunset spread across the horizon. Taraji began to speak of the times being very challenging, and the fact that we needed to give the lessons in *A Course in Miracles* even more attention than we had been giving them. The four of us agreed to start the lessons again, from Lesson #1, for the whole year ahead.

Soon we were in the air, headed back to Los Angeles. There was a man in the seat next to us working on his laptop computer, obviously with spreadsheets that dealt with financial matters. Taraji was very impressed, and made sure that I noticed the man doing his work on the plane. We were not long in the air when Tara Singh asked me, "Where is the money from the workshop?" My heart sank. I was under the impression that the coordinator in Florida was in charge of that, and responsible for getting the money and the accounting back to the Foundation in due time. I said, "I don't know, Taraji, it is back in Florida with Maria." Well, he read me the riot act. "You must be an idiot. We left Florida and you don't

196

even have the money. This is sacred money for the Foundation. How could you be so careless? How would it have been if I said that to Krishnamurti?—'I don't know' about something so essential?" I was shocked and again felt as if I were about two inches tall. There was nothing I could do but take the admonishment and call Maria when I got off the plane.

It seemed as if a short few hours later, we were in the living room of the Foundation having a good meal. I had called Maria in Florida and asked her to send the seminar proceeds right away by FedEx—and I paid the shipping bill. But I was still feeling a bit devastated, even amidst a joy of celebration that Tara Singh was home. There was a quizzical buzz in the air about canceling Puerto Rico. More and more, Puerto Rico came up in the conversation. Taraji described the people there, the leisurely lifestyle, the climate and the spectacular seaside, the good food, and his history of going there to do workshops. He made it sound like a kind of heaven on earth. Then he said, "You know, we cannot leave them stranded. We have to go. They have worked so hard to have the seminar. We cannot let them down." Wow, this was a whole 180° shift from what he was saying in Florida, about the danger of traveling. My head was spinning, but I knew it was not my place to contradict the teacher. There was some deeper lesson in this that I was meant to receive, even though it seemed like too abrupt a change of plans.

"OK," I said, "let's go then." One of the staff looked into the tickets to PR from LA and back. Because we had forfeited our previous tickets from Florida to Puerto Rico, we would have to purchase all new tickets. When we were presented with the cost we were a bit shocked. Because it was such short notice, the price of the tickets was more than double. But it seemed like the right thing to do. The staff offered to book the tickets, when Tara Singh insisted, "He is a student, and he must pay his own way," meaning me. I felt a lump in my throat—cornered again, and I had to act fast. "OK, no problem, here is my credit card." I could not say no. Something in me knew that I had to go with the flow and not make my thoughts of "lack" real, even though it was going to cost me a couple thousand dollars more.

The next day we were headed for San Juan. Picked up at the airport, we were whisked away by a contingent of Tara Singh's friends and students, and taken to a posh high rise apartment building right on the beach. We went up the elevator to the 20th floor, and more friends were waiting for our arrival. A man who was a stockbroker owned the apartment, and it was available for our use while in San Juan. Spaciousness abounded, and we had a spectacular view of the beach and ocean. One of the ladies had prepared food— papaya and mango—and we were all in the joyousness of a family reunion. It seemed everywhere Tara Singh went there was this joyousness. Even people on the street came up to him, people who had done his seminars years ago elsewhere, expressed their gratitude and delight to see him again. There was an atmosphere of unlimited possibilities swirling around us wherever we went. It was wonderful to be a witness of this genuine elation.

The workshops was held over the weekend, and proceeded as planned. I was in charge of the audio equipment, making sure that Tara Singh's lectures were all properly recorded. Nearly every lecture he gave was recorded, and this was considered a very sacred charge of the Foundation's function. Traveling with Tara Singh on this trip was also a "service." I was to help in the actual nuts and bolts of seminar production. Nothing was too complicated. But this time I was very clear that I had to oversee the money from the workshop. To my dismay, though, the accounting was in an absolute shambles. This was a "manyana" culture—"do it tomorrow"—and nothing was written down, who paid what, who did not pay, or even who was attending the weekend. I scrambled to make order of chaos because I knew it was my butt that was on the line. So I stayed after the first day just to get it straight. It took me a couple hours with one of the assistants who was actually American, and therefore spoke perfect English. She was married to a Puerto Rican businessman, and had a good grasp of numbers. "Where have you been?" Tara Singh inquired after my long absence. When I told him I was making sure the money was straight, he acted like I was being overly fastidious, implying that was the job of the coordinators. Well, that was the way it was with him. He put you through the wringer, and then it was all over, like nothing ever happened. I think the "wringer" was a teaching device to see if you would crack or react, or bail out. He gave his students a "shock" to process them out of their thought. If you could "take the heat," then your mind would, in the end, be that much clearer of the ego reactions, fears, motives, justifications and defenses. It would be that much closer to stillness and silence, that much closer to an authentic attention and peace within.

We completed our work in Puerto Rico and stayed on a few more days to visit with friends. It was a glorious time there. We were treated like royalty. The man who provided the apartment in San Juan also took us to the Four Seasons hotel for dinner. And also, one of Tara Singh's students was a dentist. She had done extensive dental work for him on previous visits, and now needed to do some follow up work. We drove to her town of Ponce and stayed in her home. She, her daughters, her mother and sister had attended many Easter retreats in California. Now she was married to Ted, an American man who had actually lived at the Foundation for many years during its first beginnings. Now he was living in Ponce, Puerto Rico, with Annie, the dentist, and her two daughters, and her parents and sister next door. Taraji loved this family. Annie did all the dental work he needed and never charged him a penny. Ted, a long time student of Tara Singh from the early days at the Foundation, had moved to Ponce to start a new life. He set up a machine shop for his business, which was his area of expertise. We stayed with this family while Taraji had his dental work checked.

One of Annie's sisters had learning disabilities. But this did not stop the family from bringing her along to the workshops, so Taraji had developed quite a bond with her. We went over to the parents' house to see them and the sister. It was a moving moment. The two embraced like long lost friends. I began seeing a deeper side to Tara Singh. He had

compassion for all people, not just for some special people. He treated everyone with the same dignity that he would have treated Nehru, or Gandhi, or Mrs. Roosevelt—or even Krishnamurti. He was a man for all seasons and for all people. If ever the word humanist applied to anyone, it applied to him. We left Peurto Rico with joy in our hearts. He was right. It was worth the extra money we spent on airfare. I returned to Philadelphia and dug back into my work and contracts, basking in this three-week experience with Tara Singh that seemed like three years. That was always the case. Because the energy level was so heightened in his presence, one felt like he lived years of experience with Taraji in a very short time, compared to the same time spent in a day-to-day routine. There was nothing routine in relating to a Master such as him. He was always in the present moment, like a wild and majestic lion, and one had to be at that level of acute attention to be with him in his leonine self. He had no other way of relating. Time spent with Tara Singh was never casual, as I mentioned, nor without a particular teaching purpose.

It was not long after I returned from Puerto Rico in the middle of November that I received a call from the Foundation. It was late at night and I was at my studio when I took the call. The staff put Tara Singh on the phone with me. "There has been an accident. Ted has been hurt very badly, and we must go back to Puerto Rico." Now there was a silence in the room I could cut with a knife. I had not quite recovered financially from the last trip, and now I was being asked to go out again. I thought it over. "When will you go?" I asked. "Immediately," was the answer. Again, I was in the middle of a contract that would have to be delayed. "It is a life or death matter," Tara Singh insisted. "OK," I said, "I will meet you in San Juan as soon as I can." I said it without thought. It was as if another energy took me over, an energy that could forget about all the excuses that the limited ego would like to insist are valid, and ACT out of a real state of love, a real state of rising to meet a very authentic life challenge, a very urgent crisis of necessity. I was on the plane to Puerto Rico the next morning.

The American lady who was married to the businessman met me at the San Juan Airport. She took me to the posh apartment. There was Tara Singh, and two other friends of the Foundation, Steve and Richleigh, who were Ted's close friends as well. The four of us came down to support the family in Ted's hour of need. Tara Singh embraced me with delight, and said, "You made it, you did not listen to your limited thought. Now we have work to do." Ted was in the middle of a very long reconstructive surgery. Annie, his dentist wife, was beside herself. It turned out he was crushed under a forklift at his machine shop, and his whole pelvic area was broken into many parts. Ted was in a coma, and the doctors did not think he would make it. We were there to see otherwise.

Soon we were all at the hospital. We all flocked into the waiting room outside the surgery area to get the news. The young surgeon came out, looking rather serious and glum. "The surgery was a success, but we are not sure he will pull through. He is still in a coma, but his vital signs are improving. Should he make it, he probably will not walk again." Annie began to cry of course. Had Tara Singh not been there to comfort her, I think she would have been hysterical with grief. But there was always an air of calm in Tara Singh, especially in a crisis. He was the coolest person "under fire" I had ever met. He took in what the doctor said, but had his own conviction that things would be different. "I am determined to see things differently," Lesson #21 in *ACIM*, was his truth. And the force of his conviction could move a mountain and alter the course of dire circumstances.

Within a few days the doctors were saying Ted would live. But there were still no guarantees about his ability to ever walk again. So we could at least take a breath that his life would be spared. A great relief came over us in this moment. We all had to face the fact that we had pressing things at home to tend to, and that our return the next day was wise. Now that Ted was "out of the woods," we knew our presence there had made a difference. The next day we embraced the family, Annie, the children, and said our goodbyes. It was not easy, but we knew things would be better, day-by-day. I returned to Philadelphia; Tara Singh and the other men flew back to LA— mission accomplished.

Or so I thought—mission accomplished. Within the week I had another call from my teacher. "You know, now it is the family I am worried about. Annie is still upset, can't work. Ted is still in a coma, and the doctors are saying again he may not make it. We have to go again. Can you come out here to LA, then you and I go to Puerto Rico to see what we can do?" I was stretched. I was shocked. I was exhausted. I was nearly out of money. Furthermore, I had promised my family I would be with them for Christmas less than a couple weeks off, and I had already booked my tickets to Kansas City. They would be devastated if I cancelled. I told all of this to Tara Singh. "But we must go," he reiterated, "there is nobody else, and Annie is the one I am concerned with now." It was a plea as if from the Christ Himself. I could not say no, but I did mention to him that I had to be back in Philadelphia on December 23ʳᵈ so I could get my flight to see my parents and sister in Kansas. "OK, Let's go," he said with a tenor of absolute urgency.

I flew to LA on the next flight, then Tara Singh and I headed out for San Juan the next day. He was right. Annie was a basket case. Had we not gone she probably would have had a mental breakdown. We gathered our strength and settled in an apartment, still owned by the stockbroker, but in a more modest part of town. Then we planned to go to the hospital to see Ted, who was now in an intensive care unit, still in a coma. We gathered for a long time in the waiting room. It was not so easy to get into the intensive care wing, especially for someone not part of the immediate family. But as usual, the word "impossible" did not apply to Tara Singh. He was quietly determined to see Ted, and see Ted that night. As we were waiting, he began to discuss Ted's situation. He gave me a commentary on Ted's karma, of the cause and effect reasons why this "accident" occurred in the first place. He explained:

"Ted was a man who liked to work. He had mechanical skills, and a sense of order and direction. This is what made him good in business projects, especially things to do with machines. He liked to manufacture things, figure them out, get the job done. Now, when he came to Puerto Rico, he did not like the people too much, especially the ones he had to hire to help in his business. They were not so driven, not as productive as he was. They were more interested in relaxing, having a good time. They could not work in the same way. But he was not as patient with them as he could have been. He got frustrated. He could have met some higher people we know, refined people at the top positions in businesses, but he was not interested. He did not even learn the language. He became bitter about the whole situation, and then more frustration came, until he decided to close his business. This is when the accident occurred, at the height of his frustration. Do you see how anger and frustration brings on something worse? You have to see this is what karma is: the cause and effect of one's own thinking."

There, in a couple of minutes, Tara Singh had Ted's whole case in a nutshell. But nevertheless, he was determined that Ted would pull out of this, and that he would be absolved of any of this "karma" that had brought about such a terrible consequence already. After explaining this clearly to me, Tara Singh and I were admitted to the intensive care unit, where Ted, a large man, was lying in a coma fighting for his life. I will never forget this day, because our lesson in *ACIM* was "There is nothing my holiness cannot do." (Lesson #38) From this lesson, I was silently reciting the whole time we were with Ted, "In the situation involving Ted's accident and his recovery, there is nothing my holiness cannot do." I just kept reciting this line, as Tara Singh tended to Ted. He rubbed his feet and stroked his hair. At one point he said his name out loud, "Ted, Ted...Ted," repeating it like a Sanskrit mantra. It was as if Tara Singh was compelling Ted back to life. He was calling him back from a distant shore; a distant land that he knew in his heart Ted was not ready to go to, not finished with this life here that he was leaving so incomplete. We stayed for about ten minutes. I was silently repeating, "There is nothing my holiness cannot do," and Tara Singh was gently massaging Ted. Finally the nurse bid us to leave the unit, but not before I could see clearly with my own eyes something quite remarkable. I had just witnessed Tara Singh raising a man from the dead. Ted would live. And Ted would even learn to walk again. It was clear to me, because Tara Singh had just willed him to do so in my presence.

Back in the apartment we spent some time with Annie. We calmed her down but she was still unable to go back to work. Her parents were tending to the children. It would take days to restore her mind to some real stability, and I was getting nervous that we would not have enough time to bring the situation to a close. On the day before we were to leave, it looked like we were not going to make our flight the next day. This would mean I would miss my flight back to Philadelphia as well, and then miss my flight to see my family for Christmas. In the car to the hospital that day, Tara Singh was very challenging. "Love is very testing," he said in his customary poignancy directly at me. I shrunk, as I could tell he did not give a damn if I made it home for my flight. All he cared about was the crisis at hand, not some sentimental Christmas party that was awaiting me back home. Who were the people really in need here? When I thought about it carefully, what would Jesus, the man we were honoring on

Christmas, do in this situation? Go to a celebration, or stay and raise the dead, or pour a healing balm on the hearts of the afflicted? So I saw what I had to do. I had to call my family and tell them I could not make it on time. I did not know when I would arrive in Kansas. It was not easy. My father was upset. My sister threatened to disown me. My mother listened to my reasons, but she was disappointed. I saw the emptiness of a conventional faith. Mostly, it is centered around traditional appearances. It has no meat at all to respond to a real need. It is mostly based on only what makes us "feel good." We missed the flight back. I was surrendered to another will, greater than my own.

So yet again, Tara Singh had me cornered. To be true to my Higher Self meant I had to let go of all my other concerns, even if it made me look bad in the eyes of others. I would have to "bear the humiliation" directed at me by family members in order to rise to real conviction in myself. It was not an easy lesson. I cried that evening when I had to tell Taraji my family wanted to disown me. He was compassionate. Now that I had "passed the test" he told me how proud he was of my actions. He said, "Your family will probably never understand these higher states of inner conviction. It is like you have learned how to fly the plane, and they have never gone near it. You will never be able to explain to them what it is like to fly the plane. You will not be able to explain to them what has happened here. Don't even try."

We left the day after our planned departure from Puerto Rico. I had missed my flight back to Philadelphia, and subsequently to Kansas City. I was exhausted and stunned, yet

I knew there would be a boon in this whole experience that I would grow to cherish in years to come. I could use my bonus miles to get to Kansas, and I actually could arrive on Christmas day, thus keeping my word on both sides of the crisis. Tara Singh did not mention again that my trip to the family was less important than helping those friends in need. We had put the needs of the people in crisis first, and met them. We had gone down to save Annie and Ted from any more painful demise. We had in fact, "raised the dead." And now on the flight to Kansas City I sensed that there was another mortification that I would need to avert, or perhaps even endure—the disapproval of my family. I could not expect them to understand these "life lessons," which only a teacher of life could disseminate. Life is challenging, and Tara Singh had taken me through a challenge in the past month and a half the likes of which I had never known—and somehow I passed through it the wiser. I overheard Taraji saying to another about me, "He will be as wise as a serpent, and as gentle as a lamb." Perhaps he was right, and I had a different destiny my family could never comprehend. So, into that destiny I travelled on that Christmas day of 2001 having been a witness to a genuine resurrection.

❖ *Chapter 19.* ❖

Second Trip to India

There was some talk between us that we were incomplete with India. Certainly Tara Singh wanted me to have the full force of the background he inherited from such a rich cultural and spiritual heritage, so there were some things we still needed to do together there. For himself, he was concerned about two things: his family property back in the village—and some money he had deposited in a bank in New Delhi. For me, he held out one last pilgrimage to the Golden Temple, which was the Sikh's greatest jewel: the holy shine and religious seat located in the Punjabi city of Amritsar. Amritsar was the Mecca of the Sikhs, and both Tara Singh and I felt we needed to go there together. I had an intuition that I had spent several past lives as a Sikh. International travel often gets one in touch with the ancient memories we hold in our subconscious reservoir that in some way formed our destiny in this lifetime. So the Golden Temple became our focus. Of course there was a large picture of the Golden Temple in the front room of the Foundation, which inspired us onward to make the journey.

We planned the trip in two parts. First, we would stop in England and see the professor and his wife, Tara Singh's older sister, and then we would proceed to India. While in India we would visit the village where the ancestral home was to be settled, preferably by giving it to some charitable interest in the town. Also, we would settle the bank account in New Delhi, with the notion that the money would go to support the Ramana Maharshi ashram in the south of India. And after those two things were completed, we would go to the Golden Temple in Amritsar. This was the plan—or so I thought.

As often was the case with Tara Singh, there was a bigger plan that was not quite apparent from the beginning, but would unfold in the moment and offer its own teaching lessons, its own challenges, and its own unanticipated miracles. The second trip to India was such a plan. The lessons were there, but none were in the form I expected, and the pilgrimage to the Sikh's holiest temple was one in which the gold of the heart proved ascendant to any physically constructed structure of worship. The best-laid plans often go awry. But in our case there were many insights to be had from the discrepancies between what we had planned, and what actually transpired.

We arrived at Heathrow Airport after a twelve-hour flight from Los Angeles, absolutely wiped out. But this time there were no joyous relatives to meet us. We had to catch a bus to Nottingham and travel another five hours to Tara Singh's sister's house. We maneuvered ourselves to the right bus stop, proceeded northward, and arrived in Nottingham sometime late in the evening. Our host and hostess were there to meet us in their Mercedes Benz, and we were grateful just to be horizontal soon after the proper greetings and cup of hot tea with a light dinner.

The conversation the next day was mainly centered upon the family estate back in India. The last visit his sister had paid to the place revealed its dilapidated condition. She was heartbroken over it. But what was the best thing to do? Would Tara Singh's children be involved? A phone call to his son revealed that Taraji had legally signed over the property to his children many years before. So in effect, it was theirs to do with as they may, even if that meant letting it deteriorate into ruin. They had given a local school permission to use the property, but that was most recently. Be that as it may, there was nothing Tara Singh could do. His children were the rightful owners now.

This did not seem to settle the matter in Tara Singh's mind, though. He was hoping the property could be useful, not just sitting fallow. So when we continued on to New Delhi, this was still a lingering issue. It pressed on his mind. On our flight to India we were still considering a trip to the village, to the ancestral home. But then there was a crisis I did not anticipate. Taraji became ill on the first day of our arrival. He complained that he was weak in the legs, and could not walk very well. What was I to do? In a foreign land, unfamiliar with the system—but I had to act.

I remembered a doctor who was at the ashram many years ago when I had visited India with Sondra Ray. His name was

Dr. Arvind Lal. I went to one of the telephone STD stations that are closely scattered across all of India and asked to look for the Dr. in the New Delhi phone book. The man was very helpful, and he was able to locate Dr. Arvind Lal at Connaught Place. I wrote down the address and returned to the room. Soon I had Tara Singh in a taxi on our way to the Dr.'s address. When we arrived, I went into the place and saw Dr. Lal's mother, who I remembered very well. I introduced myself, told her my situation with Tara Singh, and asked to see her son. She was gracious and sent me upstairs to his office. He had not remembered me, but when I filled him in, he was very helpful. Though he ran a pathology lab, he referred us to a general practitioner's office just around the corner, who happened to be a Sikh. So I took Tara Singh there for an examination. The exam was thorough, but he could not find a thing wrong with Tara Singh's health. He said it was probably temporary exhaustion from the long travel, and that we should have a couple days of rest, and then proceed along to the Golden Temple as planned. He prescribed some medication for relaxation, and we went on our way.

That day we moved to a better hotel near the Shivaji Field Hockey Stadium, into a room overlooking the playing field. It felt secure and quiet, much cleaner than the previous hotel, and the beautiful green playing field was a balm to the eye. The practice teams would be out on the field during the day. It was a mesmerizing sight to watch them play, and often the grounds keepers would spray water on the field with large hoses—streams and streams of water.

Tara Singh rested, and I was considering our next move. He did not appear to be improving. Still weak in the legs, we tried to go to the Bank of India branch to sort out his accounts. It seemed next to impossible with the Indian red tape. I called the Foundation and spoke to the accountant. "Is there a Bank of India in Los Angeles?" I inquired. Yes. "Could Taraji's account be sorted out there, and funds sent to the ashram in India?" Yes. OK—that problem was solved.

As Tara Singh's health and energy became more and more fragile, we both began to question the wisdom of taking on arduous travel to other towns and cities. It seemed the main practical issues of the family estate and the funds in the Bank of India were already solved. The estate was in the hands of Tara Singh's children, and the funds were safe and more easily accessible from the Bank of India branch in Los Angeles. So the last reason for the journey, the pilgrimage to the Golden Temple was the only reason to stay on. We pondered this for a couple of days, awaiting Taraji's health to return. But it did not return.

I remember the moment in the hallway coming back to our room after breakfast. There was a story I recalled from the account in the book *Journey Without Distance* by Robert Skutch, about the scribing of *A Course in Miracles* by Dr. Schucman. Dr. Schucman and Dr. William Thetford were instructed to go to a distant city to locate a church. When they arrived at the designated address, the church had been torn down and did not exist. In the airport on their way back to New York, Dr. Schucman saw a lady who was obviously distraught, and needed her help, which she offered. After the incident, Dr.

Schucman had the insight she shared with her colleague. It was not a "physical temple" that they were to find on their journey, but rather a "temple of the holy spirit, which was in a holy relationship." The lady in the airport in need, and Dr. Schucman's response to her, was the real "temple" they were sent to find, not a building that did not even exist.

I shared this story with Tara Singh. I said to him in the elevator to our floor, after settling our hotel account, "Taraji, the real Golden Temple is our relationship. It is worth more to me than anything else in my life. I do not need to go to see the Golden Temple in Amritsar. It is right here in our holy relationship." There seemed to be a relief that came over us. With his health in jeopardy, it did not seem wise to go any further. We came all this way, and the three main reasons for our trip had now evaporated into thin air. All was well, and all was complete. My only mission with Tara Singh at this point in our journey was to get him back to Los Angeles as quickly as I could, and to get his health restored.

We went to the airline office the next day, and within 24 hours we were on a plane back to London. We had an overnight break in the journey, so we stayed in a hotel room near the airport. The next day we proceeded home to the USA.

This second trip to India with Tara Singh was not an easy pilgrimage, nor did it end up looking like what I had envisioned. Yet, for that one realization in the hotel elevator in New Delhi, it was worth a thousand trips to the Golden Temple in Amritsar—perhaps even a million. The holy relationship, to which A Course in Miracles gives so much emphasis, was at the root of the teachings Tara Singh had

215

given me. It became clear that the whole point of my seventeen years spent with Tara Singh was to bring this holy relationship into application. It is the whole point of life itself. "To Love my Father is to Love His Son." (Lesson #246) Many want to know God in some deep way, yet it is through relationships with our fellow human beings that we will receive this sacred "knowledge." I let go of all my pictures of holiness and righteousness in that elevator in New Delhi. To meet the needs of my brother first and foremost, to safeguard his well-being by our return to safe haven, was my real second trip to India and the Golden Temple.

❖ *Chapter 20.* ❖

Keeping it Alive

By 2003 the work of the Foundation, and subsequently the work of Tara Singh, was winding down. The major figures that had been part of the action of the workshops, retreats, publications of books and tapes were no longer living near the Foundation in Los Angeles, so the staff was what now down to what I would call a "skeleton crew." Just the bare bones of what had been there years before, when I first made contact with Tara Singh and the Foundation, were keeping the Foundation alive. The two main retreats, Easter in the spring and Yom Kippur in the fall were still on the schedule, but local workshops around the country had all but ceased. Tara Singh, though he spoke about wanting to spend some time in silence, also found it hard to give up on the idea of regular seminars and sharing.

My friends who lived in or near Philadelphia—Kiki Vekkos, Clarke Van Sant, Alexander Barnes, and Paul Meistering—were willing to help with producing Philadelphia events. So we scheduled them and got to work. Tara Singh's following in the Philadelphia had at one point been very strong, but since many had studied *A Course in Miracles* for so long, they had lost interest, or had moved on to other things, and we had to work doubly hard to bring the people to the workshops. But we pulled it off and kept Tara Singh's wisdom and teachings alive. With the help of Kiki Vekkos and other friends, I managed to produce two weekend workshops in the Philadelphia area in 2001 and 2002.

On one of the occasions of his visits to Philadelphia, Tara Singh and I travelled to Lakewood, New Jersey, to meet his friend Dr. William Kelly. Dr. Kelly had been a good friend and doctor of Taraji's since the inception of his work with *A Course in Miracles* in the early 1980's. He witnessed the formation of a non-profit foundation and all of Tara Singh's years in Los Angeles. They met while living in Virginia Beach, being part of the Paul Solomon Fellowship, a spiritual community based on the psychic readings given by Solomon. Dr. Kelly, now a homeopathic doctor and a D.C., was very active in the psychic work of Paul Solomon at that time, and befriended Tara Singh who was also teaching at Solomon's Fellowship.

After spending three years in silence in Carmel, California, Tara Singh went to Virginia Beach, guided by an intuition that the work of Edgar Cayce would be important to him. Taraji was approached by William Kelly in a park, on his way to Virginia Beach. William came with a reading on tape from Paul Solomon—in which this gifted psychic was saying about

Tara Singh, "He has been brought half-way around the world just to be here."

Our trip to New Jersey was one of reunion, and also for Taraji to have a physical examination from Dr. Kelly. We went to the office first, underwent the examination, and then proceeded to Dr. Kelly's apartment for the evening. I drove behind them in my car doing my best to keep up to their speed, which was well beyond the posted limit. It felt as though they were trying to leave me in the dust. But I managed to keep up, and we arrived for the night, spent some time in conversation, had a good breakfast the next day, then we left for the Philadelphia Airport to catch Tara Singh's flight back to LA. Barbara Michael, one of the Foundation's staff, met us at the airport. She had been visiting her parents in the Philadelphia area. Barbara still lived in LA, and was marginally involved with the Foundation after many years of full time, dedicated service.

On another visit to Philadelphia, we held a workshop in a large house in Chestnut Hill, owned by Clarke Van Sant, an architect and fellow *ACIM* student. Afterwards Tara Singh and I travelled to Washington D.C. in order to see the Lincoln Memorial together, which Taraji considered to be one of the most authentic temples in the USA. He highly regarded Lincoln as one of our greatest beings, and he wanted to share this experience with me—a visit to our nation's most honored ground.

As we were traveling down Interstate I-95 from Philadelphia through the forests of Maryland, Tara Singh was in another state of being—and so was I. It was as if a heavenly aura engulfed the land, and all the trees and fields, the rivers we crossed, and even the cars and roadway itself took on a beauty that was hitherto unrecognized. "It's like a dream—it's like a dream," Tara Singh kept saying about the awesome beauty we were witnessing. There was a feeling of heavenly bliss in the car and in all of the visions of a beautiful world.

We stayed in a hotel not far from the Mall in Washington. The room was spacious and looked out over the iconic government buildings. We had just settled and brought up our things when Tara Singh said, "I would like to show you the pranayama." This was a surprise I had not anticipated. Often Taraji mentioned this very sacred way of breathing that the yogis in India had spent thousands of years perfecting. It was considered the "Raja," the "King" of all yoga. This was not something he shared with students who were not serious. So I had to take a moment to integrate this offer. What came up in my mind was that I may not be ready to take on such a serious and sacred responsibility. Letting this go, I flowed with the dynamism of the moment.

Lying on the bed, Taraji gave me the instructions. "Make yourself like dead, with your hands at your sides." I did what he said. "Lay there for about five minutes." Five minutes seemed like five hours to me. I could feel myself relaxing into a deeper and deeper calm. As I sank into this state of profound peace, Taraji gave me the breathing instructions, and I followed his directions exactly. The whole pranayama practice took about 25 minutes. At various times, I had to hold the breath in for a certain number of counts, feeling fear that I would not have enough air—but after a few rounds this fear

220

dissipated and my mind came back to calm. Deeper and deeper into this calm I went, until at the end of the pranayama process there was a grace in the room I could feel in myself, a peace so profound and all pervasive than I had ever experienced. This was the jewel in the crown of Taraji's teachings, and he had just shared its blessing with me. After fourteen years of association with my teacher, I had merited this boon of trust, this gift of God that had been the pillar of Raja yoga from ancient times. Our bond was now sealed with this sharing. Our holy relationship was just ascended to a new level of mutual respect and absolute trust.

That night we had dinner outdoors- in the hotel restaurant. It was a balmy evening. We discussed the future of the Foundation's work, and the future of Tara Singh's work. The work was winding down. Many had left the Foundation, and now the workshops were also all too infrequent. Tara Singh was yearning for a period of silence and aloneness, yet at the same time, he still wanted to be productive and share the *Course*. These were some of his concerns. I listened with respect, but I had no answer for the situation. I was committed to bring him to Philadelphia a couple times a year. And there could be the two longer retreats at Easter time, and in the fall for Yom Kippur. The rest of the year he would have for meditation and silence. This was the status quo at the moment. He had taught me to just look at the facts; just look at what is so. My situation was that I was married, had a householder's life, and was committed to finding my truth, in that context of this life and work. I was an artist as well, maintained a studio, and my artistic creativity in painting was important to me too. We let this all soak in as we looked at it.

The next day we drove towards the Lincoln Memorial. We parked the car on the street, and walked quite a distance toward the majestic Greek building that was off in the distance at the west end of the Mall. There was an air of a temple in the Memorial, even though it was dedicated to one of our most well-known political figures. We ascended the steps and entered into the Presence of the man who had been the spearhead for the end of formal slavery in America, and maintained the union of the United States. Tara Singh felt

without Lincoln the United States would have still been divided into north and south, two separate entities that would have prevented its evolution and growth.

In his early years in India, Taraji's association with Jawaharlal Nehru revealed that this Indian statesman revered Lincoln so much he had a life-sized sculpture of Lincoln's hands on his desk. The non-violent fight for the freedom of India from Great Britain was partially inspired by Lincoln, and by Henry David Thoreau who wrote the essay "Civil Disobedience". Thoreau, and that essay in particular, had inspired Gandhi to begin his non-violent revolution. In this hallowed hall of Lincoln's energy, Taraji and I soaked up the silence. The spirit of the man was very strong, and I felt blessed to be experiencing it for the second time in my life, this time with my teacher who was introducing me to the deeper essence of one of America's true founding fathers.

After this experience, there was nothing more to be said. It was time to head back to Philadelphia and to complete the eastern tour. Driving back through the Maryland landscape was equally elevating. The beauty of the panorama was upon us, surrounding us, and greeting us at every turn.

Keeping our relationship alive was another force of nature that went beyond the confines of events and travels, but permeated our awareness of everything around us. Like the moments outside of time in India, these moments I had with Tara Singh in my own homeland had an awesome beauty. We lived in a technological age of prowess and affluence, which had produced systems for everyday life that made existence a joyful and easy experience. The car and the road became part of this ease and facility as we swiftly rolled through the grandeur of the great outdoors. The bridge over the Susquehanna River was long and wide. What a feat of engineering to be able to cross this formidable body of water as though it were just a small stream. In the elevated atmosphere of American ingenuity Tara Singh and I held together a bond that transcended, yet included so acutely, everything in our immediate and sensory world. With the sharing of the pranayama in Washington DC, I had received a great spiritual gift that put me in touch with the most actual and grounding necessity of human life itself, the very breath that is the most essential life connection possible. Without breath there is no human life. Gratitude begins with the first breath. And it was on this trip to Washington DC, to see the temple of the greatest liberator, Lincoln, that I received my initiation into the greatest liberation. The years spent with Tara Singh yielded in the flowering of my own Self —a relationship with my own eternal breath of prana *keeping it alive*.

❖ *Chapter 21.* ❖

In My Own House

Completely Letting Go

I realized the importance of a real teacher was to awaken me to be who I really am—to introduce me to my true Self-Identity. I spent a lifetime constructing a "self" that, along with the "good," contained all of the conflicts, problems, limitations and sorrows of living in this world. I endured them, somehow, with some promise of nirvana *later on* in my life. I lived by thought, which was mostly preoccupied with the past, dissatisfied with the present, and to some degree anxious about the future. I thought about becoming better, becoming a more ideal person with an improved situation just ahead of me, as I would chase the next reward, the next carrot of gratification that would evaporate into an ephemera of memory—memory of a *peak experience*. This true teacher, Tara Singh, took away my self-deception. He dismantled the "self I had made up," leaving me to face the emptiness and absence of a partial and *conditioned self* that had taken me years to construct. I now had less and less to "achieve" now that I had been touched by a spiritual master who automatically simplified my life. The things that had meaning for me no longer mattered. This real teacher had "nothing to teach" in the sense that he "took away" what I already knew. What I "knew" was full of problems, so he removed the mental belief systems that filled my memory banks, which manufactured my unhappy and problematic experiences. In short, any true teacher will attempt to undo the "self I had made up." It was not my real Self, but was the only self I had known.

If we who are serious about Self-realization through *A Course in Miracles*, and give real attention to the first ten lessons in the *Workbook of ACIM*, we discover Jesus is doing the same thing. "Nothing I see means anything."#1 "I see only the past."#7 "I see nothing as it is now."#9 "My thoughts do not mean anything."#10 These lessons are designed to undo our memory, our accumulation of thought we store as "knowledge," and to bring us to an empty state of mind, which allows our real mind to flower and emerge into our awareness. But as much as we seek enlightenment through various religions, practices and gurus, we are still left in our own house. Someone said, "Did you ever notice whenever there is a problem, you are there." So you take yourself with you, and whatever problem you experience, you always had that problem- just waiting for release of the thought forms that caused it.

There were lessons I still needed to receive from Tara Singh to stop my own thought—the culprit of all problems. On one occasion he wanted me there at the Foundation. I was totally out of money from all the previous travel we had done together. I mentioned I could not come; I did not have the airfare. He said, "The Foundation will pay for your airfare." "OK," I said, "then I can come for a few days, a week or so." So I booked the flight and put the tickets on my credit card and flew to Los Angeles. I arrived at the Los Angeles airport and Taraji was waiting there for me in the baggage claim. We hugged and were glad to be together. Back at the Foundation we had some intimate time together in the Prayer Room, on our morning walks to the Art Museum, and with some friends who still lived very near the Foundation.

There was a lesson I was to receive that had probably been fully orchestrated by my teacher. One of the lessons Tara Singh taught was to be absolutely impeccable about your word. Consistency of word and deed was the beginning of spiritual wisdom. All the great masters taught this. One must make his word a law unto itself, consistent with higher laws. This is what gives the word the power—that it is always true and connected to the Source of truth. So this lesson was to be given to me in a manner that would be unforgettable. At one point I asked the last remaining staff member at the Foundation, a young woman who had been there for a number of years, if Taraji had mentioned reimbursing me for the airfare. She said he had not mentioned it to her. OK, I thought that was strange, as we had had the conversation prior to me agreeing to come out. I dropped it and did not mention it again after that.

But in the middle of the night, about 1AM, Taraji came bursting into my room. "You have not an ounce of gratitude, whatsoever. You are treated like a prince here at the Foundation, and you have the audacity to ask the Foundation to pay for your airfare. Get out. Pack your bags and in the morning—I want you to get out of here." I was stunned, as I took on more shock to my system. I did not defend myself. In the morning I arose early, took my shower, and packed my bag. I proceeded downstairs to the Prayer Room. Taraji and the young woman were sitting there, awaiting my arrival. He asked me to hand him back the mala beads he had given me that came from the Ramakrishna Mission in India. He gave them to me around the time he taught me the pranayama. I took them off and handed them back. He showed me the door, and as I was leaving he handed me a painting I had given him, "Here, take this. We don't need it. How will you be?" I did not get into too much talk about the whole affair. "I will manage," I said, with some certainty that was true. I left for what I thought would be the last time I set foot at the Foundation. It was a bright Southern California morning. I had my roller bag, another carry on, and the painting as I headed out on my own.

Still in the shock of it all, I began to walk toward Wilshire Boulevard. "What was I to do now?" My flight back to Philadelphia was not for a couple of days. I felt like something in me was awakening. I did not blame Taraji for being "unfair." I did not defend myself. And I did not regret asking for my airfare to be reimbursed. I felt it was important for me to stand up for myself and ask Taraji to "honor his word," the very lesson he was meticulous about teaching all of his students. If this meant my time was finished with him, then that was what it meant. I was not happy or sad. I was not self-righteous or guilty. In fact all the opposites of thought were coming to an end in me. I could see the things in my world with my senses, but there was stillness in them that emanated from my own stillness. I did not know where I would go. Perhaps I would hang out in a park for a couple of days. Perhaps I would take a taxi to the Beverly Hills Hotel, and treat myself. The two had no difference. I walked on, until I arrived at a modest hotel a few blocks away in which people who were visiting the Foundation often stayed. I checked into the hotel and ascended the stairs to my room. It was a joy to be alone. I was looking forward to a good rest, a time in which I did not have to be at attention, or in the vortex of a stark teaching. I lay down on the bed and soon passed out, as I had hardly slept a wink that night.

It had been less than an hour when the phone rang. It was the lady at the Foundation. She said they would come and get me shortly, and that I should meet them outside the hotel. Well this was a turn I had not expected. I gathered my things and went to the front desk to check out. I paid for my short time there, and then waited for them outside by the street.

Back at the Foundation, not much was said. No apologies were handed back and forth. "We have to make it work," Tara Singh said. I think that was his way of saying, "You passed the test." I did not get angry; I did not resist the teaching; I did not make demands for my airfare; I did not defend myself; and I also stood up for myself, for my own conviction that honoring one's word had to be my truth. I was even willing to confront the teacher, and even myself, on this point. The next couple days at the Foundation were quiet. Taraji talked about the inherent unwillingness of *thought* to let go. I felt that I was letting go. And he was giving me real life lessons in which letting go was not only necessary, but inevitable.

There was a time in which he asked his teacher Krishnamurti, "Does life take care?"—to which his teacher replied, "Yes, when you completely let go."

"Well," I asked myself, "how close was I to completely letting go?" When I finally left on that visit to return to Philadelphia, Taraji handed me a check for the reimbursement of my airfare.

I'm Going Home

It was not long after this visit I got a call from the Foundation that the house at 902 Burnside was being sold, so Tara Singh and the Foundation would have to move. The landlord was moving on. The Foundation would have to be packed up and a new place would have to be found. This threw everything into another vibration. There was a woman still living at the Foundation taking care of the basic accounting, Tara Singh's personal care, and the general correspondence. But she was the only one out of many who were still formally living at the Foundation along with Tara Singh. And even she had some inklings of leaving.

I had planned to bring Tara Singh to Philadelphia in early April of 2003. So prior this planned visit I went to the

Foundation to see him. He was in a new house not far from the old location, in the Miracle Mile district of Los Angeles. 917 Genesee St. was the address of the new house of my friend and Master. Much had to be let go of during my visit prior to the move. Many of us were there to ease the transition, clean out the garage and move the essential things. When the final move was made I could tell the Foundation was in a transition that was huge. Tara Singh was concerned, but also accepted that life was always kind to him. He moved to the new place with the grace of life providing him with all that was needed for this next phase of his life and work.

In March of 2003 I went to the Foundation to check in on my teacher and prepare him for coming to Philadelphia in April. There was an atmosphere in the new place that matched the old. A prayer room had been installed in much the same way as the one before it. The Holy Beings were still at the heart of the place and Tara Singh was still the keeper of the Altar and the vibration of *A Course In Miracles* as given to him by Dr. Schucman.

But the work was coming to a close for him, and this was disconcerting. He began to lose his memory. He became more concerned about what would happen in the future. We would walk to the green park around the Los Angeles Museum of Art and discuss this. "You are needed at the Foundation," he would say to me. But I had made peace with my life in Philadelphia at the time. "I can come back and forth, Taraji, " I said, "But I have my life in Philadelphia." I told him. I could feel him being a bit disappointed with me. "But you are needed." There was a silence. But we were of two different minds on this matter. I would have had to let go of everything to be at the Foundation, and at that point I could not do it. He was losing his short-term memory fast, and I did not trust myself to be able to handle that situation either.

The woman who was taking care of Tara Singh had been at the Foundation for seven years. She was being challenged daily by Tara Singh in the Prayer Room about her motives. Though she had given all these years to the work, she was starting to lose patience with Taraji and his confrontational method of teaching. I was to make arrangements for Tara Singh to come to Philadelphia in a couple of weeks. So there was anticipation that the situation would gain more clarity when he came to visit. But then something happened that totally threw me for a loop. We were sitting at the dinner table and Taraji was sharing, as he often did during the meal. He was sharing on the importance of accepting things exactly as they are, being free of wanting things to be different than they are. He spoke with a certainty, "When you truly wake up and do not want anything, you realize you already have everything." There was silence in the room. Barbara Michael was at the table also. The other lady was still eating her food, not listening with much attention to our teacher. Barbara and I were more and more still, more and more focused on Tara Singh's words, as the woman across from us, sitting at Tara Singh's right, kept chomping her meal. Suddenly without warning, Tara Singh took a swing at her and slapped her on the back of the head. "What are you doing? Have you no dignity? Are you just going to go on chomping away like an animal?" There was an upset in the air I had never felt to this degree. "I will not put up with this" she said, "I am leaving the Foundation." This was a real crisis. There was no one left at the Foundation now. The last "Indian" had fallen. I was discombobulated. I had never witnessed Tara Singh physically striking someone, and was not so sure I could accept this as a teaching method. I had heard about teachers of old doing such things with their students, but this actual event jogged me to the bone. I was thrown into a crisis the likes of which surmounted anything I had ever dealt with in my years with Tara Singh. The young woman left the Foundation, heading for a friend's house nearby. I was sent there to retrieve her keys, which I did.

When I returned, Barbara was there in the living room. I went into Taraji's room with the keys. "Here they are, Taraji." We went into the Prayer Room and sat. He said, "You better watch out, I feel you moving away from me." I could feel his words cutting into me. Were they true? I was in shock, and I could not seem to pull myself out of it. I called some other friends to let them know the status quo. When Taraji finally went to bed, I was exhausted from what I had witnessed. Barbara was still there. I said to her, "Barbara, I have a flight back to Philadelphia in the morning. Taraji is scheduled to come to Philadelphia in about two weeks. I am going home and prepare for him to come." She assured me that things would be OK and I should catch my plane as planned.

I did not get much sleep that night. I awakened early and caught the shuttle to the airport at 5AM. I was listening to the part of myself that would have to allow life to take care in a way that was perfect for the situation. For me, I knew I had things at home which needed my attention, and I was not to judge anything that had just occurred: I was not to judge the woman who seemed disrespectful and who had just left the Foundation; I was not to judge Taraji for the harsh way he corrected her; I was not to judge myself for deciding to keep the scheduled time of my flight back home. I had to trust that life would take care in this situation if I completely let go, and that Barbara would be there for Taraji until he could come to Philadelphia in a couple of weeks. It was not until later that I would be shown that life had another plan that I was not in control of, and it would provide yet more lessons in my holy relationship with Tara Singh. In a few hours I would be back in Philadelphia in my own house, for better or worse, standing in my own conviction that I was exactly where I needed to be. The life lessons that were being given to me were huge, and I had to flow with something that was beyond my "understanding." "I do not understand anything I see." is Lesson #3 in *ACIM*. Taraji was giving me that lesson in my face, yet again. I knew I had to be independent of the Foundation, stand under my own roof—not under another man's roof, even my teacher's. But at the same time I had to be attentive to the situation in Los Angeles.

I called Barbara daily to see how things were going. She seemed OK. Taraji was enjoying her company. I could assure him that in a couple weeks he would be in Philadelphia, and we would be together for a workshop. This made him happy. And I was immensely happy to be in my own house. My decision to come home on that day was also my decision to accept whatever consequences this decision would have for me. When one is cornered, he must act. And this was the second time I had to say "no" to my teacher. He had said, "You are needed at the Foundation," and I had stood up for my own intuition to be in my own house, in my own life, in my own destiny. At that point I was in shock, even fear of what was in store for Taraji and me. I did not yet realize this decision to go home would lead me to a destiny that would be independent of Tara Singh's, my Master and teacher. I wanted my freedom more than anything else, even if it was the freedom to be in the prison house of my own making. I was not ready to walk out on everything I had made. So my "unwillingness" was still alive. It was still the ruling nature of my thought. Though I knew I was not yet fully liberated, it was of my own accord that I would be free or not free. At least I knew this much: I was the master of my own destiny. I could sink or I could swim on the merits of a plan that would be given in the form best suited for me, being in my own house.

❖ *Chapter 22.* ❖

Inherent Unwillingness

Prior to meeting Tara Singh there was uncertainty in my life. I was split between what my life was, and what I thought my life "should be." This split was the root of sorrow to which Buddha referred to in His 'four noble truths.' The four noble truths are that the nature of existence is suffering; the cause of suffering is craving, or desire for something to become what it is not already; the end of suffering is the cessation of this craving, of this desire; the way to end desire is to be spiritually disciplined in a practice of right living.

When I returned from the Foundation to Philadelphia I was more accepting of my place in life. I was getting closer to the desire-free state of being. Tara Singh was in Los Angeles. I was on the other side of the country in Philadelphia. Our lives, though we had made strides in establishing a holy relationship, had aspects that seemed worlds apart. I knew there was something up, there was something happening in

Tara Singh's life that was unprecedented—and something in my life unprecedented. I was inherently unwilling to go to the Foundation and be Tara Singh's caretaker. I had hoped that Barbara would fill that role. She had no other ties. This was presumptuous of me, and it was not to be. I began to make the plans for Tara Singh to come to Philadelphia. I called the people who would support me in this endeavor.

When I was about to arrange the flights, I received a call from one of the Board members of the Foundation. "Cancel the workshop," was the message, "Tara Singh is in no kind of shape to travel there." This was a disappointment, but I could not over rule this respected Board member's decision. There were attempts to bring in caretakers to the Foundation to help Barbara with Tara Singh's daily care. These attempts did not go so well. Tara Singh did not want any "outsiders" in his space. He was not accepting the fact that he needed care, and that he needed help other than Barbara to keep things going. Some other friends went to help, but no one showed up to stay permanently.

Then I received news that was very disconcerting. On Good Friday, April 18th, 2003, some of the Foundation board members in Los Angeles took Tara Singh to the UCLA Psychiatric unit for evaluation. They had decided his condition was unstable and that they needed to provide him with medical care, which they were convinced he needed, and with managed care facilities in the long term that would provide for his day-to-day needs. I could not get my head around this action. It felt like a betrayal to me at the time. Tara Singh's life was not his own, now. It had been taken over by people who were well meaning, but acting from the conventional response. None of them were willing to keep him at the Foundation because that would mean moving there themselves to care for him. None were willing to do that, including myself. So how could I judge them? I could not. But I was judging myself, the one who had got the closest to him.

Tara Singh's short-term memory was going. No one used the Alzheimer's word, but he had been losing his memory for a while now. Soon, he was taken to a managed care house. I talked with him on the phone. He did not like it one bit. He had been removed from the Foundation, which had been his home and place of work for over twenty-five years. He had been separated from the Prayer Room and the Altar, which seemed like a violation to him and me. And he was now on medication, hardly having ever taking any allopathic pills his whole life, which was obviously a shock to his system. I was beside myself with grief. I could not imagine how things had come to this point. I could not accept the fact that my teacher had human frailties. I could not accept the fact that there was not much I could do in the momentum of these events. I could not accept the fact that my inherent unwillingness to leave my life behind and move to the Foundation to take care of my friend and teacher had resulted in these consequences. I had some loose ends to complete on a contract, but as soon as they were complete I loaded the minivan and headed out to California to assess the situation for myself.

It took me four days to reach Los Angeles. I headed straight for the Foundation. I slept in the back of the car to save time and money. A married couple who had been Tara

Singh's students years before were now living in the Foundation house on Genesee Street. On the day I arrived, they were not to be found. I called my friend Kiki who had been visiting Tara Singh recently. She told me I would find the key under the back door matt. I let myself in and unpacked my things, and then drove to find the place where Taraji was being kept. It was not too far, on a tree-lined street, in a small house that had been converted to a managed care facility for the elderly. There were about six or eight residents in the house, and Tara Singh's room was in the rear of the house, having its own outside veranda with a garden and a swing, chairs and a garden table. There were others with Tara Singh when I arrived. He was sitting on the bed, absorbed in a calm energy. Our eyes met, but he was in a different quality of stillness that took no heed of me. The others in the room were listening to what he was saying, and I came into the middle of a lecture. I sat in one of the chairs and observed. The place was very bright and clean, very neat, and Tara Singh's room and garden quite beautiful. I had the impression that this was a good place for him, one in which all his needs were being adequately met. My thoughts, that his move out of the Foundation was a violation, began to subside. I even started to agree that managed care was what Tara Singh needed at this stage of his life. He was beginning to have so much memory loss and confusion at times that he needed professionals to care for him. Part of me saw the necessity of it, but another part of me could not accept this "separation" of him from the Foundation, from the Prayer Room, and from the Altar, which he had so faithfully maintained for so long. It was like separating the man from his source of power. It would have been like removing Ramana Maharshi from his ashram by Arunachala. The American way of life justifies institutional care over real love, and then calls this expedience real compassion. I include myself in this critique. We are all gripped by our situations in life, which prevent some other action to take place. So we do the best we can with the medical and institutional care giving systems available. But is this real compassion? Perhaps it was, in Tara Singh's case, but part of me thought this solution that everyone was extolling as a miracle was just rotten.

The next day was Taraji's birthday, so many were there to see him, even the Foundation board members who had been responsible for his admission into managed care. I noticed I did not like meeting them, as I did not fully accept their decision or their manner of making that decision. Tara Singh was not informed ahead of time that this was what they were doing. In fact, on Good Friday he was told they were just taking him for a ride, all the time having planned his admission into the UCLA Psychiatric ward. It felt like an expedient deception to make their plan go smoother. It felt like a lie at the base of their "good intentions."

After the party, I took Tara Singh for a walk, and then for a ride in my car. He was disconcerted about where he was. In fact he was drugged up pretty heavily, and not so clear. But he did know he was not at the Foundation, and he wanted to go back there. He pleaded with me to take him back to the Foundation. My heart was wrenched. I knew that to take him back would mean I would have to DROP EVERYTHING ELSE in my life, and never go back to Philadelphia. The inherent unwillingness to do this was strong in me. Part of me wanted to do it. Part of me did not want to do it and put my own life in crisis. Part of me did not trust myself to be able to handle his care and demands. I could not accept the situation as it was, but I could not take the action that would be required to return with Tara Singh to the Foundation. I told Tara Singh he needed to be where he was in the managed care place. He would need this care in months to come. He was losing his memory, and this was the solution for his living situation now.

It was not easy for me to say this. Part of me felt guilty and cowardly that I could not give myself totally to his return to the Foundation. I held these feelings in abeyance by justifying the opinions all the others had about his state of mind. They had convinced themselves that this was the right decision. They had convinced themselves this was the only decision that made sense. They had convinced themselves that this was "life providing" the right solution to the "problem." Part of me knew this was a total expediency, a total justification, and wanted to fight for a different option. But the bigger part of me, the inherent unwillingness part, went along with the status quo and accepted that Tara Singh's fate was to be in managed care, and that this fate was actually the best thing for him and all concerned. It did not feel miraculous to me. It felt conventional and in compliance with the limited thoughts of the brain, of the ego, which Taraji had worked so hard to free me from. I was no better than all the rest. I had accepted the appearances that this was the best solution. It met the needs of Tara Singh and it kept me from having to make a cataclysmic change in my own life, in my own situation. I could not move to the Foundation to take care of him, and I knew this when I left him just a few weeks before with Barbara. But it still felt like inherent unwillingness was ruling my life, not the Christ consciousness of miracles that I had studied so long to apply.

When I saw the board members who made these decisions, I said what I sensed was only partially true. "This is the best solution for Tara Singh. All his needs are being met." The part that no one was addressing was that removing Tara Singh from the Foundation was a violation of Divine Laws at a deeper level. No one, including myself, was willing to make that whole, unequivocal surrender to move to the Foundation to take care of Tara Singh. He had taken care of hundreds in the course of his twenty five years at the Foundation, feeding them, uplifting them spiritually and mentally, sheltering them—and not one person could give that unequivocal care back to him in his hour of greatest need, including myself. Within a few days I was on my way back to Philadelphia. I had accepted the status quo, and Tara Singh remained in the house that was to be his home for the next few months.

The teaching was very strong. It could not be denied, though it was a hard pill to swallow. The ego is inherently unwilling to give itself up. It sees problems, and wants solutions that are the most expedient and undemanding of itself to change. It often hands them over to *experts*. I was not willing to let go of my life in Philadelphia. I did not have the determination to move to Los Angeles and care for my teacher and friend who had given me everything bright and beautiful I had received through our association. I went along with the status quo, the "prevailing, worldlier wisdom" of the other board members who were being "objective" and "factual." They were insisting that miracles were being worked on Tara Singh's behalf. I was convinced they were not miracles; they were calculated results of an inherent unwillingness we all have to totally surrender and give ourselves to another. It is the condition of those who have not "completely let go." It was my condition and the condition of all the others in Taraji's close circle. We used the conventional managed care system because we had resistance to "give all to all," to give all to the one who had given his life so totally for our enlightenment. We were all too engaged in other life choices and entanglements.

Tara Singh made it clear we were ruled by "unwillingness." The ego says it wants to be enlightened; it seeks enlightenment, but as the *Course* says, "makes sure never to find it." We are addicted to the search, but the closer we get to the release, the "complete letting go," we "chicken out" and maintain the status quo, and use that as the reason we cannot go any further. I was enmeshed in my life as a householder in Philadelphia. This was my status quo. I was attached to that whole complex life of maintaining properties, a small business, a marriage, an artistic need to have a studio, etc. This was more than I was willing to give up and face the unknown. The unknown would have required me to "completely let go." And like all the others who came and went to the Foundation to study with Tara Singh, the only one who had mastered this teaching given to him by Krishnamurti, was Tara Singh himself. My letting go was only partial, not complete.

Therefore my inherent unwillingness was stronger than my acceptance and trust that life would take care if I surrendered totally. I was not ready to make this step with Tara Singh, or anyone else. I still viewed it as a sacrifice. It looked like jumping into the fires of total self-annihilation—which it would have been—of the little self I had made up. The self that faced annihilation was not my real Identity anyway. But, like everyone else, I justified my unwillingness with reasons that looked good, and even wise. Tara Singh's basic physical needs were being met, but where was our heart in all of this? None were willing to face this absence of the heart in the decisions that appeared to have the force of necessity and practicality behind them. We were all inherently unwilling.

❖ *Chapter 23.* ❖

The Mystic's Detachment

Later in that year of 2003 I visited Tara Singh in the place where he had been ensconced. By this time he had been put on quite a regiment of drugs that were purported to be necessary for balancing his condition. I could see he had declined both physically and mentally. He recognized me, but I suspected the drugs he was being fed were making him groggy and somewhat more incoherent. In effect he was in a "chemical straitjacket," in my opinion, that was deemed necessary to keep him calm and passive.

His diet was not good. They were feeding him junk food. This was something so far from the impeccable diet he kept at the Foundation. We sat at the dining room table as he ate an ice cream cone. His speech was sometimes slurred and his words were not enunciated. Again, I had never seen him like this. How much was it a deterioration of his mental condition, and how much was a result of the medications he was being given. I did not know as I was not part of that aspect of his care, nor was I authorized to ask for that information. I was present as his friend now, but not as a caretaker.

As his student I asked myself, "How could this be?" He had been so vital and alive all the years I had known him, and now he was not in his power at all—it seemed to me. But he was, in a much different way. The mystic's journey is to be unaffected by the external. To be totally detached from the conditions of the world would be of paramount importance to the mystic. He could even be taken advantage of quite easily because his innocence does not account for defenses, calculations or psychic protections. Tara Singh was such a mystic, and he was certainly letting all things be exactly as they were. It was mainly my internal reaction to the situation that I had to deal with. I did not like seeing him in this state of helplessness, but it seemed this was exactly what I was meant to see. He was returning to this helplessness state of total innocence, total surrender, total detachment, even from the body and its concerns. Tara Singh was still teaching me great lessons even in situations of his managed care. I did not like seeing what I saw, but it was forcing me to face myself, and face the fact there was nothing I could do but accept the status quo without a judgment. I could not judge myself, or Tara Singh, or the managed care staff, or the ones in charge of making Tara Singh's decisions for him. He, and the situation I found him in were leading me to the mystic's detachment. I witnessed this detachment in him, but I also witnessed it in myself, which I suspect was the real lesson here. There is a lesson in ACIM, "Today I will judge nothing that occurs." Lesson #243—and I was being given a huge opportunity to practice it while I was with Tara Singh throughout his time in managed care.

I would go every few months to see him. The next time I was to visit, he had been moved to another facility. It was recognized that he was being too heavily medicated in the first facility, so the move to the next place was an improvement. When I visited this time, I had brought him a woolen shawl I had purchased at the Woolrich store in upstate New York. Shawls and blankets were very revered gifts in Tara Singh's eyes. He used them frequently, and I was glad when he received the gift with much joy. It was intricately woven with a beautiful plaid pattern, in autumn colors, with a very refined weave. He wore it on the second day I visited. Much more himself, not on so much medication, I had a real heartfelt connection with him on this visit. The facility was high on a hill in West Hollywood. We sat together in the lounge, looking out over the entire city of Los Angeles. We did not say much to each other, but we appreciated the togetherness. I would stay a few days, and that was about all I could bear to witness. It was hard for me to relate to him in this condition of helplessness. Of all the people I had met in my life, Tara Singh represented pure Life Action to me. And now I had to see him in a different light. I had to forgive myself, him, and all others involved, for the status quo of this situation. It was not easy. At times I wanted to lash out at the ones calling the shots. I wanted to "blame" myself for not doing more. I did not want to accept the situation as it was. These were the things I went through internally.

I saw Tara Singh only once during his stay in the second

facility. He was moved to a third place, Belmont Court, on Highland Boulevard near the Hollywood Bowl. In 2004 I visited him a couple times there. He was now in a section of the facility that was a "locked unit," for those with severe dementia. Apparently this was considered necessary for his safety as he would sometimes try to wander off. The place was very clean and neat. The people seemed professional and caring. It was a top-notch facility. My friend Kiki Vekkos had moved to Los Angeles to be closer to Tara Singh, and rented an apartment a couple blocks from the Belmont Court facility. Another friend, Esther Witte, had also dropped everything to move to LA, and spent time with Tara Singh daily. I stayed with Kiki when I visited. In December of 2004 I went to stay for a whole month to be with my teacher. Kiki was back on the East Coast visiting family, and her apartment was free.

During this period there was a visitor. Tara Singh's daughter from Belfast came to see him. She was very dissatisfied with the situation, but at the same time not in a position to do anything about it. The people at the Foundation did not wish to have much contact with her or Taraji's family, so I was asked to pick her up at the airport and keep her in the apartment next to Belmont Village. She was not so happy that her father had been taken away from the Foundation, but once she saw his mental condition, she understood the reasons for it. "He does not remember who he is," she said to me after her first visit. I did not have this impression. When I visited Tara Singh I felt the same energy I always did. He may have lost some ability to put sentences together, but the things he did communicate always showed me he was perfectly aware of the deeper meaning of things. I felt that it was the medication that was making him less lucid, not his state of mind in itself.

Shortly after Taraji's daughter came and went, the huge Tsunami hit Thailand and India on December 26th 2004, striking and killing over 144,000 people. This was a shock, and hard to fathom, that in one day such a force of nature could end the lives of so many souls. Here I was focused on one soul, my teacher, doing what I could to ease my pain, and possibly his transitioning out of the role I had for so long held him in, that of my mentor and spiritual teacher. He was still my teacher, but I was receiving the lessons of detachment that the mystic school of my relationship with him was inexorably giving to me.

I would spend time with him a few hours a day for the month I was in Hollywood. It was a time in which I had to accept that his physical health would probably not improve, and that he was going to be here, or in a facility like Belmont Court, for the remainder of his life. I recall sitting with him in the well-appointed hallway of his unit, and he said to me, "People come here to die. It is in the vibration of the very walls of this place." That was not the voice of a man who did not know what was happening to him and those around him. So, for me Tara Singh remained the one person in my life who always spoke the truth, no matter what it would look like to others. He was a mystic, and so he was totally detached from the status quo of his external situation. He related to the joy within, and to the stillness and silence of the mind that was ever connected to the Divine Force of life, regardless of all the apparent death energy all around him.

❖ *Chapter 24.* ❖

Sleeping in the Van

There were times when I could hardly bear the thought of Tara Singh's situation, when I had nowhere to put it in my mind. It seemed he was languishing away in a place that was unrecognizable to the stature he merited. He was a king amidst commoners who recognized not his royalty; he was a man free of motives amidst those who had only known motives; he was a teacher of life in an environment in which everyone was moving in a meaningless march toward death. By now he was well entrenched within the system of managed care. Those in charge of his situation were convinced this was the best and only solution for his state of being, and no other solution seemed at all possible. Some would visit him and say his mind was gone. But I would visit him and find his mind was still sharp, in the sense he knew exactly what was happening to him and those around him. He had entered a childlike state, just as the figures in Elephanta who had gone into a trance of total detachment. He was not affected by the external situation when it came to his inner knowing. Others had a totally different experience with him—his "difficult side," etc. But I was spared this experience. When I would visit there would be an uplifting energy of open possibilities and freedom. I did not see him bound to an illness of memory loss; I saw him as taking another step toward his absolute freedom from thought, from all limitations of any kind, including the apparent physical limitations of his status quo.

In 2005 I visited him once more in the Belmont Court facility. It was much the same experience as it was before. We would sit in the hallway of the unit in the easy chairs and be quiet—not saying much—and appreciate each other's company. Sometimes we would sit in his room, and other visitors would come and pay their respects. It looked as though he was "fitting in" to the routine of this environment, but at the same time he seemed light years away in a place beyond thought, beyond words, and beyond all perception itself. One thing was certain for me; he had not ever for an instant lost his ability to invoke a state of stillness and silence. Always, within a few minutes of sitting with him, a blanket of peace would come over me, and there would be another atmosphere that was not present before—one in which the "peace of God," to which *A Course in Miracles* refers to so succinctly, was bought into my awareness. By being in the presence of Tara Singh and this Christ energy I was always uplifted. The external situation was the external situation. It had no ability to detract from the inner power that Taraji wielded. This inner power, which he had gained from his years of spiritual practice and association with great beings never left him. A light was shining in him, regardless of his memory loss, his difficulty with speech, his weakening physical condition. I felt fortunate to be in this presence, always, and at one point I knew this man was my Master for this reason. He could invoke stillness and silence and help me hold them in my awareness.

In the winter of 2005 I received an email from one of the Foundation's board members. Tara Singh had been moved to Iowa. One of my fellow Foundation friends and board members, Melanie Coulter, who had been in charge of his care with the various facilities, and who had also worked for many years in this field of elderly care giving, had come to Los Angeles with her husband Marvin to take Tara Singh back with them to Iowa. Melanie worked in a managed care facility in Stuart, Iowa, and she would now oversee Tara Singh's living situation in that place. The facility in Iowa, which I had seen before when I attended a Tara Singh workshop in Melanie's area, was an older building, not so modern, and in the old style of linoleum floored hallways with hospital type rooms on either side. It was not as upscale as Belmont Court, but the fact that Melanie worked there, and would have a direct hand in Taraji's care was a huge plus. Later Melanie spoke to me of the challenge she faced in moving Taraji to Iowa. Though he went along without too much resistance, he was well aware he was going to a cold climate, and to a facility that was older and not so cheery.

Kiki Vekkos and I planned to visit Tara Singh in the New Year in Iowa. I drove my van out to meet him, and rendezvous with Kiki when I was there. My parents and sister lived in

Kansas City, so I went to visit them for Christmas, and then drove up to Iowa afterwards. The weather was turning very cold, and the Iowa fields were starkly empty, as the winds blew across them in a wintry gust of a bone-cutting chill. I reached the facility in Stuart in the evening, a day before Kiki was to arrive, and I went to find my teacher and friend. It was the first time I was not so sure he recognized me. His demeanor towards me was cool, and I could not tell what lesson he was trying to impart. Melanie was there in the front office, and after a short visit with Taraji she came to join us. There was a sense that she was in charge, and that he looked toward her for a cue, for a sign that I should be asked to leave after a certain time in my visit. Though we walked hand in hand down the hallways, and spent about an hour together, I got an intimation that I was to leave, and also not be dependent on Melanie for a place to stay. I had planned to stay in her house with Marvin not far from Stuart, but now it seemed inappropriate to linger and join her later. I took my leave.

By now it was into the night. I drove to the Super Eight Motel parking lot, but I could not go in. I was in the deepest doldrums of my whole seventeen years spent with Tara Singh. It felt like I was being rejected. Terrible thoughts went through my head. It felt as though I was being thrown out onto the trash heap of Tara Singh "casualties." Of all the people who had come to *eat the fish and the bread*, but who had never returned, I was now questioning my role in this difficult situation. My teacher was being "crucified" in a slow process of wasting away, mentally and physically, and now I felt like the "villain" who had set the whole process in motion by declining to go to the Foundation the couple years before to render him care. These were the "thoughts of self-immolation" that were running through my head. I felt my life was worthless and wasted—and that the very person who I had held in the highest regard was now cutting me off from his inner ring of counsel and influence.

It was a rough night. I drove my van west, down Interstate I-80 away from Stuart, in a state of delirium. Where was I to go? What was I to do? Then I turned off at the next exit, ten miles away, and parked the van on the side of the road. It was pitch black, not a light, nor a car in sight. I spread out the blankets and sleeping bag in the back of the van, curled up into a ball, and tried to go to sleep. Occasionally a car would pass by, and the van would fill with the brightness of shining headlights. The temperature was dropping, and I was lying there feeling absolutely dejected, as though my life was forfeited. I was not suicidal, but at the same time I felt if I had frozen to death that night, I would not be less off, and perhaps even more the better. Finally I did fall asleep, and I was awakened in the morning by the pinkish gray light of dawn, and the increase in traffic along the remote country road.

I remembered I was to pick up Kiki at the Des Moines airport that day, so I turned the van around and headed back Interstate I-80 toward the city. Soon there was a loud thumping noise in the front end of the vehicle, as if one of the wheels was out of kilter. I stopped the van and on closer inspection, I appeared that I did not have a flat tire. Driving back to Stuart, I went to a garage. Their assessment was that I had a "broken tire." Apparently, some of the inner steel belts had disintegrated, thus causing the thumping noise. But they did not have a replacement size of tire I needed. I would have to continue into Des Moines to make the repair. How indicative of my situation with Tara Singh. I could not move forward. All my movement with him in my spiritual quest of awakening had come to a halt, and even my mode of propulsion that kept me rolling forward was now broken, disintegrated from within. I was in the dark night of the soul, with no vision of salvation from what seemed like my helpless and hopeless situation.

It took about an hour for my van to limp into Des Moines, and find a tire shop that could under take my repair. On the way to the airport I found such a place, and pulled in to buy and install the necessary new tires. Then I proceeded toward airport to arrive at the proper time to meet the flight of my friend Kiki. She was always a balm to my spirit, like an unconditionally loving grandmother. She always had an insight or a perspective that would lift me up and out of my doldrums, especially now, in this time of my most critical moments of self-doubt, of self-judgment, and feelings of unworthiness. I had to let go of my attachment to Tara Singh. I had to accept the facts of how things had transpired. I had to accept his possible rejection of me. I had to face the end of my dependence on a man whom I had placed somewhat on the pedestal of idealism that was of my own making. I was now having to face the fact that he was a man with the frailties of other men, and that his life was coming to an end, and that I would, at some point, have to face his death, his exit from his body. I felt like I was dying too and perhaps his situation was my own—marooned in a world that did not feel like home. But, nevertheless, we seek for that thread, an etheric presence of peace that leads us out of the labyrinth of discontent that composes the bulk of human existence. This thread of a presence was invoked in every moment of stillness and silence Tara Singh imparted. It was far more real that the most empirical scientific proof, yet more fleeting than the melting snow on a sun warmed late winter day.

Kiki and I drove to Stuart and checked into the Motel Eight. In the afternoon we paid a visit to Tara Singh in the community center that cared for the elderly, just down the road. We found him in his room. It had been made as comfortable as possible. He had some of his favorite books; a TV and some nature videos that he so much enjoyed; a simple bed; a lounge chair and a couple simple folding chairs for guests. He was lying on his bed when we arrived. We had brought some flowers for his room. When he saw us he greeted us like long lost friends. We embraced. He was so glad to see us. He was delighted we came all this way. It was as if the night before had not occurred, and our meeting that ended in a kind of cool rejection was just a figment of my imagination. My guilt had projected the whole scenario, and now that I was more in the acceptance of "what was, exactly as it was," instead of my yearning for it to be some other way, I could now forgive myself and enjoy the blessings and forgiveness of my friend and teacher.

Kiki and I walked the halls with him, had a meal with him, and sat with him. The stillness and silence in the room brought on the presence, as it always did in the vortex of Tara Singh's energy. We basked in the peace of this presence, and then took our leave. Later, Kiki and I faced the fact that Tara Singh was probably preparing himself to make his transition soon. I mentioned what Taraji had said to me a few years before, "I would not want to die in America." He was well aware of the status quo in America that sequestered old people away in managed care facilities. He felt it was symptomatic of broken families, busy life styles that did not permit the reverence for the elders, and a whole different approach to life that discounted the old and their contribution to society in all their productive years. Yes, the old were "managed," but they were certainly not revered and respected. People like Melanie were doing their best to provide this reverence and respect, but she was the exception, not the rule. She had been touched by the light and presence of Tara Singh, which were rarities in this field of caring for the elderly. So this arrangement was in lieu of the fact that Tara Singh had no family nearby to care for him and take him in. The sad fact was that many of the residents did have families nearby, but still put them in this "old folks home." We have been in the momentum of managed care facilities—the business of taking care of the old—for a few generations now. And it seems there in no going back. Thus we have created warehouses for the old, "where they go to die" as Taraji so succinctly put it to me during his time in Belmont Court.

"I do not want to die in America." It was a statement seared in my mind like a directive. "If not here, then where?" I thought. Tara Singh spoke of the elders in India, of even his own mother, who on a certain day, when she saw her life had been productive and complete, chose the day of her own death. She literally took a conscious departure from her body on that day, singing songs of joy! "Was this to be Tara Singh's way?" I questioned. That evening I went to see him in his room again, alone this time. We sat in the silence of the presence. I had to get off my chest any remaining guilt I felt about all the things that had transpired in the past three years of his time in managed care.

I told him it had been difficult for me to witness his declining health and vitality. I felt guilty I had not come to the Foundation to allow him to stay there. I confessed I was afraid of that option, and that I was unwilling to take that on. I told him that I went down along with him. It was like a decent into hell, the past few years, witnessing his decline. Though I did not have the solution myself, I could not really accept this conventional way of dealing with his loss of memory and the need of nursing care. There seemed to me something brutal about it, something blind to real compassion. I was not judging others, but perhaps it was myself whom I was judging the most for not doing anything about the status quo. When he asked me to take him back to the Foundation early on in his removal into managed care, and I refused, I felt I had "sold out" to helplessness and expediency, like everyone else had done. I felt I was going down, and that I had hit rock bottom. All of these things I confessed to my friend and teacher.

He listened very attentively, as he always did, without any reaction or comment. Then the presence came into the room like a descending atmosphere of silence and stillness. We sat for a moment in this aura, and then he embraced me. "We will only go up from here. We will only go up from here." He repeated it to make sure I got it, "We will only go up from here." Now there is a lesson in *A Course in Miracles* that says, "God has condemned me not. No more do I." Lesson #227. The light had come into my life via Tara Singh. He did not *condemn* me, or anyone else, for any of actions toward him. He did not hold any grievances toward me, nor did he hold any grievances toward anyone else who had acted with the intention of his "best interests" in mind. Even though they may not have perceived their "best interests," or Tara Singh's, he held no judgment about them, their actions, and the subsequent consequences of their actions upon him. For him this was his truth: "The light has come. I have forgiven the world." Lesson #75. He had totally risen above it.

By then I was crying tears of joy. My teacher had given me the boon of total absolution. Throughout my few years of soul wrenching doubt, guilt, depression and discontent, he had never once held anything against me for my actions, or lack of actions. In fact, he acknowledged me for seeing past the self-deception of expediency. He knew that I knew this managed care solution was not the highest thought. It was not the miracle everyone was saying it was, even though he was steeped in the miracles of his detachment and non-reaction. The miracles were on his side, and I was now brought into the vortex of this awareness that absolved me instantly of all error. The LOVE he had for me came pouring into my heart and I was lifted out of my despair. We sat in the energy of this Self-acceptance. In those very intimate moments, I was receiving one of the final acknowledgements from him that I would have in our worldly life together. I was back in the good graces of being his student, and friend, in the Holy Relationship that set ours apart from all the rest. And it was this model of complete forgiveness that he wanted me to receive so that I could give it to others and myself. "By grace I live, by grace I am released. By grace I give, by grace I will release." Lesson #169. And so I ended that day in the total embrace of my Master of miracles. Tara Singh had imparted to me the miracle of forgiveness that wrapped me totally in the grateful awareness of the Atonement, and the Christ who is in charge of it.

❖ *Chapter 25.* ❖

Rallying the Family

I asked him about this statement "I would not want to die in America." I needed more clarity on what he meant by that. The soul has a destiny in this life, and this destiny includes where and when one is born onto the stage of human events, and also where and when one leaves that stage, and under what conditions. We talked briefly about this statement, and it became clear that Tara Singh's destiny was to incarnate in Mother India, meet great beings such as Gandhi, Nehru, Gyani Kartar Singh, the head of the Sikhs, then come to America and meet Mrs. Roosevelt, Justice William O. Douglass, and other great leaders—and then to renounce it all for an inner life of the spirit, and meet such great beings in this realm such as Krishnamurti, the Teacher of the Dalai Lama, and Dr. Helen Schucman. Then he was to have his work of sharing *A Course in Miracles* through the auspices of the Foundation for Life Action, and later the Joseph Plan Foundation. He would have students and be their spiritual mentor; he would write books and give lectures on the subjects of inner awakening, self-reliance, having a life style of spiritual practice, and living in a sacred manner. Now he was in the final phase of completing his mission, and what was this completion to be like in the oeuvre of his many life actions?

If "I would not want to die in America" was Taraji's true sentiment, then where? I asked him about this. India was where he started this life, and it was Mother India that was calling him back as the place of his final transition. This was not going to be possible, I said, without the help of his family. In fact, I was certain the other board members in charge of his care did not agree to this. They thought it was a "crazy idea" of a man who was not clear anymore, who had lost his power to reason. India, even as an integral part of Tara Singh's final piece of destiny, was half way around the world. How does one say they want to make their transition in a particular place, on the other side of the planet, without sounding totally crazy? It made sense to me, but to the powers that be, it seemed not only impossible, but downright *insane*.

We sat in the stillness of this vision, and let it soak in for a while. In the front lounge area of the facility, we sat at a lunch table and considered the next step. I told Tara Singh, "I would have to contact your family. I am willing to do that. Without their help we could not get you to India." It was like a "last request" that Tara Singh was making. He knew his time left was short, but his yearning to go back to India was strong.

This would be our last meeting. After our conversation, and my agreement to contact his family, I left the same day to return to Philadelphia—a two day drive from Iowa. Saying my goodbyes to Kiki, I mentioned to her this discussion with Taraji about his wish to return to India to make his final transition. She was supportive of me exploring the possibility. Knowing that his mother had taken a conscious departure, it was not so far-fetched in my mind that he would be planning a similar kind of passing.

Back in my home in Philadelphia, I looked up the addresses of Tara Singh's relatives in England and Ireland. I composed letters to them about Tara Singh's request to return to India, and sent them off. I called the Ramana Maharshi ashram in Thiruvannamalai to explore the possibility to take him there. They were not open, given his condition of memory loss. Within a week or so I received e-mails from Tara Singh's sisters that it was not possible for them to help. They had other family responsibilities. When I called Tara Singh's son in Belfast, he was also closed to the idea. In fact he was clear that he did not want to have anything more to do with his father. He said that it was his father's Karma to be in the place where he was. So, none of my overtures to Taraji's family requesting help to take him back to India were of any avail. During this period, I received a communication from the Foundation's acting head of the board to "cease and desist" from writing to Tara Singh's family. The ones in charge of his care did not appreciate, nor agree, with exploring this possibility of taking him to India to make his transition. They held me in contempt, I sensed, for even considering it. As each response came in, I could tell that this was not meant to be. His family members were leaving Tara Singh to experience this fate, to languish away in his current situation. It was going to be America where he would spend his final days. They did not have it in themselves to disrupt their lives enough to take him back to his homeland. There were too many uncertainties. The two people who could have done it, Tara Singh's son and daughter, were totally in judgment of their father and unwilling to get beyond it, even for this one final request.

I had to write to Tara Singh the results of my inquiries. I included a gift of a Pendleton Indian blanket that I had purchased when I was a boy. It was one of my most prized possessions. I also sent a woolen sweater I had brought back years ago from Ireland. It was my favorite. The news that I hoped to report, that I was able to "rally the family" to get him back to India, was not to be. The family would not be rallied. No one would come over from his family to help him with his last wish to make his transition in India. That was the status quo.

I took a long look at this whole issue of his family, or any family for that matter. The family mind is based on tradition, convention and conditioning. People in the family mind are focused on their immediate needs and conveniences, and seldom want to disrupt their lives and routines. The family mind is often fortified with fear and an insurmountable desire to hang on to past grievances, or securities too comfortable to disrupt. I felt like I had failed to "rally the family" on Tara Singh's behalf. I had even prompted the disapproval and reaction of the other Foundation Board members. But I did give this possibility of taking Tara Singh to India one last exploration. The family refused, but that was also a completion in its own way. The "gold of the heart" which Tara Singh had taken them a couple years before, and to which I was a witness, was now forgotten in his hour of need. Their fear and grievances—which got the better of them—or their own family situations that they deemed more important, had influenced their decision. Perhaps they thought the whole idea was "crazy" as well.

I was resigned to the outcome, yet somewhat sad. I had done the best I could to rally the family. I had taken it as far as it could go. There was nothing more I could do legally to get Tara Singh back to India. Only his children or sisters could have over ridden the authority of the Foundation board members in charge of his care, and they had decided he was in the *right place*. So I had to accept this as the final life lesson, and as Tara Singh would often say from Lesson #268 in *A Course in Miracles*, "Let all things be exactly as they are." And this meant, there was no *family to rally*. It was time for me to face that fact and just let go. Where he was now *was* the right place for him to be.

❖ *Chapter 26.* ❖

The Word He Is Gone

As Tara Singh received the word his family would not come to take him back to India, my sense was that he was complete with them. He was also complete with this incarnation and his mission. Though it was obviously not in his destiny to make his conscious departure, or Samadhi, in India, it was my destiny to try and grant him this request. So it was a completion of sorts for me as well, when the last conversation with his son transpired. It revealed that Tara Singh's children still held huge grievances toward their father, and there would be no reconciliation of this personal conflict in their minds while their father was still alive. So be it. That was not any of my business beyond relaying the request Tara Singh intimated to me to make his transition in his Mother India. This was told to his family, who all declined.

It was then apparent that America would claim him as one of their immigrant sons. He had come to the USA to bring the light of a different truth, a different reason, to these shores of a vibrant melting pot of possibilities. He had brought the great tradition of a spiritual imperative, which was India's heritage, to the heart of the New World. He had come "half way around the world" to impart the peace of God, a "call to wisdom," the silence of mind, and *A Course in Miracles*—as the pillars of a force that could transform a nation. He came for an inner revolution of the spirit that would transcend all other causes for freedom. It would be a freedom that liberates us from the conflicted self and all the thought it had accumulated. This was something beyond any other external revolution. It was a revolution of the soul to make contact with its true Self Identity. And it was a revolution to happen in America.

Tara Singh would often comment how, after World War II, America was on top as the leader of the free world. She had spread her economic and political influence beyond her shores. Then she moved through the decades of the "cold war" and now she has been faced with new challenges of a global interdependence in this new millennium. China is on the rise as a world power, and America has been embroiled in the "war on terrorism" that has sapped her funds, polarized her citizens and government, and compromised her world-class status as the main upholder of global commerce, and also as the main proponent of civil liberties and freedoms. As Tara Singh had put it, the "future of mankind" depended on which direction America would choose to go as a nation and a world leader.

There were two energies Tara Singh described at the root of the American "identity." When the Europeans came to these shores, these two energies were in play, and ultimately in a battle for dominance, even today. One was the "gold rush" energy of grabbing all the "gusto" that could possibly be grabbed; the other energy was "in God we trust." The founding fathers attempted to imbue God's blessings in the laws and vibrations of the land and at the same time keep the "separation of church and state" as a check and balance which would actually insure our religious and ideological freedoms.

America had risen to the top of economic and technological dominance after the 1940's, and therefore achieved affluence and prosperity that far exceeded that of any other nation or people. But it had also fallen into the "gold rush" energy of greed and self-interest that was undermining its original purpose as the torchlight of freedom and economic and social opportunity. The concentration of power was now becoming more and more in the hands of the few, and these few had manufactured a "military industrial complex" that wise leaders had warned against in their foresight. They warned of an exhaustion of resources this vying for world military dominance would bring about. In lieu of an economic and technological dominance, what was the greatest gift that America had to offer the world in real terms of uplifting other peoples and nations? Technology was an amazing resource and offering, but it seemed to come also with a fear and greed for more world dominance of resources. America had become the "policeman" of the world without the world really asking of it this role. It had become the biggest exporter of military hardware on the face of the planet, exceeding even Russia for the past ten years. What kind of gift was this? "Go for the gusto" meant go for the building of a corporate network of world dominance that would be supported by the most sophisticated military ever seen in human history. We could, by the middle of the cold war, totally obliterate the planet and the entire human population with nuclear weapons, hundreds of times over. This was how imbalanced our greed and fear had become—in the name of exporting "nation building" and "democratic freedom." There was certainly something wrong with this American picture.

Something must have been stirring in the bowels of the nation that was reigniting the true destiny of America. In the late 1960's, at the height of this turmoil of function, a most unexpected event of monumental proportions was unfolding in New York City, between two of the most improbable individuals—two clinical psychologists at Colombia University. One of them, Dr. Helen Schucman, began receiving direct communications, in the form of an inner dictation, from Jesus. With the help of her colleague, Dr. William Thetford, for six years this dictation was taken down by its scribe, and then transcribed by her friend. This became one of the most revolutionary spiritual scriptures the world has ever known, *A Course in Miracles.* So now the vibration of America underwent a shift. In the midst of the greatest surge of the "gold rush" energy in America also occurred, almost simultaneously, as if on cue, the formation of the "greatest sacred gift" America had ever produced. "In God We Trust" was now in its ascendency in the form of *A Course in Miracles.* Tara Singh referred to it as "A Gift for All Mankind," and it came out of America, out of the busiest city in the world. Somehow, amidst the middle of the most turbulent times of civil and racial unrest, and at the height of the "cold war," this gift had assured that America would ascend to the role of a spiritual powerhouse, much in the same role India had been for eons before. It would revolutionize how we thought of religion itself, and weave the necessity of "In God We Trust" into the very fiber of our culture and world contribution.

Tara Singh was a bridge between the East and the West. Born in India, partially raised in Panama as a boy, then sent back to India in order to be a witness to India's struggle for independence, he met pre-eminent men and women at the center of a world stage. Without much formal education, he was destined to be a protégé of the Sikh leader, Gyani Kartar Singh, in whose circles of influence put him in touch with the prime minister of India, Jawaharlal Nehru, and Mahatma Gandhi. He came to America in the 1950's as an unofficial ambassador of India's new freedom, and then met Americans of eminence, Mrs. Eleanor Roosevelt and Supreme Court Justice William O Douglass. In New York he was instrumental as an early liaison of the United Nations between Mrs. Roosevelt and the first UN representative from India, Vijaya Lakshmi Pandit, and the sister of Nehru, who later became the first woman president of the United Nations.

While living in New York City, Tara Singh had his first predestined meeting with Mr. J. Krishnamurti, the world teacher who had been groomed by the Theosophical Society to be their messianic figure. By then Krishnamurti had renounced all organized religions and groups, having walked out of the Theosophical Society, and this role of world savior. His mission was to set people "unconditionally and absolutely free" from all dogmas and belief systems that kept them from realizing their true potential and nature. When Tara Singh met Krishnamurti in the mid 1950's he was transformed from within, and knew he could not go on pretending that politics and governments could solve the real problems of mankind, which were mainly internal issues of the mind and quality of a person's inner thoughts and character.

Krishnamurti spoke of the necessity to come to a "still mind," one that was free from conditioning, from fear, from the accumulation of relative knowledge. Within minutes of meeting Krishnamurti, Tara Singh's life was transformed. He left the world of politics and entered the realm of absolute truth. Studying yoga in India and following Krishnamurti's teachings led him to meet the teacher of the Dalai Lama, for whom he cared for in the last years of his life. Then Tara Singh spent three years in silence in Carmel, California, to explore the real possibilities of coming to a still and silent mind, so emphasized by his teachers. Having come to this peace within, he then met Dr. Helen Schucman in the late 1970's, and was taught by her for two and a half years the deep significance of *A Course in Miracles.* This book would play upon the evolution of America, the individual, and humanity in general. These true words of Jesus would transform Tara Singh and awaken him to his true life's function, which was to be a teacher in the spirit of the *Course's* inner calling. He was ordained by Dr. Schucman to "give workshops." Before her passing she said to him this directive, "I leave you the *Course,* and it is for the rest of your life." It was with this blessing from its scribe that Tara Singh became one of the most authentic voices in America

271

during the 1980's and 1990's of the true importance of this work. Not content with intellectual "knowing," his years in silence enabled him to impart the inner transformations necessary for the individual to bring the *Course's* principles into application. Tara Singh possessed the Voice that could communicate the authenticity of the Christ Mind the *Course* represented, which he shared in his workshops for over 25 years. And thus for 17 years of that action, and the few years after its completion, I was transformed and blessed by his care and influence. He was my Master who led me to the miracles of the stillness and peace of God within. Because he had received it from Krishnamurti, had confirmed it with his years of silence, and tested it in terms of his tutelage with Dr. Schucman, he rose to the level of the One Voice, and was ordained to impart its truth as described in *A Course in Miracles*. Many others who taught the Course had greater intellectual knowledge and understanding of the material, but none had the "juice" of application that flowed through the very veins of this man transformed and enlightened by his meeting with the Absolute. It was a state of mind he attained, because of his determination to transcend thought, which the first lessons of the Workbook are so insistent upon doing. "My thoughts do not mean anything," is Lesson #10. Tara Singh had attained this emptiness of mind, and therefore had received the energy required to transmit it. And when the *Course* says, "My Father gives all power unto me," in Lesson #320, it certainly applies to this man from India to whom "nothing was impossible."

It was not long after my meeting with Tara Singh in Iowa that I received word from the Foundation that he had been moved to another facility, one more equipped to handle his declining health issues. Within a few weeks of this move, I received the word he was gone. The winter was still lingering in the air. I was half expecting the call, but it was still a hit to my heart to know this was the end. My years with Tara Singh, the most spiritually rich and transformational, challenging and confronting, had come full circle. Now I would have to stand on my own, and find what I had in myself to give. The rehearsal and the preparation were over. The man who had "given all to all," and to me, was now off to other dimensions. He entered my heart and never left, but his departure from a body marked the end of an era. I had surrendered, as much as I could, to this Holy Relationship, which resided now in the rarified ethers of my mind, and in the grateful cells of my beating heart.

❖ *Chapter 27.* ❖

Final Resignation

The death of Tara Singh created a vacuum at the Foundation. There were things that had to be decided and done with the million and a quarter dollars left behind in the wake of his passing. Though this was not his "personal money," belonging to the Joseph Plan Foundation (a 501 3C federally approved non-profit educational foundation), it was still a good deal of funds to have to manage along with the future direction of the Foundation. I was on the board of directors along with a dozen or so others Taraji had selected. But the control was already in the hands of a few, the same who had made Tara Singh's managed care decisions. The first order of business was to plan a retreat in Montecito, California, at the Casa De Maria retreat center where Tara Singh had given his first workshop. After his passing there was a spirit of honoring Tara Singh's work, his blessings, and his life—through gathering together and through the showing of his videos. Also, for we who were close to him, there would be a scattering of some of his ashes on the grounds of Casa De Maria, and also in the Oak Grove in Ojai where Krishnamurti had given his talks. In the summer of 2006 I made my plans to attend this memorial retreat, still in the shock of his Samadhi.

My friend Kiki had bought a place in Ojai, not far from the Oak Grove. After the memorial retreat I would go there to spend a few days and catch up with her on the news, as she was not attending the retreat. It was wonderful to be in the vibration of aloneness. I arrived in Los Angeles the day before the retreat began. I was determined to make this experience one of joy, not one of grief. I treated myself well, as Tara Singh would have wanted me to do. I had booked a room in the Hotel Bel-Air, one of the most beautiful hotels in the city. Nestled in hills of Bel Air, its grounds are breathtaking. It has a quietude that is deep and profound, which pervades the place. I had one of the most restful nights there I had ever spent with myself. I imagined Taraji would have appreciated the surroundings, as he had an impeccable appreciation for aesthetic beauty. The gardens were world class, having some of the best examples of an arboretum, well-tended by a staff of many. A meander through the paths and grounds revealed a swan lake. The blessings of beauty were commensurate with the honoring of the man I had been so close to for most of my adult life. He had opened my eyes to an inner glory, and this night in the Hotel Bel-Air certainly was in keeping with that glory. Affluence, he would say, was responsible for most of the man-made beauty that was in the world today. The wealthy are the ones who have the means to create extraordinary things. They do not need to calculate and scrimp, but rather create a vision of magnificence that does not compromise. Everything at the Hotel Bel-Air spoke of this refusal to compromise. It was not extravagant, but elegant; it was not decadent, but dignified; it was not showy, but majestic; it was not superficial, but clearly functional for the guests.

This night in the Hotel Bel-Air put me in a whole different vibration. It reconceived myself to a new dignity, one in which I could hold my head high in an environment of absolute serenity and beauty. Even though I was not in the economic echelon that could sustain this level of expenditure over a long period of time, the one night in this external paradise was a boon that I felt Taraji's hand was upon. He would have appreciated the vibration of this Shangri La of aesthetic sophistication, even though it was expensive and exclusive.

He was not into denial of anything. In fact he was one to explore many things in life, many sensational things, even in the midst of the affluent, so that at the end of his life he could say he had no unfulfilled desires.

I walked the grounds the next morning, and had a good swim in the pool. It felt like Divine Leisure, about which Taraji had spoken so much, was upon me. I entered a depth of appreciation. My senses were intensified in this gratitude of observation and the scenes I was observing rose to meet this thanks I felt within. After twenty-four hours in the Hotel Bel-Air, my mind was totally quiet and divorced from the concerns of back home. I was well prepared to meet the occasion, which was to honor the memory of my teacher, without actually meeting him in the flesh. This was new to me, as I had grown accustomed to the presence he invoked, and wondered if this same presence would be there for the workshop, even with his person absent.

By late morning I was headed toward Montecito to participate in the retreat. Situated near Santa Barbara, Montecito has a wealthy residency, and amidst the wonderful estates is Casa De Maria, formerly a Catholic Convent but now a retreat center for other denominations as well. Also in Montecito is a Ramakrishna Mission that Taraji had taken us to on many occasions. It is a center for the Southern California Vedanta Society. I was feeling the nervousness of meeting the persons who had taken charge of the Foundation. Doing my best not to judge, but rather appreciating their role as overseers, not only of Tara Singh's managed care, but now as the Foundation's ruling officers, I met them at Casa De Maria for only the second time since being with them on Tara Singh's birthday in 2003, three years earlier. It was a cool meeting, but I was willing to let all my grievances go and accept the fact that they had a destiny with Tara Singh, as I had, but in a totally different way. It was not my role to be so involved in the organizational aspects of Tara Singh's work. It was my role to get close to the man, even intimately involved in his family affairs, and at the same time retain my relationship with him as the student, and he my teacher. As far as the "organization," I was to be a witness, not a participant.

The workshop went on for three days. Some of the videos of Tara Singh's lectures were played on a big screen. The presence that he was so adept at invoking was strongly there. This was good to know that his energy was still just as potent in his sharing, even in absentia. I had a relaxing three days. There was a board meeting of the Foundation, and the officers were re-elected to their positions. These people had been at the Foundation in the years when Tara Singh was in his most productive phases. They had invested time and money to be there—and the Foundation gave to them as well, in terms of Tara Singh's daily wisdom. They were the rightful inheritors of the organization. I could see my role dwindling, though I would stay on the board for another year. Most of the decisions were made by the officers prior to discussion, then, presented to the general board for approval.

The ashes of Tara Singh were spread on the grounds of Casa De Maria. I participated in this ceremony. Some of the people close to him were given a hand-full of the ashes to spread. We all went our own ways through the gardens, and released the powder as we were inspired in our silent walk. A completion beyond thought was happening. Certainly Taraji's presence was there, very strongly. I think he would have appreciated our efforts to honor him, but at the same time see any sentimentality in it as well, and root it out. He was a living presence, and this honoring of ashes was perhaps a meaningless ritual in his eyes. Perhaps it was really more for us, living without him now, so we could feel connected and *right* in our sentiments. There was certainly no harm in it, and perhaps there was some merit in it. Yet in the end Tara Singh's true memorial was the Holy Relationship he had with each of us in our hearts, and that was a completely living thing that no mortuary ritual could come close to paying homage. The living of his truth in our lives and in our minds was the true testimonial—and that would take a vigilance and commitment in our future years to come. What would we do with the Holy Relationship he had given to us all? That was the real challenge and legacy that Tara Singh put forth to us, even after his Samadhi.

We completed the retreat, said our goodbyes, and many headed for Ojai, to the Oak Grove, where one last homage would be paid to Tara Singh at the site where his teacher, Krishnamurti, had given so many talks to the public. I traveled to Kiki's and the both of us went over to the Oak Grove to meet the rest of the people from the seminar. A few words were spoken by various people; we all sat for a while in the silence of the Oak Grove, and that was basically the end. I did not see any of them again, except for Melanie Coulter on a couple of occasions, because she lived in close proximity to my parents in Kansas City; and Dr. Bill Kelly, because he lived near my home in Philadelphia. Of the ones in charge of the Foundation, we had a couple of conference calls per year to handle Foundation business, but even these were feeling to me like a formality, and not a heart connection.

Because I did not feel the connection to the others or to the mission as they perceived it, I felt the need to move on. My connection to Tara Singh himself was my heartfelt truth, so that was what I maintained. It was even beyond words now. I did not feel the need to listen to his lectures through recordings, nor read his books. It was like the man himself had entered me, and that was something so beyond words that all the preparations for that visitation and melding were now as distant and as unnecessary as the actual miracles I experienced with him that undid my thought, and brought me to the state of inner silence. Now the silence was worth more to me than the words. My own inner silence was more profound to me than the words of Tara Singh that brought me to the silence. Without a doubt he was my teacher, he was my Master, yet now I was standing *in my own house*, in my own destiny to see what it was I had to extend to the world as a result of this Holy Relationship.

It became clear to me that I was not a team player. Not that I had an issue with teams, and the necessity for teams. Tara Singh could not have done his work in the world without a dedicated team of close students to help organize and carry out his workshops, as well as publish his books and lectures. But I had not been a part of that team, and my function, even after his death, was not to be a part of the organization that carried on with the JPF business. It took me a over a year to see this, as I did not want to be disrespectful of Tara Singh's decision to put me on the board of the JPF in the first place. But the ones in charge were ten times more equipped than me to handle organizational dynamics and workings.

Tara Singh was not a secondary man. He was not a team player. He was under no man—except the Masters from whom he received his power and instructions. And even they turned him loose to find his own way. And he imparted to me this same determination: to be under the ceiling of no man, no organization. It was not my bailiwick, nor my desire, to be a superfluous member of a governing body in which I felt no passion, and in which I felt I had no voice. The Joseph Plan Foundation Board could not replace the direct spiritual guidance of Tara Singh, so I saw the best thing for me to do was to gracefully resign.

The Joseph Plan Foundation goes on disseminating Tara Singh's books and recordings, and giving a few workshops on *A Course in Miracles* every year. For any serious student of *A Course in Miracles* I highly recommend the teachings of Tara Singh over all others. His books and recordings are like the "Gold of the Heart" you will not find anywhere else. You can read a hundred books on *A Course in Miracles*, but none will even take you close to the silent mind for which the *Course* is designed to impart to you. Tara Singh is the *master* Dr. Schucman left in charge when she took her own Samadhi: "I give you the *Course*, and it is for the rest of your life." Those were her words to him, which he faithfully fulfilled. There was no "absence of felicity" in his Holy Relationship with her, nor hers with him. They never saw each other as "personalities." To each other, they were prime players in this offering of *A Course in Miracles* to the world—"A Gift for All Mankind" as Taraji described it. You may go here for books and tapes of Tara Singh's offerings, as well info on JPF retreats: http://www.josephplan.org/home.html

In the fall of 2007 I resigned from the Joseph Plan Board. It was my final resignation in an era of my life in which I had received the lasting boon of a Holy Relationship. Tara Singh opened my eyes to the proper approach to *A Course in Miracles*. He offered me the miracles of compassion, the Miracles & Miracles that made my whole life into a lasting Miracle. He was the Master of my unspoken words, the one who tore open my heart and brought my chattering brain to silence.

❖ *Chapter 28.* ❖

Two Years of Limbo

Tara Singh's passing began a new era in my life, but I did not know what it was. Much in the same way, when Krishnaji told Tara Singh, after his years of silence, "Now that you have it, how would you like to express it?" Tara Singh told me that he did not know the "how" part. He was not even sure that he "had it." What was it he had? When he assured me in Iowa, "We will only go up from here," in his room in the old folks home, what was that? I did not know. At least I knew I was absolved in his mind of any shortcoming on my part. There was a sense in that statement that the past was gone. What I did or did not do on his behalf to keep him at the Foundation did not matter. What was the action, right or wrong, of putting him in an institution because of his failing health did not matter. What mattered to him and me was our Holy Relationship that was something beyond the body, and all of its concerns. Though his physical health was failing, the health of our relationship had been sealed by that one statement, "We will only go up from here."

When he passed there was a sense that an era in my life was finished. I had "seen it through to the end." Now I was left in the space of aloneness. I was married, and had been for 28 years, but that relationship was strained. I lived my life, working as a small contractor building high-end kitchens and bathrooms, painting in my studio, having a small circle of friends with whom I had a negligible social life. There was a feeling that I would rather be alone in meditation than in the normal exchange of business and "bla-bla-bla." There was a poem of Rumi's that I liked. It talked of the gazelle that ventured up the mountain to partake of the sweet grasses of the highland meadows that could not be had at the lower levels of the plains. He went there alone and experienced the clear Joy of nourishment far more complete and whole than anything he had known. This grazing in the alpine meadows put him in ecstasy, for days on end. Then when the winter was coming upon him, he knew he would have to descend to the plains again, rejoin the herd, and eat the common fodder to which all the others were accustomed. It was a kind of agony. None of the other gazelles even knew of the sweet grass, so they could not understand his suffering. Once he had tasted the meal of enlightenment, the ordinary food of mere survival did not nourish his real needs.

This was my dilemma after Tara Singh left his body. While I had my relationship with him, the sweet grass of stillness and silence was easily accessible through his strong tutelage. I had someone to relate to who saw deeply into the real meaning of life. When he passed, I was alone it seemed, without his hand on my shoulder. I would have to find it inside, in a deep inner connection to this man who had transformed my life and expanded the parameters of my consciousness. It was almost impossible to explain this relationship with anyone who had not risen to the heights of the alpine meadows and eaten the sweet grass of this profound gift of life. The Holy Relationship is not something fully realized in the more conditioned movements of routines and habits. People may not even rise to it in their family ties and relationships. In fact these predictable patterns of relating are often the block to rising to this other way of living, this other kind of relationship free of motives and thought. Who would even value it? Most people live lives of "quiet desperation," Thoreau had said. So, now that Tara Singh was gone from my life in body and personal presence, what was my relationship to this other way of living in the ecstasy of transcendence, so easily accessible while I was with him?

I spent the major portion of my workdays on my customers, and the projects I contracted. I had developed my craft over years of practice, even to the point that I saw it a part of my spiritual life. The challenges of perfecting one's craft were faced and met, to the degree that perfection at this point was natural and easy. The steps of the craft were mastered, even the communication skills that were involved in the management and definition of the final production, the final art form. There was no competition either in me, as I had achieved a reputation of quality that preceded me. People were glad to have my services because they knew something

285

beautiful would unfold in the end. All this was good, and it nourished my sense of being productive, but it was still not what Tara Singh had in store for me in the statement, "We will only go up from here." I was still stuck, it seemed, in *a life of the known*. It had become mechanical and routine. Though there were some creative moments that stepped outside the predictable confines of repetition, I was not fully using the spiritual capacity I had inherited from Tara Singh. I was "staying at the survival level," wasting my life energy in ways I did not even fully realize. I was an incognito mystic in the midst of a conventional life of maintaining and ordinary life of mortgage payments, car payments, 9 to 5 routines of a small business and property ownership—with a little time thrown in for my creative life in the studio, which really was not going anywhere in terms of recognition in the larger world. I had plenty of time to spend in quiet, reading the lessons of *A Course in Miracles,* listening to Tara Singh's tapes and videos. But there was a point in which even listening to his words spoken on tape did not fulfill my need to find my own way up. "We will only go up from here," remained an enigma, a final instruction, a challenge to rise in my own way to a purposeful life that was non-conventional—and a gift for mankind.

I was well aware I was not fulfilling this great inner need. I was settling for the same crumbs I had always settled for—the crumbs of survival. Work hard, pay the bills and spend some time alone to tinker with distractions and hobbies, but essentially make no difference in the greater course of life. I was in limbo. At least when I was with Tara Singh I felt my life had some transcendent purpose, but now I was surrounded by the herd that had never tasted the sweet grass of profound silence. I could come to it myself in periods of doing nothing, to some degree of stillness and peace surrounding me in my meditation room, but this was not something I shared with others. I did not even mention it to my wife. We had no dialogue whatsoever about what had been the most significant relationship of my life. In fact, I could feel her resentment and anger that I had given Tara Singh a deeper attention than I had given to her in our marriage. But our relationship had not offered the sweet grass of transcendence to the degree I had achieved with Tara Singh. It had its beautiful moments, but for the most part they were within the confines of a conventional life. We fooled ourselves in thinking that we were "artists" and therefore not the same as regular folks, but in the end our lives were just as conventional and routine as everyone else's, with some rare moments of escape into aesthetic appreciation and attention.

I was never too much of a "businessman." I did not approach even my craft with as much business prowess as I could have, to have made my contracting endeavors grow and thrive in ways that would be expected from the years I invested in them. Granted, I had become precise and artful in my exchanges that always produced successful projects, but I was never attached to increasing and expanding my results. Perhaps I was never committed to that kind of "success"—of projecting and pursuing financial and entrepreneurial goals that the normal creative person would take on naturally. Something of a life of renunciation was more akin to my inner workings. I was more in admiration of an Indian mystic,

Ramana Maharshi, than a self-made billionaire like Bill Gates. Both had their contribution to the direction of humanity, but the mystics' path of non-doing sang more to my heart than the draw of the marketplace to accomplishments in the business realm. It was an inner life I wanted, and this did not require the ambition of success to drive the cogs of my inner motivations. I was motivated, as it were, from my seventeen years with Tara Singh to value stillness and silence more than any other "acquisition" in the pursuit of real happiness.

But there seemed to be a limbo of discontent hanging over me in the period after Taraji's passing. I did my work without real passion. Before, the reason to earn money was to pay the bills and to fund my time with him; after his death it became just to pay the bills and keep the properties maintained, the rental house rented, the roof from leaking, and the car and house insurance and taxes paid up. I was the master of my small kingdom I had made, but this kingdom seemed more of a burden than a glorious domain. There was no sweet grass there, no alpine meadows of transcendental nourishment, but only the dry bland fodder of the languishing plains. I was in the doldrums of a routine life of survival, with no idea of how to "go up from here."

My marriage was cracking and beyond the point of mending, I felt. I was not even certain I wanted to mend it. We had grown apart with different priorities. Tara Singh's edict to "simplify your life" went on deaf ears in our household. We were not simplifying anything, it seemed. In fact the demands were getting more and more exhausting, more and more complex in their necessity. We spoke of simplifying, but nothing was ever done to make this happen. I was beginning to resent the burdens of maintaining an estate of properties and things I did not even want. There was no fire in my counterpart to transform the status quo. In fact, I could feel inertia in just the opposite direction. And I was buckling under this weight in a state of deep depression.

I had some friends who could hear my discontent. One happened to be a customer of mine for whom I had done various projects. She had a business of her own, an expensive dress shop for wealthy Main Line ladies. She had taken a liking to my artwork and to my life. She also employed my wife as her gardener—and this is how we met. I admit, this female friend became my emotional confidante. I knew my marriage was really over, but I did not have the energy to end it. I had someone to talk to, finally, with whom I could share my stories of *eating the sweet grass* with Tara Singh. To this friend, I could share my deeper spiritual longings that I had not been able to share with my own wife for years. Tara Singh had become my "secret sharer," my confidante, my confessor. But now, in the limbo period after his death, this role was taken up by a Jewish, dress shop lady from the Philadelphia Main Line. She was even willing to hang some of my paintings in her dress shop. How cool was that. I knew it could not go anywhere in terms of a real intimate relationship because she was happily married with three grown children. But it was a source for some little warmth that was otherwise void in my life. So this friendship sustained me for the period of time between Tara Singh's death and the life action that began what I was to do with the rest of my life.

To "only go up from here" was not so much in my awareness at this point. The seeds of my future had been planted, but they had not yet broken ground with healthy new sprouts. I was grabbing for anything that looked like an inner understanding of my deeper need to be heard and respected for whatever aspiration I still had left in me. The flame ignited by my seventeen years with Tara Singh was still lit, but growing dim. This one friendship kept it alive for me. This one friendship, though perhaps dangerously close to crossing a conventional emotional boundary, proved my saving grace in this limbo of a wasteland I was living in. It set the stage for an action that far exceeded anything I could have ever imagined or calculated as my destiny in life.

In the late fall of 2007 this destiny was about to take shape and shift in a way unimaginable. I received in the mail a flyer for a workshop, produced by my rebirther I had known and worked with in the 1980's. The workshop was one given by Sondra Ray, the lady with whom I had gone to India in 1987 and 1989, and the one who had introduced me to *A Course in Miracles* over two decades before. Somehow I knew I was meant to go, to pay my respects to this lady who had opened my eyes so much, who had set me on an inalterable course of life that put me in touch with the likes of Tara Singh. Though these two had never met, I could see the hand of divine destiny weaving these two strands of my background into a fabric of shared spiritual gifts, which now composed my life and hearkened my deepest inner yearnings to know my real Self. I did not waste time to sign up for the workshop, and sent in my check made out to Sondra Ray.

The workshop, simply called "The Money Seminar", was held in hotel conference room in downtown Philadelphia. There were about 30 people attending from various cities on the East coast. A few people from New York were there. A few familiar faces from my "old days" in the rebirthing community were there. Sondra Ray was just as I had remembered her—clear and vivacious, simple and direct in what she delivered. The processes were interesting, and got me to look at my relationship with my own prosperity issues. I had always had enough money, but I could not say I had mastered it to the degree I would call myself "successful" in terms of accumulating "wealth." One of the processes was to write down on one side of the page how "poor people" think about life and money, and on the other side of the page write down how "rich people" think about life and money; then to consider on what side your affiliations and beliefs fell. I could see where I had inherited certain beliefs about wealth, or lack of it, from my parents and family. It was good for me to look at them in order to become conscious of my common "patterns."

Towards the end of the seminar I heard that Sondra was giving private consultations in the days following the workshop, so I booked to have one of these. Because one of the suggestions in The Money Seminar to increase one's prosperity was to tithe 10% of one's income to something or someone who is spiritually uplifting in your life, I had already decided that I was going to make a tithe to Sondra Ray during this visit for the private session. I had just been paid a sizeable completion payment for a contract I had just finished, so I would start my conscious tithing practice here. The payment had been for $12,000.00—so I made the check out to Sondra Ray for $1200.00—which was the suggested 10%.

I arrived on the Monday after the seminar in the morning and had my "face to face" meeting I had wanted. We talked about my life. I explained my relationship with Tara Singh for the past 18 years—and my continued study of *A Course in Miracles*, Ho'oponopono, a Hawaiian spiritual practice we shared in common. I also shared the fact that my marriage was over and I was living alone in one of my houses I owned by my art studio. I remembered the session well. Sondra seemed very interested in my artwork, what I had been doing for so many years after the India Quest, and rebirthing. But the crux of the session centered on uncovering what she called the "personal lie." This is a deeply submerged negative thought one has about himself that affects the outcomes in his life. As I shared about my life experiences, especially about Tara Singh and the final years in Iowa, and my feelings about falling short in his care, we uncovered some deep seeded thoughts of "guilt" that I had been carrying for a very long time. It was important to look at this "guilt" in order to let it go.

After the consultation it was time to pay for the session. It was then that I expressed all of my gratitude I felt to Sondra Ray. "You know," I said, "if not for you I would never had known about *A Course in Miracles*. I would not have gone to India, Hawaii and many places in the world. I would not have known about Ho'oponopono. And I would not have met Tara Singh. Much of the spiritually important things in my life would not have proceeded and grown so fully. And by the way, I really heard what you said in the training this weekend

292

about tithing to those whom lift you up spiritually to be all that you can be—so I am tithing to you this $1200.00." There was a pause. I think Ms. Ray was a bit shocked. Then she said, "Wow, this is great, I really needed this money to pay my taxes!!!" Well, what she did with the money was no concern of mine, but one thing I was certain of at this point—the limbo I found myself floundering in after Taraji's Samadhi was over.

❖ *Chapter 29.* ❖

The Nashville Connection

In Lesson #47 of *A Course in Miracles* there are a few lines that accurately describe what I felt about Tara Singh, my teacher. They sum up his personal character as it presented itself:

> **"There is a place in you where there is perfect peace. There is a place in you where nothing is impossible. There is a place in you where the strength of God abides."**

Of all the people I had met in my life, Tara Singh embodied these qualities, and that was why I gravitated toward him as my teacher, friend and mentor. Now I was finding myself gravitating toward another who I felt had the same qualities, yet in a different form, a different expression of this holiness within—*Sondra Ray!* She was dynamic in ways that got my attention, and I noticed the same crystal clarity in the way she spoke, in the way she questioned, in the way she gave shape to the basic issues in life. After the weekend seminar and the private session, I knew our destinies had reunited and that we had some kind of action to share together—but it was not quite clear to me what that action was.

In Tara Singh I saw for a fact—"nothing is impossible." In Sondra Ray I saw the same thing. With these kind of people life action did not stop short with the obstacles of thoughts like "I can't," or "What would the neighbors think?" I knew something was rumbling in the core of my solar plexus for some kind of major shift and change in my life. With the re-entry of Sondra Ray this rumbling reached a crescendo of a deep abiding mantra that would redirect the whole course of my life—"Om Namah Shivay." This was the mantra of Babaji. This was the mantra that He said was more powerful than an atomic bomb. This was the mantra that He purported would "destroy" all ignorance. Years ago while in India with Sondra, I had received a copper, brass and silver bracelet with this mantra in Sanskrit, inscribed across the face of it. For years it had been tucked away somewhere, but suddenly it reappeared a few months before Sondra arrived back in my life, as if to prepare me for this reunion. I began wearing it again after 20 years of absence. This was no chance coincidence. I noticed I was wearing the bracelet when I received the flyer in the mail that Sondra Ray would be teaching a class in January in Philadelphia.

After our session we lingered in the living room of the Philadelphia Rebirthing Center. There was a fire in the fireplace. I noticed Sondra's Ho'oponopono book out on the coffee table, the Hawaiian form of spiritual cleansing she had introduced to me over 20 years ago. Obviously from much use, her book was tattered and worn. I made a comment about it. "Yes, do you know where I can get a new copy?," she asked. I did know the lady who was the head of the *Foundation of I, Inc.* in Philadelphia, the organization that produced the Ho'oponopono events in the USA. I could contact her and ask if it was possible to get a new book. So after agreeing to this, we said our goodbyes and parted our ways.

I sent Constance Webber an email regarding Sondra Ray's request for a new book, and cc'd Sondra. Soon I received a call from Sondra—"Connie invited me to her apartment to pick up the book on Wednesday, but none of us here know where she lives. Can you drive me there on Wednesday around 5PM?" It seemed my time with Sondra was not yet complete. "OK, I will pick you up at 4PM, as the traffic will be heavy and it may take us an hour to get there." I was a little on edge about this trip. I knew that there was some subtle "disapproval" in the Ho'oponopono community of "rebirthing"—perhaps going all the way back to the days when Sondra and Morrnah Simeona, the founder of this modern version, were close associates. Morrnah was Sondra's true teacher in this art, and Sondra had also written a book on Hawaiian spirituality, *Pele's Wish,* that was pretty far out there. So I had a little apprehension going to the meeting, not knowing if there were still some subtle *differences* that had not been resolved.

I covered myself by putting a life-sized portrait of Morrnah Simeona in the front seat of the car. She was the "head" of this lineage, and I needed to invoke her presence in the car on the way to this meeting. "Wow, where did you get that picture!" Sondra exclaimed when she got into the car. I explained I had kept up with my practice of Ho'oponopono over the years, and kept this picture of MS in my prayer room at home. She was surprised, to say the least. Within the hour we were in downtown Philadelphia.

Connie Webber was gracious. Her apartment, high on the twenty-something floor of the Rittenhouse, one of Philadelphia's most exclusive residences, overlooked the Art Museum, the Schuylkill River, the University of Pennsylvania, and the expansive Fairmount Park. We had a short chat as I noticed she had put out some "food tools," which are certain edible tools that initiate the Ho'oponopono process. Sondra discussed her life. I listened and observed. After about twenty minutes, Connie rose up and approached a credenza in the living room. As we all arose, she handed Sondra a new Ho'oponopono manual, and said, "This is from Morrnah. As far as I know, you are the only one who she gave permission [outside of the *Foundation of I* that disseminates the class and information] to share the process in public. She gives her blessings on this book for you." That acknowledgment was all I needed to rest my mind about Sondra Ray's relationship to Morrnah Simeona and the Ho'oponopono process. It was of the highest caliber.

After the meeting we had dinner at one of the fine restaurants on the square. Sondra's assistant from Paris was joining us, who felt like a chaperon. After the meal I handed Sondra one of my many handwritten journals and said, "I would like you to read this." It contained some recent writings and small watercolor paintings and drawings. On the cover page it had a picture of a lone tree springing forth in the midst of a starkly expansive lava flow in Hawaii. Inside the cover it said, "Dedicated to all new life that springs forth from the fertile debris of ruin." That line expressed the sentiment I had in that phase of my life, after the ruin I felt inside from the death of Tara Singh and the death of my marriage. Apparently my relationship with Sondra was leading me to that *new life.*

Sondra received the journal and said she would read it. Also, I became clear that it was time for me to commit to another trip to India, to Babaji's Ashram, where she took a group every year. It turned out she was going there in March, so I had plenty of time to prepare myself for the journey. As she was describing the India Quest of recent years, I interjected, "I am going this year." It came out of nowhere, like some force other than "me" was making the decision. We were all a bit shocked at the table, but also elated that new possibilities were opening up.

Asheville, Nashville, and a new beginning—

I received another phone call from Sondra Ray a few days later. "Why don't you join me in Asheville, North Carolina, in a couple of weeks, for Babaji's Samadhi Day," which was February 14ᵗʰ, Valentine's Day. "You can stay with my friend, Toni Toney, where I am staying. " The whole thing sounded very exciting, and also stretching my comfort zone. But I agreed to go. I would have to rent a car, because at that point I only had a work van for myself—too cumbersome to drive to North Carolina.

As I was passing through the Smokey Mountains of North Carolina in a blizzard, I called our host, Toni Toney to get some last minute directions. She pleasantly gave the directions in her slight southern draw, saying "darlin' this" and "darlin' that"—and told me where the key would be under the matt, because she and Sondra would be at a book signing. And at the end of the conversation she said, "And just come on in, darlin', and put your things in the back bedroom with Sondra. That is where you will be sleeping." Well, this was too fast for me, although I knew there were Higher Forces bigger than me running the show.

I was anxious to arrive soon, as the snow was falling furiously and the evening was drawing in. I pulled in the same synchronistic moment Sondra and Toni drove their minivan into the driveway. We spent the evening around a fire. Toni prepared an evening meal for us while Sondra and I caught up on things. When bedtime came we just continued our conversation in our pajamas—it seemed so natural and flowing. We just happened to be in a bed. There was innocence and restraint, respect and spiritual intimacy the likes I had never known. It became clear to me this was turning into a relationship that would be my destiny to follow.

The next day, during a breathing session at an evening lecture, Sondra asked me if I would come with her to Nashville, her next stop on the tour. I was hesitant, because it seemed like I had many loose ends in Philadelphia to handle before India Quest. As I was breathing away when a powerful energy came over me and I could practically hear Babaji saying, "What are you waiting for? Go for it!" So I reversed my decision not to go—and Sondra was delighted to have me along for the weekend workshop there. We drove my car and arrived at her organizer's house. It was a telling moment, because Sondra noticed I still had my wedding ring on. I could not get it off. My finger had grown around it and I had not had it off for thirty years. I asked the woman organizer, who was also an artist, if she had a pair of diagonal pliers which are used to cut metal wire. She did. So I took the pliers and cut the gold ring off of my finger. It made a sound that was startling to us all, and the pieces flew across the kitchen floor. I went into a spontaneous rebirth, and Sondra had to see me through it. All the guilt of leaving a thirty-year marriage was coming out of me. But I had to go through it.

During the weekend workshop in a Unity Church, I heard Sondra's friend Toni read her love poetry about twin flames. She was a gifted poet, and the words seemed to be describing what was awakening in my relationship with Sondra. By the second day of the training I was certain. I asked Sondra to marry me in India. "Wow," she said, "I need to get my head around this." After a while she said, "The answer is yes, but we need a year together before we can get married. I want to invite all my friends and it will not be enough time for them to make it to India this year," which was in less than two months away.

So our relationship was sealed in Nashville. I went home to prepare to leave Philadelphia for good, to make my way to India in March, and return to Los Angeles after that with Sondra. There was a lot to complete in the divorce. It was not easy for my ex-wife to accept the fact I was really moving on after thirty years. It became easier for me though, when I realized I did not need to hang onto anything. I called Sondra and asked her, "How would you feel if I arrived 'naked?'"— With no assets from my past life in Philadelphia. She said, "I think that would be great, not to bring anything from the past." Giving away my claim to the assets would speed up the process—in fact I would not have to return to Philadelphia, ever, regarding my old life. I sold a lot of my tools from the studio, and soon left Philadelphia with two suitcases for LA, not to ever look back. Before I left I called the divorce lawyer and said, "Give her everything."

❖ *Chapter 30.* ❖

The Golden Temple

I said to Sondra, "I want to go to the Golden Temple after the India Quest is over." That would take a few more days. We got our driver, Narender Gupta, to take the journey with us from New Delhi. The drive to Amritsar took about ten hours—a long day in the car, especially on India roads pocked with potholes. But there was something I felt was incomplete in my attempts with Tara Singh to go there on our last trip to India. This trip had sealed our holy relationship as the real "temple" of the Holy Spirit, and took me to heights I had never known, but I still felt a trip to the Golden Temple to honor this bond was in order. Though I could not make it with Tara Singh in the flesh, I could take the journey for him, somehow, and for myself. Together we could go in spirit to honor the roots of this Sikh religion which was the source of his spiritual tradition, and which also provided the intense spark of interest that had ignited me into a spiritual life way back in 1984 with Yogi Bhajan.

Indian roads are good and bad. There is an intermittent flow of easy traffic on the more modern sections of roads— then the slow creeping crawl through the congestion of small towns and villages, sharing the road with bullock carts and pedestrians, slow and cumbersome vehicles filling the route to capacity. The heavy congestion stirs up clouds of dusty atmosphere. We were happy to be in the confines of a clean, air-conditioned mini van, insulated from the outside drama of the Indian diorama.

Arriving late in Amritsar, we came to the hotel and welcomed a good shower and a bed. Early the next day, Narender fetched us to take our final pilgrimage to the Golden Temple, in the center of town. I was in a quiet mood, taking along my copy of *A Course in Miracles* and a picture of Tara Singh. We parked the car in a very congested neighborhood as we approached the outer walls of the temple complex. Going through the gate there was a rush of open energy, a light that descended upon the place and my heart. It formed an expansion immediately in my mind, as the Golden Temple sat glowing in the middle of the water tank, connected to the outer walkways by a narrow causeway. Larger than a football field, the water tank provided a tranquil oasis for the soul. Soon we were at the water's edge. I placed a few drops of the holy nectar on the picture of Tara Singh, and said a quiet prayer of thanks to him for all he had given me. Now I felt a full circle in my life was coming to an end. My meeting with him, nearly twenty years ago, was flowering and coming into its full power within me. My connections to the Sikh religion were making total sense: through this affiliation I had met my real live Master in this lifetime—teaching me the most pertinent scripture of Christianity in these modern times, *A Course in Miracles*.

Interestingly enough, he passed along a lineage that was as unexpected as the so-called "atheist,", Jewish in background, scientific intellectual by profession, Dr. Helen Schucman, who was to be its scribe. Who would have considered a Sikh from India would have been Dr. Schucman's prize, yet uncelebrated, best student—perhaps only *real student*. She herself, not wanting the attention of a "teacher," was barely accepting this role of the founder and rock of a tutorial spiritual lineage. For most practical purposes, she, and the student she produced in Tara Singh, remained well hidden as the epitome of a Teacher/Student Relationship of the holiest kind.

"The Holy Spirit's temple is not a body, but a relationship."
(ACIM Text, Chapter 20; Section VI; 5-1)

So why is the Golden Temple such a holy place? Obviously it is a physical form, a "body" of some sort. Yet, what is this body being used to communicate? It is communicating the potential of a holy relationship. To make real contact with the Golden Temple, or any temple for that matter, one has to transcend the form and arrive at the soul essence of it. One has to arrive at the Holy Relationship that it makes apparent: one has this with the Sikh Gurus who had mastered the art of the Holy Relationship, whose root is Love; one has this with the people who are pilgrims visiting this site; one has this with the profound architectural qualities and proportions formed by this remarkable and beautiful structure; one has this with the elements of space, air, fire, water and earth that compose all physical manifestation; one has this with the sacred songs and recitations of the holy scriptures in the Golden Temple itself; one has this with the relationship of the servants who feed the people throughout the day; one has this with every living creature that has visited the Golden Temple in the past, present and future; one has this with the Divine Forces that are behind the whole flowering of the Sikh religion and its holy expression.

The function of a temple is to connect us with Higher Forces of creation, with each other, and with our Self. At the altar, the central heart of the temple, an energy is transmitted in which a person can meet his true nature and lay down any distraction that prevents him from knowing he is one with God. This is the purpose of a "temple." Usually the life of a sage or an enlightened being is associated with a temple, one with whom we have a holy relationship. This holy being aids us in our relationship with divine forces and with each other, and imbues the temple with real spiritual power. In the Golden Temple of the Sikhs, the presence of the ten Sikh Gurus, Guru Nanak through Guru Gobind Singh, are held in the central structure along with the most sacred Sikh holy book. People cross over the waterway of life to the central core of the Golden Temple that holds the Altar to the ultimate truth.

Dr. Schucman, in her incomparable book of poems, *The Gifts of God*, writes about the real function of a temple, to hold the sacred Altar.

"DEDICATION FOR AN ALTAR

Temples are where God's holy altars are,
And He has placed an altar in each Son
Whom He created. Let us worship here
In thankfulness that what He gives to one
He gives to all, and never takes away.
For what He wills has been forever done.

Temples are where a brother comes to pray
And rest awhile. Whoever he may be,
He brings with him a lighted lamp to show
My savior's face is there for me to see
Upon the altar, and remember God.
My brother, come and worship here with me."

(Gifts of God, Page 93)

The Golden Temple of the Sikhs, or any church or tabernacle or synagogue or holy shrine, is meant to get us in touch with the holiness within us and our brother, with our Self we share with the brother—and in this honoring of the Self we share, we remember God and our divine nature. In this way do we end the "separation" we feel in life from each other and with God, our Creator. *A Course in Miracles* says, "To love my Father is to love His Son." Lesson #246. Without loving the brother first, how can we know the God who created him and us? This is why the true *golden temple* is a holy relationship I have with my brother—and ultimately with my Self in God.

We go to worship Jesus, or Mohammed, or Buddha, or Moses, or the holy Guru Nanak, but who we are really going to worship? It is our Self we share with all our brothers. The temple, and its most sacred altar is inside of us—just as all of our brothers and sisters are inside of us as well. To love them is to love our Self and God, equally.

Certain practices of the Sikhs were imbued in Tara Singh's mission. He fed the people. And here was the root of that practice at the Golden Temple. Pilgrims purchase a Prasad, a kind of honey-wheat pudding to be taken and offered at the Temple. The people cross the causeway and enter the sanctuary, giving their offering of Prasad, then on their exit receive a portion of the Prasad back for themselves. After paying their respects of worship they proceed to the Langar Hall, where thousands of people a day are fed for free. High officials and lowly street sweepers all have to sit in the same humble places to receive their meal. All people are fed. None go hungry. Worshippers sit on woven grass matts on the floor, and await the men serving from the buckets of food. They can eat as much as they want; the men come around and refill the plates. There is abundance beyond comprehension. Hundreds of people are served at a time—then hundreds more. Literally thousands are served in a day. The Golden Temple is a place that nurtures the people in every way, on every level of mind, body and spirit.

Sondra, Narender and I, after crossing the causeway, gave our gift of Prasad and entered the Golden Temple. We sat for a while listening to the sacred songs, the bhajans being played around the Holy Scriptures. Then we took our leave, and as we passed out of the temple we were given back a portion of our Prasad. It was deliciously sweet, and imbued with the energy of full appreciation. We felt uplifted by the sweetness of it. Soon we found ourselves sitting in the Langar Hall, on the grass matts that stretched for yards, in rows upon rows, across the floor of the hall. Soon men came to serve us our food on plates made from woven leaves. Rice and dal and cooked vegetables, with chapattis' formed our meal of the day. We savored it in silence. It was the completion of a whole experience of the Golden Temple. I could feel the energy of Tara Singh around me, and the satisfaction that I had made this pilgrimage in his honor to partake in the aura of this most remarkable shrine on earth, the Golden Temple, which was the physical metaphor of our Holy Relationship we shared together for over seventeen years in the flesh. Now it was to be elevated to the level of a freedom that transcended time, religion, bodies and all forms of physical encounter. Our bond would be sealed in eternity in this visit to the Golden Temple. This visit would serve as a remembrance for the core of my devotion, *A Course in Miracles*, which brought us together, through the lineage of Jesus and Dr. Schucman, meandering by means of a Sikh as my master, into the very purpose of my destiny—to awaken into my true Identity of my Self in God.

❖ *Chapter 31.* ❖

"Into His Presence"

There is a most remarkable prayer in *A Course in Miracles*. To plumb the depths of it one would actually come face to face with the Christ in one's Self. It is probably unlikely that a person could go to this depth without the aid of a true teacher, a master who had already made contact with its essence, its actual truth beyond just the verbal idea of it. And this remains the challenge of a true seeker of truth throughout the ages: a holy relationship is needed with the master in order to liberate the seeker from his own thought. Why, you might ask? Because, I could say, thought cannot know the real truth, the whole truth, which is beyond the words and the meanings of words. Truth is beyond words. It is a presence that is palpable, actually attainable, when the projections of thought are dropped. And for this renunciation of thought, a real teacher is needed. One needs a master to shock them out of thought, which is as persistent as the forces of nature.

The prayer is from Lesson # 157 in the Workbook of *A Course in Miracles*. It is a prayer that was often sited and sung at the Foundation where Tara Singh lived and taught. What I can say about it is this —for Tara Singh these were true words, realized words, and by that I mean he had plumbed the depths of them and eaten the kernel of truth they represented. Because of this he was able to share the stillness and the silence of that truth with his students. He could invoke the actual presence, and he and everyone in His Presence would feel it. He could transmit the essence of the words—beyond the words. He was able to communicate this state of being beyond thought itself, in which the presence grew stronger and stronger in the hearts and minds of those he touched. The prayer itself, such a pinnacle of true spiritual heights of *A Course in Miracles*, puts us in the presence of Christ Himself:

"Into His presence would I enter now." Lesson #157

"Into Christ's Presence will we enter now, serenely unaware of everything except His shining face and perfect Love. The vision of His face will stay with you, but there will be an instant, which transcends all vision, even this, the holiest. This you will never teach, for you attained it not through learning. Yet the vision speaks of your remembrance of what you knew that instant, and will surely know again."

So, for someone who has not met a real master in the flesh, how would he or she make this real contact with the Christ presence beyond the words? How can they make contact with this presence right NOW—here and NOW? It has to be possible.

A Course in Miracles assures us that "I need but call and You [God] will answer me." Lesson #327   How can we ask for and receive this presence? How can we enter into it, and have it be an authentic encounter, and not just wishful thinking or some pretend self-hypnosis? Let's give it our attention *right now*.

First we have to see that we are not in the awareness of this presence in our everyday lives. Our minds are preoccupied with thought, mostly with past thoughts that keep us distracted from the presence. This is the status quo of our thinking. We have a thousand concerns that are not the Christ Presence, and these concerns keep us distracted. Can we drop them for a spell? Can we put them on the shelf and say, "No, there is something higher I would like to devote my attention to, something more pure and loving, more peaceful and serene, free of all problems." When we really want this as our truth, there is a space in our mind that starts to open up. Our thought begins to slow down, and the space between our thoughts begins to widen. The emptiness of our mind, like the very sky across which the clouds of thought move, begins to open up and be clear, free of the distraction of the moving formations of clouds and storms of thought.

In this space is the presence. It is a space free of thought, of concern, of doubt, of belief. It is a space that is holy—that is empty and free of wanting. It is even free of wanting the presence. It trusts that the presence is there, but that no efforts

311

can bring it into awareness. In fact, it is a "surrender of effort" which can invoke it. It is like saying "Nothing I see means anything." Lesson #1. Not even my wanting of the Christ Presence means anything. And in this space of "nothingness" the Christ Presence rushes in.

We can then become renewed, with a new mind. We can then become willing to "enter into the now" where the presence is, without the conditions of our thought. Then awareness begins to dawn in us: but true awareness is the "unawareness of everything, except His shining face and perfect Love." When you want to see Christ's Love and shining face "above all else" (Lesson #27), then you will. But you cannot bring with you any grievances. You cannot see Christ's face if you do not see it equally in your "worst enemy." You cannot leave one human being outside of your vision, because you can only see the presence of Christ with the vision of Christ. You, who are in essence as equally holy as the Christ—can only see Him, experience HIS PRESENCE—using His vision. And this means you have to let go of all your thought and forgive everybody and everything. "My thoughts do not mean anything." Lesson #10. When you have dropped your thought, even for an instant, the Christ Presence can enter into your awareness. You are now "unaware of everything," except this presence.

"The vision of His face will stay with you, but there will be an instant, which transcends all vision, even this, the holiest."

We are getting closer to the essence of it, but not quite fully there. For me the face of the Christ, and the face of Tara Singh are one and the same. He taught me to see the Christ in my brother. He taught me even to see the Christ in the person I disliked, the person who treated me poorly, and the person on whom I instilled my judgments. In this universality of acceptance, there is a vision of the "face of Christ." You cannot have it without this acceptance. Even the worst person you can imagine, Hitler or a Genghis Khan, who did terrible atrocities, perpetrating the most inhumanity to man, must be seen in the light of this pure vision. You must forgive them all, because they "know not what they do." In this total relinquishment of any judgment, you can have a vision of Christ's face. Yet, even this, the holiest of visions, can be transcended. Even this vision, that requires your full acceptance of the Atonement, the full forgiveness of all mistakes, your own and all those of others, will be the precursor of an instant of vision even holier.

Thought stops. This Holy Instant contains no thought. You still notice your senses and their objects, the world about you and all the people and things that inhabit it, but it is all One. No differences, no distinctions, no this vs. that, no conflict or discrimination. Only the Peace of God exists. In this state, "The Peace of God is shining in me now." Lesson # 188. This becomes your truth, your reality—if only for an instant.

"This you will never teach, for you attained it not through learning. Yet the vision speaks of your remembrance of what you knew that instant, and will surely know again."

Who can rise to this? It is not to be "learned" in a book. It is to be lived. Can you let go of all judgment—of yourself and others? They are the same. You cannot judge another without harming yourself. You cannot judge yourself, without holding your brothers back as well. Can you rise into the *presence*? Can you enter into it? Are you willing to let go? Do you trust it is possible, and that the Christ is there to help you?

Only the Christ can take you there. This cannot be taught, nor learned—but only *lived*. You have to be willing to live into Christ's Presence—to have the vision of Christ's face, which is in all faces—and even this, the holiest, must be transcended. The Holy Instant is beyond thought, beyond the senses. Most likely, none of us have had it, or if we have had it, only for a few seconds. But as the poet Kabir has said, "Five seconds of this holy vision are worth your whole life."

You may not be able to retain it, to cling to it, but those five seconds you will never forget. They will transform your whole life. And you will never forget the grace, the absolute grace they bestowed on you. And though they have passed, this grace is a state of being, a holy instant of your certain experience that you shall "surely know again."

❖ *Chapter 32.* ❖

Completion of a Circle

The completion of the circle of my relationship with Tara Singh had its final flower at the Golden Temple in 2008, but it began much earlier. What does it mean to be complete? We have all kinds of relationships in life, meeting hundreds, even thousands of people. What are these circles of relationships that seem so important to our development and evolution as human beings? Sometimes a relationship is formed with a figure of history we have never even met, and becomes more important than those with the flesh and blood characters that people our lives. Sometimes the person in flesh and blood we encounter for a very short period of time remains more impressionable than the persons who have been in our life from birth. The circles of relationships can involve many similar characters at the same time, like a collection of classmates that graduates to another stage in life. This circle can vanish like a mirage, and none of the members ever seen again. Sometimes though, there is a significant "circle" which is so essential to our destiny in this life, that it becomes the sole and principle focus of one's whole being and reason to be. It contains within it the full spectrum of color that spreads across the palette of infinite possibilities that go into the painting called "our life." It is the macrocosm of the whole, the unit of measure, the "circle of influence" which determines our very fate and very life action. When this is recognized as such, one gets closer to the essence of love, of devotion, of true appreciation for all that life has to offer. This "circle" emerges as the greatest figure of existence, not static, but ever drawn in the gesture of a meeting—the arcs of two minds converging to form the one ultimate demonstration of a Holy Relationship. Two cease to be two, but rather become the One that perennially binds all living things into a single life. This is the ultimate completion of a circle. It appears as though an *end*, but in fact it is just a real *beginning*. It appears as though a *means*, yet it is as well the very *end* it has at its roots a very divine purpose.

This is a relationship of mastery. In appearances there is a Student and a Master. In essence the relationship, predetermined, is an acceptance of divine roles that are set in a place and time of a dimension beyond the confines of conventional measurement. The teacher is the Teacher, because there is the Student. The student is the Student, because there is the Teacher. There is an exchange of wisdom that is not of thought, not of a curriculum established by any motives either may have. The whole unfolding of its action on earth is a matter of a Divine Destiny unprecedented and unplanned by the human brain. It is a Circle of the highest order, one on which religion itself is based. It is a demonstration of Love, made manifest, in an Action of Life that serves to be an example of Love's flowering for all time to come. It is the real geometry of existence, the real figure of human measurement sought after by the most serious aspirants. It is the divine example that serves to guide humanity in their darkest of hours. It has its antecedents. Socrates had his Plato. Buddha had his Ananda. Jesus had his Peter. Muhammad had his Ali. Sri Ramakrishna had his Vivekananda. And Dr. Schucman had her Tara Singh. These are all Golden Circles of the highest order. And for me, as the student of Tara Singh, real or only imagined, I had my Golden Circle of influence that transcended all other relationships. It was blessed and surrounded in the holiness of predestined proportions. The completion of this circle was merely an acknowledgment of its very nature, the Teacher/Student relationship that made my awakening possible.

In the fall of 2005, when Tara Singh was still in the Belmont Village Senior Living Center in Hollywood, I paid him a visit. There was one day that struck me as particularly significant. We were sitting on one of many comfortable couches in the hallway of his unit, and as usual there was an atmosphere of stillness around us that was very palpable. Out of the blue I said to Taraji something like, "All things in life have a beginning, a middle and an end. It seems like now our time together is coming to an end." That his transition of dropping the body was looming in the very near future seemed inevitable. This kind of "limbo life" that Tara Singh was living at that moment did not seem fitting of his stature as one of the most brilliant minds of the age. Being marooned in a brain that was losing its capabilities to remember daily facts and receive accurate impressions seemed hardly the fair outcome of a life dedicated to the acute awareness of a universal, and yet a very grounded and practical philosophical and religious capacity. I was having trouble accepting this phase of development in our relationship. I was having trouble accepting the fact that Tara Singh was losing his mind at some level, and our time together was in a totally different phase of evolution. Though he was still "my teacher," the lessons were now of life and death inadvertently, beyond anyone's apparent control, and in the hands of God and Higher Forces. The reverence I had for him as my teacher never ceased, yet the kinds of exchanges we had were almost wordless now, and something beyond explanation.

He looked at me with a knowing that what I was saying was true at some level. His physical life was coming to an end and our relationship was being played out toward the completion of a cycle whose purpose was the transmission and sharing of a Holy Relationship that existed far beyond time, bodies and personal expectations and effects. Often Taraji had said, "Just be a witness." Of course he meant not to judge any situation, but to just observe the various factors playing out— and that this "life action" would inevitably contain the lessons any of us were to receive. Well, this piece of my lessons was hard to accept, hard to remain a witness to, without the judgment of "unfairness" that seemed to accompany my view of Tara Singh's downturn in mental and physical health. Perhaps, then, it was selfish of me to imply an end, when

318

really it was my non-acceptance of his situation, and my own, that actually wanted relief in the form of a timely and what appeared to be a predictable "end." Tara Singh himself had told me he received a reading from a clairvoyant in India who indicated he would live to be 86. He was now in that year. Would the reading play true? Usually he did not mention these kinds of predictions casually, and a few years before he had made this fact known to more than a few of us who were close to him.

When I received the call from Johanna MacDonald that Taraji had been moved to Iowa, to be in the facility that Melanie Coulter managed, there was a sinking feeling that something was "in the air." Tara Singh is planning his "exit," I thought. What seemed to be the perfect setting for his current situation, the Belmont Village facility, in a perfect climate of the country, was now being traded for an "old people's home" of an older style, dreary in stature by comparison, in a climate of downright winter that Taraji intentionally avoided most of his latter life. He was being moved for some good reason, even though it may not have been for the reasons everyone thought.

As I mentioned, Kiki and I went to see Tara Singh in Iowa in the early days of 2006. My attempts to rally the family to get him back to India for his transition failed, most likely for good reason. Yet part of me knew his time was coming to a close on these physical planes, and I had to prepare myself for his "leaving." When I sent him my favorite sweater I bought in Ireland with my father and a Pendleton blanket I had from all the way back to my early teenage years, there was something of a surrender of myself, of two of my most prized and sentimental possessions, perhaps even symbolic of important pieces of my psyche. I knew these "gifts" were important for him to receive. Moved to a more modern facility near Des Moines, Iowa, I called to make sure Tara Singh had received these items. "Oh, he is wearing the sweater now," said the resident nurse, I recall. It made me feel something wonderful, that he had received my offerings and my presence was somehow wrapping him in the woolens I held so dear.

Shortly after sending the sweater and the blanket, and noting his glad reception, Tara Singh passed away in March of 2006. I had called the facility the weekend of his passing, and knew he had stopped eating and drinking. Though I sensed his time had come, I was still holding out some irrational hope that his situation could change. Perhaps this is what we do in the face of "death." We do not go gently into that dark night in our minds, though somewhere in our bodies we give up the ghost, and succumb to what we have been conditioned to believe is the "inevitable."

It was a completion of a Golden Circle. I had met the man who was to become my teacher for seventeen years—on a cool spring day in Stony Point, New York, on Good Friday of that year of 1989. He had taken me to heights of my being I would not have otherwise discovered, without his guidance and tutelage. And now he was gone. Everything, it seemed in life, was to have a beginning, a middle, and an end—and this was the end. I had to accept it, though I did not like it. I had to somehow integrate Tara Singh's death and the last few years of his decline. But it was harder than I could imagine. The lines of this circle were coming to a closure in spite of me, in spite of my acceptance, or non-acceptance that "this was so." Yet the ramifications of our Holy Relationship were most definitely living on, and even moving on in spite of what I thought. This relationship had its own "dynamics," even beyond the body and personality of a man I held so dear. With the completion of this circle began the action of a new one and the role of Tara Singh in my life would continue to unfold in ways that were unfathomable to the human brain of thought and limited recollections.

❖ *Chapter 33.* ❖

ACIM for These Times

Tara Singh told me directly that *A Course in Miracles* was probably not meant for these times; it was more advanced than the human psyche could possibly fathom. But there could be a few individuals who could benefit and come close to what it is saying. When he asked Dr. Schucman if she thought anyone had brought the *Course* into application, she mentioned Mother Teresa. And in the same conversation she mentioned the state of human affairs on the planet as "Bad....bad....bad." Similarly, when someone had asked Mr. Krishnamurti how many people had actually heard what he was saying and had been truly transformed by his message, he said, "Only a handful—four or five." The next question, if so few, then why did he continue to give talks for over 60 years? He replied, "It was the only right thing to do." So whether the human psyche was ready or not, *A Course in Miracles* came to these planes out of a great need; and because of the need, Dr. Schucman incarnated to aid humanity along in its process of waking up. So in actual effect, the essential message of *A Course in Miracles*, which is one of complete forgiveness and Atonement, is for these times. It will lead the student through and "undoing" process to an encounter with inner peace that ensues from the absolute knowing of the God created Self. This is very much needed, and has always been needed. Therefore, out of this necessity, Divine Forces made it available for the ones "with the ears to hear."

"Having the ears to hear," was greatly stressed by Tara Singh. Over and over he would almost plead with his students, "Who has the ears to hear?" And this was not an intellectual knowing he was talking about. It was an application beyond thought. It was a total realization of the words, which was a state of being beyond the words. Plenty of people studied scriptures over the centuries, hovered over holy books, made arguments for and against the principles contained in these sacred writings—but so few had risen to the actuality of what the words were saying. So few actually had "the ears to hear." Many could read to learn, but not read to be totally transformed and transfigured.

A Course in Miracles is not for the feint of heart, nor for the casual seeker. It is not to be merely learned, but it is to be lived and applied. It is for the one who has come to utter disillusionment with the insanity we call "normal" in this world. The first lesson is obviously a total cataclysm of belief— "Nothing I see means anything." Who can read that lesson and come to such emptiness within, without feeling totally annihilated? But who is being annihilated? Is it not the selfish, fearful, petty, put together, insecure personal self we made up, who has never known real joy, real happiness, real unconditional love in this lifetime? It is this false self that has to "die" in order for us to have the ears to hear another Voice within ourselves. This Voice, the Voice of *A Course in Miracles*, beacons us to discover a nature that is true, that is Created and original, that is the basis for our real Self Identity which is our inheritance to know in the present. *A Course in Miracles* wakes us up to know who we are as God created us. It is a Course in absolute Self knowing, Self-realization. Its purpose is similar to the purpose of all the spiritual Masters who have come and gone— to awaken the individual out of his lethargy of sleep, his forgetfulness of peace and joy. It is to impart *perfect happiness* as our real nature.

A *Course in Miracles* is for these times, presented in terms and language for these times. We live in a psychological age, one of great scrutiny of thought, of language, of communication of events and images through media and social networks. Never before has our potential for real inner change been so great. Never has the issue been made so abundantly clear as to what the real problem facing us is—the problem of separation—facing us as a human race, and facing each individual man, woman and child that walks the planet. We have become separated from nature, from our creative Source, from our neighbors, from our families and spouses, and from our God created Self. We are in an identity crisis, and have been for a very long while—perhaps for eons. A college education, learning more skills to fit within the economic and social systems, does not necessarily solve this one "problem" of separation, nor give us a sense of our boundless Identity as God created souls. We are in a crisis, whether we are willing to admit it or not—and *ACIM* is one good and clear means of solving that crisis.

Never has there been such a *Course*. It is a "self-help" curriculum that "removes the blocks to the awareness of Love's presence." (*ACIM* Introduction) It defines a different way of living free of conflict, strife, and grievances, and makes it available to us. It even offers us the dissolution of the belief in "death" that grips humanity like a boney vice-grip of inevitability. Yet, similar to other revolutionary phenomena that came to change the course of humanity; this quiet Voice of truth can be drowned out by the din of distractions and the momentum of self-destructive tendencies. It's Voice of reason is spoken to deaf ears. We have had *A Course in Miracles* in our midst for nearly forty years now, and who is truly with it? Who has the ears to hear its profound message, and live by it? This is still the challenge of human kind, to hear and integrate the highest thoughts of its pinnacle of evolution. The mystics and the sages rise to the realization of these states of absolute Joy, Peace and Love and attempt to communicate their true essence of being to the rest of us. But unfortunately we remain fast asleep in our tendencies of fear and limitation. Our eyes remain blind, and our ears deaf to the spiritual truths of the ages.

A Course in Miracles, like the words and life of Jesus 2000 years ago, remains only a potential in us, not an actualization. And to overcome the inherent unwillingness to truly make a shift in consciousness, we would need miracles, and the determination to have the ears to hear. Surely these miracles, these "shifts in consciousness," are offered to anyone willing to give *A Course in Miracles* their body, mind and soul. It would take this kind of total surrender to make a difference, and a reverence for the *Course* as the authentic Voice of the Christ in these times. *ACIM* is, in essence, the "second coming" of the Christ that is actually dawning in the very person who is reading it. It is a tool of tremendous awakening to the one who can see it for what it is. It actually leads you to your very own Christ nature, your True Self Identity that is your destiny to fully realize in this lifetime.

I often say in the talks I give around the world on the *Course*, reading it seriously is akin to actually having a conversation with Jesus. It is like He is sitting in a chair in front of you, and you are having a dialogue with Him. It is that direct. One does not need a middle-man to interpret or to mediate between you and Him. You do not need a church, or a priest, or a religious belief system of any kind. You could even be an "atheist" and still have this transformative conversation with one of the most profound states of mind you will ever encounter. As Sondra Ray has said, reading *A Course in Miracles* is like "Drinking the Divine." It is holy nectar that will nourish you beyond any sustenance you could possibly imagine. Tara Singh described it as Jerusalem, Mecca, and the Holy Ganges River all rolled into one. It offers the holiest of the Holy Relationships possible—that between your brother, your sister and your Self, and in that completely forgiven relationship you find the Peace of God.

Though it may not have been written for these times, *A Course in Miracles* is *here*, and *here now* to stay. It transcends time all together, and, like all the Voices of Truth throughout the ages, it offers a viable means for a sleepwalking humanity to wake up. It offers a means for you to wake up. "How long would you like to remain asleep?" is the question. You can awaken into a new awareness now. Jesus is here to hold your hand and lead you to your Self Identity within, this very instant. Why not take advantage of His help that is provided today, right now, in *A Course in Miracles* for these times?

❖ *Chapter 34.* ❖

Masters and Miracles

The need for a teacher, or a spiritual Master, is almost essential to living. We are barely awake as it is, conditioned in the belief systems of thought that are from our familial, cultural, and personal programming. A Master is one who has freed himself from all of that, and usually as a result of having his own life teacher who aided him or her in this release and awakening. It takes a miracle, a shift in awareness, to be free from this conditioning. This person I blundered into, Tara Singh was my "master." my teacher of the miraculous. It was a relationship most likely predestined; one I had already "signed up for" before I came into this incarnation, and one that would demonstrate to me the highest potential of my own holy Self. Tara Singh was *off the chart* of beings I met in this life that awakened me. He had nothing to teach, per se, or to "add" to the self I had already made. But he did have a lot to "take away" in the subterfuge of erroneous thoughts I had accumulated for lifetimes. He was my "destroyer of illusions," the one who removed the darkness of my conditioned brain, and placed me in the care of my own Christ Self. For this kind of relationship, what would one pay? It is worth more than one's whole life to have such a blessing.

When Taraji told me I was "stuck at the survival level" and that in order to free myself I would need "miracles," I knew he was telling the truth. I was not so certain what those miracles would be, but I was certain about the first part—I was most definitely stuck at the level of survival. So I remained open for those *miracles* to unfold. The stories I described in this book have demonstrated to me that there is a Higher Intelligence moving and working in my life—in everyone's life. This benevolent force, this benign energy wants the best for us, the highest possibility of our human divine potential to be realized and true for us right now. For this greater potential to be realized, miracles are needed. The examples and experiences of these *miracles*, these *lessons*, do not always appear as a bed of roses at the time, yet, in hindsight, the evolutionary shifts are phenomenal. In the East they often call these lessons "leelas," or divine lessons pre-arranged by the guru to get you through some stuck pattern in your life—in order to liberate you from it. One rarely sees a leela coming, but in the midst of the difficulties being played out, gets to purge the lesson and pattern out of his or her system. One is then free forever of the pattern, having seen it clearly, perhaps for the first time ever, and having taken full responsibility for its results. Ignorance is thus overcome. One is then awakened from the "dream" of separation and the consequences of the errors. One is totally *forgiven*. I became aware that survival was not the way of a meaningful life, and that having

329

something of my own to give would always be consistent with Divine Laws. Tara Singh, my master and teacher, awakened me to these facts. Who else would have? The compassion of the true teacher is infinite, to save us from the ill effects of the very self we have made, the ego that we think is our only option in a complex life in which we are entangled.

Miracles are ultimate love expressions. Masters are masters of one thing—unconditional love. And this does not mean unconditional sentimentality. Often they are tough characters. They are as tough on the ego as the ego is tough on us. They have to be. Because of our inherent unwillingness to wake up, to make a fundamental change, the true master has to *shock us* out of our lethargy. And the shocks are not always polite or pretty, but they are always helpful. This is why people run for their life from a real teacher, a real Master, because he or she will be seen as a "difficult person"—or an "angry person"—or a "demanding person." Masters are often in the form of raw diamonds. When you find one on the road they appear as a common rock, and only from the polishing of patience and determination from the student will they reveal their true luster. Real Masters are often in "disguise." They are well hidden, and keep themselves that way on purpose. They do not have a horn to toot, or a whistle to blow, or a cause to get behind. They are at peace with themselves, and with all of creation. They have nothing to prove, and nothing to lose or to gain. They are in the world but not of it. They are incredibly alive and dynamic, but on first glance, one may not even notice them.

Tara Singh told a story of how one would recognize a true Master. There are so many people claiming to be wise, to have the answers to your ultimate "self improvement," to your essential spiritual awakening, how would you know the real one, the one for you? He told this story:

"There was a man on a ship going to a Southern Indian city. He was a merchant, doing business there, and was carrying fifty pieces of gold to purchase his wares. On the way to the city a severe storm blew up, and the ship was in grave danger of sinking. Fearing for his life, he kneeled in his cabin and prayed, 'O Lord, please protect me. Please save me from this terrible fate. I will do anything to live. Just get this ship through the storm and safely to the city. I will go straight to the Guru and give him all fifty of my pieces of gold. I will give to God all of my money.' So miraculously the storm subsided with his invocation—and he was astonished that his prayer was answered. So in a somber mood he arrived at the city, and knew he had to now fulfill his promise to God, and find the Guru and give him the money. Well, there was a 'guru' on nearly every street corner. How was he ever to find the real one, the one to whom he promised the fifty pieces of gold? He was in a real dilemma. So he came up with a plan. He would take his money, and give a little to each of the 'gurus', until he had fulfilled his promise. So that is what he did. To each guru he gave a little piece of his fortune, until finally, on the edge of town, he had remaining in his pocket only a few small coins of very little value. He thought he would give even this last piece of gold to someone. He spotted an old man under a tree, sitting quietly, sheltering himself in the shade from the intense summer heat. So he thought, 'Good, this old beggar man could use the last few coins of my fortune, I will give them to him.' So he approached the old man, relieved that he had fulfilled his promise to God, and placed the coins in his lap. To his surprise, when the coins fell onto his garment, the old man looked up and said, "You promised me all fifty."

This was how the merchant found his true Master, his true teacher in life. It is something not of his thought, or of *his plan*. It could not be sought and found directly, but rather provided by a huge action of the amazing grace of life itself.

This was how I found Tara Singh, in my backhanded way. An audio-tape fell off the shelf in the bookstore: *"Bringing A Course in Miracles into Application"*. Who would have noticed it? Who but me, who had been introduced to *ACIM* years earlier by Sondra Ray? And having been exploring Sikhism myself for a couple of years, how would a Sikh, representing *A Course in Miracles*, be completing the circle of influence this action of life was providing? These were all *miracles* in themselves. I could not have aligned these coincidences in a thousand years. So I blundered into LOVE without even seeking it. This is how they came to me, my *Miracles with my Master, Tara Singh*. These were my *Applications of A Course in Miracles*.

It says in the *Principles of Miracles* at the very beginning of the *Text of ACIM,* miracles should not be under our "conscious control," because they would be possibly "misguided." When Divine Forces are moving our life, as they definitely were with me in my meeting with Tara Singh, and in his meeting with Mr. Krishnamurti and Dr. Schucman, the calculations of the brain are not involved. There would have been no way the merchant in the story would have known his true teacher, his Master, was sitting on the edge of town, under the tree, looking like a beggar. The meeting was miraculous, and of a grace provided by *an energy* not under his "conscious control."

Such was my meeting with Tara Singh. When he saw me in the lobby after the Stony Point retreat in 1989, our eyes connected. He noticed I was wearing a Sikh bangle of stainless steel around my right wrist. He had one too, but his was made of gold. "OK, that is a Sikh kara, I see you have on," he said to me. I nodded in silence, as if to say "Thank you, I know who you are, and you see who I am, your student." And that was the miracle that set our course for the next seventeen years, and whose vibration is still guiding my life into the fruition of my mission with *A Course in Miracles*. Like my teacher before me, and his before him, Dr. Schucman, I have been given the boon of this remarkable Holy Relationship with the Holy Christ within. It is a direct relationship, having been tempered in the many years of encounters with my Master in the flesh, Tara Singh. Miracles were offered, and miracles were received. They were always beyond my "conscious control," to liberate me from a life at the "survival level." And this is a liberation for which a true Master is needed. And I am lucky in this lifetime to have this most basic need fully and unequivocally met.

The first thing I heard Tara Singh say in 1989 in Stony Point is the key to how anyone would recognize a real teacher. "I have nothing to teach. You all know too much already." A real teacher does not add anything more to your ridiculous memory. He takes away. He undoes your negative thoughts, your fears, your opinions, your pride and attachment, your anger and un-fulfillment that you have learned over a lifetime. He or she empties your mind of all its subterfuge, its unessential parts. The real Master removes all that is not Love in your life, and all that is not Joy in your life. He takes you through a set of trials that unravels your mind, and brings it to silence and stillness, free of judgments and guilt. He puts you in your glory, and lifts you higher than you could ever have gone on your own. He gives you God's grace in actuality, not merely in theory, and feeds your soul with the living nectar of truth. All this he gives, because the false is undone already in him. He has no motives. He lives by the will of God, not by his own wishes and desires.

Perhaps you may meet such a being in this lifetime. That is my greatest prayer for you, my reader. You may find him in *A Course in Miracles*. You may find him on the edge of town. But when the call is sincere, and you want that above all else, you will find this holy being, and enter into a Holy Relationship that will enrich your life beyond anything else. Then over time you will notice there is Love in your world, and you have been the fortunate recipient of miracles with your Master.

❖ *Chapter 35.* ❖

My Life as Markus Ray

I began this story as Mark Sullivan, and ended it as Markus Ray. One might ask: why did you take your consort's name, a woman's name, instead of her taking yours, which is the common social practice? Sondra Ray has been a well-known writer and spiritual teacher for nearly 40 years in the public domain. As a public figure, it did not seem fitting that she would become "Sondra Sullivan". Furthermore, we wanted to have the same name. This is unlike many enlightened couples in which each maintain their separate and different last names. We wished to be unified, but in a different paradigm that was sensible, and also considerate of the feminine name and lineage.

Also, our culture has been under a patriarchal dominance for nearly 5000 years. What has become of us in that system? We have witnessed a lot of atrocious wars and genocides in the "name" of a *just cause,* or some nationalistic or racial prejudice. We thought it was high time to shift this patriarchal energy to a more balanced version of matrimony. Not that we would revert to a "matriarchal" system. That would be out of balance in the opposite direction. But the willingness to take the woman's name could perhaps shift us to a middle ground, in which the attributes of the Divine Mother are also at work. We need the healing and acceptance of all people as one humanity—and men and women living as equals. We are all deserving of the life giving and enhancing qualities of the Divine Source from which we all came.

Lesson #184 says, "The Name of God is my inheritance." What would that be? What is in a name? Shakespeare said, "A rose by any other name would smell just as sweet." We have names for everything, in hundreds of languages. We are given a name at birth. What is in a name? Why do we have this symbol of a name, with the parents we have, in the culture we were born into? What is our real "name?" What is this "inheritance" the lesson is speaking about? Why would we value receiving this inheritance? What spiritual capital is increased, by accepting this inheritance? What is the Name that God is giving us? The lesson states:

> "It would indeed be strange if you were asked to go beyond all symbols of the world, forgetting them forever; yet were asked to take a teaching function. You have need to use the symbols of the world a while. But be you not deceived by them as well. They do not stand for anything at all, and in your practicing it is this thought that will release you from them. They become but means by which you can communicate in ways the

world can understand, but which you recognize is not the unity where true communication can be found.

Thus what you need are intervals each day in which the learning of the world becomes a transitory phase; a prison house from which you go into the sunlight and forget the darkness. Here you understand the Word, the Name which God has given you; the one Identity which all things share; the one acknowledgment of what is true. And then step back to darkness, not because you think it real, but only to proclaim its unreality in terms which still have meaning in the world that darkness rules.

Use all the little names and symbols which delineate the world of darkness. Yet accept them not as your reality. The Holy Spirit uses all of them, but He does not forget creation has one Name, one meaning, and a single Source which unifies all things within Itself. Use all the names the world bestows on them but for convenience, yet do not forget they share the Name of God Along with you.

God has no name. And yet His Name becomes the final lesson that all things are one, and at this lesson does all learning end. All names are unified; all space is filled with truth's reflection. Every gap is closed, and separation healed. The Name of God is the inheritance He gave to those who chose the teaching of the world to take the place of Heaven. In our practicing, our purpose is to let our minds accept what God has given as the answer to the pitiful inheritance you made as fitting tribute to the Son He loves.

No one can fail who seeks the meaning of the Name of God. Experience must come to supplement the Word. But first you must accept the Name for all reality, and realize the many names you gave its aspects have distorted what you see, but have not interfered with truth at all. One Name we bring into our practicing. One Name we use to unify our sight." Lesson #184

"God has no name," it says. Yet, "His Name becomes the final lesson that all things are one, and at this lesson does all learning end."

When I met Sondra Ray in 1985 and she introduced me to *A Course in Miracles*, little did I know my whole destiny was being spelled out and forever changed. The lessons were set. The meeting with Tara Singh, my master of this modern day scripture of life, was at hand. I had a different name then. It was one of my made up self, my conditioned self. The implications of this name, along with the tendencies and patterns that came with it, needed to be outgrown. All actions of life, from that point of being introduced to the *Course,* contributed to this process of outgrowing and "undoing." My teacher, Tara Singh, was a master of "undoing." He provided me with the means for self-honesty that would expedite and clarify that process in my life.

After Taraji's passing in March of 2006, I went through the year and a half of limbo. Something *big* had come to an end, yet something *even bigger* that was to be my real life destiny had not yet begun. It was in the winter of 2007-8 that the comet of my spiritual constellations came back, live streaming across the sky of my inevitable destiny. Sondra Ray entered into my life again. I had not seen her in nearly 20 years. Yet, why was this woman all of a sudden returning into the firmament of my spiritual life? I thought deeply about it. Who introduced me to India directly, and *A Course in Miracles* in the first place? When I heard her speak about the *Course* in 1986, and say, "This is the most important book written in 2000 years," my life was never the same after that moment. What internal alchemy was set into motion in my life as a result? Without her catalytic words that sparked my interest and brought me into contact with my true master of *A Course in Miracles*, where would my life have been? What debt of gratitude did I owe to this woman who had been so crystal clear about the importance of the *Course* in my life? Of India? Of a true spiritual master and destiny?

Almost immediately after receiving the pamphlet in the mail about her upcoming seminar I decided to attend. Sondra Ray was the same dynamic Self I had encountered over two decades before. She had not changed the intensity of energy and inspiration she transmitted. I was grateful to be back in her aura of Babaji and the Divine Mother—and *A Course in Miracles*. It became clearer to me of her role in my spiritual awakening, and of my evolution as a soul on the road to the Self-realization. Everything she spoke was a truth, just like Tara Singh—no wasted motion, no casual expenditure of energy that would distract one from the urgency of realizing their true Self. She was a master in her own right, presenting the perennial philosophy of the dharma, or the "way of life." This is a devotional way of living in a sacred manner in all areas of your life. She was not just a teacher of a few self-improvement techniques. Rather, she was a master of undoing, just as Tara Singh had been for me for all those years. And I was relieved to have found her again, like a "second chance," and a new opportunity to express my gratitude began to unfold in very miraculous ways.

When I booked a private consultation with her after the "Money Seminar" in Philadelphia, I was a bit nervous of being face to face with my former teacher. There were a lot of blanks to "fill in" about the past twenty years of our absence. I hardly knew where to begin. But I started with gratitude. The tithe of $1200 was just a token of appreciation for all the spiritual blessings she had bestowed upon me. We met, and I gave her the tithe really from my heart of gratitude, nothing more. There was no other motive. I was so grateful she woke me up to the significance of *A Course in Miracles*. I could hardly repay that with money. Yet the tithe was symbolic of my huge appreciation. It would suffice. Then we had the consultation. I was at a crossroad in my life. I knew my old marriage was over, and I had even moved out of the house. What was in store for me? I was wide open.

The session was powerful, and I became reacquainted with Sondra Ray's style of internal processing. Her work with our "most negative thought about our self," which she calls the "personal lie," is at the core of the clearing process. It is the ego's chief weapon used against us, to keep us from knowing our authentic Self. It became clear my "personal lie" was "I am guilty" in the session. I felt guilty about not doing enough to "save" Tara Singh from the ordeals of his last years in managed care facilities, and I felt guilty that after 30 years of marriage, I had failed to bring that relationship into a state of true harmony. "I am a failure" was another thought, another "personal lie," which was still submerged in my subconscious mind. I was glad to have this new clarity, yet I was still unsure what to do about it.

But then life had an answer. Events kept putting me closer and closer to Sondra Ray and her mission. We went together, with her French chaperone, Shanti, to visit an old mutual friend and spiritual mentor of ours, Connie Webber, who lived in Center City, Philadelphia. Afterwards we had dinner, and a meaningful discussion about many things. We discussed India, *A Course in Miracles*, my life with Tara Singh, and the completion of many of my life cycles, including my old marriage. Also, we spoke about the Divine Mother and Babaji, and their role in the new paradigm of relationships that was to usher in awareness of the Divine Feminine, which had been so sorely neglected in patriarchal societies for over 5000 years. Sondra had just written a book on the subject, *Rock Your World With The Divine Mother*, and I was just beginning to read it. New perspectives were opening up for me.

A Course in Miracles, still within the language of a *masculine Divinity*, had very little to say about the "Mother Energy" that was so much a part of the perennial philosophy, especially in India. The Divine Mother plays a *huge* role in the spiritual life of the East—and to the detriment of the Western world, the

341

balance of these gender polarities, in the sacred sense of religious focus and practice, has all but been lost. The indigenous cultures were more equipped to keep these polarities in balance, especially the Hawaiians, yet these cultures were drowned out by the overbearing nature of the Western patriarchal and dominating forces. The conquest of the old fertility cultures, deemed by the Christian patriarchy as "pagan," literally wiped out the Divine Mother worship from the annals of religious tradition and impetus. The Divine Mother, beyond just being the Virgin Mary in the Catholic Church, was all but non-existent in the Western and Middle Eastern countries.

Sondra Ray, in her forty years of work and focus on Babaji and the Divine Mother, has become one of the major voices in this restoration of the Goddess into the minds of the people. In an age totally dominated by patriarchal politics, economics, and religion, Sondra Ray offers an alternative to balance this highly one sided and self-destructive model of worship. She embodies the Divine Mother in all of her writings, work, and actions worldwide.

It took very little time for me to recognize my new destiny was being laid out before me—and in a very rapid fashion. There was little time to waste. At that dinner meeting I committed to accompany Sondra Ray on the India Quest, her annual Spring trip to Babaji's ashram in the Himalayas. I had not been there since 1989, and I was looking forward to restoring my relationship with Sondra, with Babaji, with India, and exploring the new vicinities of the Divine Mother. In February, before India Quest, Sondra invited me to attend some events she was holding in Asheville, North Carolina. I agreed. It was here that our relationship began to really take shape as a couple. And by the time I also accompanied her to Nashville the week after, I was certain we were to be together as a permanent thing. I asked her to marry me when we would be in India in March of 2008. She accepted the proposal, but said she needed a year to prepare for a marriage. So, the decision would be to come together for a year, travel together, work together, and then keep going. This sounded like a sensible plan, as I still had things to complete in Philadelphia. Just before the India Quest, after signing over the assets of my "old life" 100% to my former wife, I left Philadelphia one last time and never looked back. I carried with me only two suitcases with a few clothes and books. My old life was over. I was complete, and eager to embark on an unknown and unprecedented journey.

So began my life as Markus Ray. Sondra Ray and I married in Herakhan, India, on April 4th, 2009. This started a new cycle of a different inheritance, in which the Name of God was put in the first place. Not as an empty ritual of chanting, "Om Namah Shivay," or any other mantra of repetition that would lull me back into a false "religious" sleep, but rather one that would WAKE ME UP even further into Christ's Immortal Presence. Babaji, the Immortal Christ Yogi of India, who is a Maha Avatar of the highest proportions, entered into my pantheon of Holy Beings in my life, with Sondra Ray, my pre-arranged consort. An ancient chapter with Tara Singh was coming to completion, and a new chapter with Sondra Ray and the Divine Mother began. The "Miracles with my Master" continue. They are not under my "conscious control." My relationship with *A Course in Miracles* deepens, as I have opportunities to share its message and significance to audiences worldwide. What could be better, to be in the Holy Relationship I had with Tara Singh, now with my own wife and teacher Sondra Ray? Perhaps Tara Singh and Babaji were behind it all along. I would not be surprised. Bole baba Ki Jai! Hail to the simple Father—and Mother, I might add. Jai Maha Maya Ki Jai!

And now I, Markus Ray, the name I have claimed as my inheritance to be consistent with my Divine consort, Sondra Ray, would end this story, *Miracles With My Master, Tara Singh*. I leave with you, my readers, this final lesson of *A Course In Miracles*. Taraji often spoke this prayer out loud to many others and me. I share it with you now—and offer it back to him who was, and still remains, my first true living Master.

> **"This holy instant would I give to You.**
> **Be your in charge. For I would follow You,**
> **Certain that Your direction gives me peace."**

> **"And if I need a word to help me, He will give it to me. If I need a thought, that will He also give. And if I need but stillness and a tranquil, open mind, these are the gifts I will receive of Him. He is in charge by my request. And He will hear and answer me, because He speaks for God my Father and His holy Son. AMEN."**
> **(Lesson #361-65)**

SONDRA RAY and MARKUS RAY on their wedding day in
India, April 4, 2009

❖ *Bibliography* ❖

1. Dr. Helen Schucman (scribe), *A Course in Miracles,* Combined Volume, Third Edition (Mill Valley, CA: Foundation For Inner Peace, 2007) Lesson #'s cited in text.
2. Tara Singh, *The Voice That Precedes Thought* (Los Angeles, CA, Life Action Press, 1987)
3. Henry David Thoreau, *Walking* (http://www.transcendentalists.com/walking.htm)
4. Henry David Thoreau, *Walden* (Boston, Shambhala Publications, Inc., 2008)
5. Dr. Helen Schucman, *The Gifts of God* (Tiburon, CA, Foundation for Inner Peace, 1982)
6. Rainer Maria Rilke, *Letters on Cezanne* (New York, Fromm International Publishing Corporation, 1985)
7. Wikipedia, various quotations cited: Sri Ramana Maharshi; Our Lady Of Guadalupe; Elephanta

❖ *Resources* ❖

MARKUS RAY :

Website: www.markusray.com
Blog: www.markusray.wordpress.com
Facebook Profile: www.facebook.com/markus.ray.169
Facebook Page: www.facebook.com/LiberationBreathing
Facebook Page: www.facebook.com/markusray.artist
LinkedIn: www.linkedin.com/pub/markus-ray/16/254/606
Twitter: https://twitter.com/MarkusRay1008
Instagram: https://instagram.com/markusray1008/
Pinterest: www.pinterest.com/markusray/
E-mail: markus.ray@aol.com

Amazon Author Page:
http://www.amazon.com/author/markusray

SONDRA RAY:

Website: www.sondraray.com
Blog: www.liberationbreathing.blogspot.com
Facebook Profile: www.facebook.com/sondra.ray.90
Facebook Page: www.facebook.com/LiberationBreathing
LinkedIn: www.linkedin.com/pub/sondra-ray/33/136/79b
Twitter: https://twitter.com/sondraray1008
E-mail: immortalrayproductions@gmail.com

Amazon Author Page:
http://www.amazon.com/author/sondraray

Joseph Plan Foundation of Tara Singh:
http://www.josephplan.org/home.html
Krishnamurti Foundation: http://www.kfa.org/
Ramana Maharshi Ashram: http://www.sriramanamaharshi.org/
Sri Babaji Ashram: http://haidakhanbabaji.com/Ashram.html

❖ *About the Author* ❖

Markus Ray received his training in the arts, holding an MFA in painting from Tyler School of Art, Temple University in Philadelphia, PA, USA. Also a writer and a poet, he brings spirituality and sensuality together in these mediums of expression. He is the author of a major work, *Odes To The Divine Mother*, which contains 365 prose poems in praise of the Divine Feminine Energy. Along with the Odes are his paintings and images of the Divine Mother created around the world in his mission with Sondra Ray. This work will be available in October of 2015 on Amazon.

Markus is a presenter of the profound modern psychological/spiritual scripture, *A Course In Miracles*. He studied with his master, **Tara Singh*,** for 17 years, in order to experience its truth directly. His spiritual quest has taken him to India many times with Tara Singh and Sondra Ray, where Muniraj, Babaji's foremost disciple, gave him the name Man Mohan, "The Poet who steals the hearts of the people". In all of his paintings, writings and lectures, Markus creates a quiet atmosphere of peace and clarity that is an invitation to go deeper into the realms of inner stillness, silence and beauty. He teaches, writes and paints along side of Sondra Ray, and many have been touched by their demonstration of a holy relationship in action. His iconic paintings of the Masters can be viewed on www.MarkusRay.com which he often creates while his twin flame, Sondra Ray, is lecturing in seminars.

Markus Ray & Sondra Ray** are brought together by the grace of their Master, Maha Avatar Herakahn Babaji. Babaji Himself said, "Markus is my Humbleness. Sondra is my Voice. Together they are my Love." As Ambassadors for Him, their mission is to bring His teaching of *"Truth, Simplicity, Love and Service to Mankind"* along with the presence of the Divine Mother to the world. They do so through seminars (like the New LRT®) and the healing practice of Liberation Breathing®, and the study of *A Course in Miracles*. They are unfolding the plan of Babaji, Jesus and the Divine Mother, which is beyond our wildest dreams! Their relationship is a shining example of what is possible through deep ease and no conflict. They can take you to a higher realm where Spiritual Intimacy©, miracles, and holy relationships can become real in your life. Their next book together, ***Spiritual Intimacy: What You Really Want With A Mate***, will be out in the middle of 2015. Their various Sacred Quests around the world with Liberation Breathing® prepare many to receive more profound levels of *DIVINE PRESENCE* in their lives, and awaken more awareness of Immortal Love in their hearts.

*Tara Singh, author, humanitarian, lecturer on *A Course in Miracles* was trained by Mr. J. Krishnamurti for over 30 years to prepare him for 3 years in silence....out of which came the blessing of his meeting with Dr. Helen Schucman, the scribe of *A Course in Miracles*. It was his intense relationship with Dr. Schucman, on a daily basis for over 2 and 1/2 years that served to ordain Tara Singh as one of the most authentic voices on this modern day scripture available in these times.

**Before her life mission as a Rebirther, teacher and author, Sondra Ray earned a B.S. degree in Nursing from the University of Florida College of Nursing, and a Masters Degree in Public Health and Family Sociology from the University of Arizona. She was trained as a Nurse Practitioner in Obstetrics and Gynecology. During her assignment in the Peace Corps she was stationed in Peru, which prepared her for world service. During her service in the US Air Force she was stationed at Luke Air Force Base in Arizona.

TARA SINGH and MARKUS RAY in Vermont
at John McClure's Bakery

TARA SINGH Lighting the Altar

❖ *Other Titles by Markus Ray* ❖

Odes to the Divine Mother

ISBN: 978-0-9916277-2-1

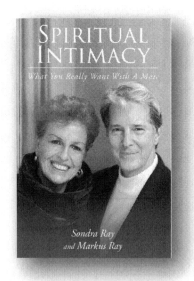

Spiritual Intimacy

ISBN: 978-1-68139-931-7

❖ *Notes* ❖

❖ *Notes* ❖

Made in the USA
Columbia, SC
31 August 2017